Paul Duncan was born at a young age, grew up and now has the body, if not the mind, of an adult. He lives two-thirds of his life in a house. Paul co-edits *Crime Time* magazine and is presently writing a biography of Gerald Kersh.

1997
No Exit Press,
18 Coleswood Rd
Harpenden, Herts, ALS IEQ

Copyright 1997 Paul Duncan & Contributors

Published in association with **Crime Time** magazine

A CIP catalogue record for this book is available from the British Library.

ISBN 1 - 874061 - 85 - 8

9 8 7 6 5 4 3 2 1

Book Design By Crow Design

THE THIRD DEGREE

THE THIRD DEGREE

CRIME WRITERS IN CONVERSATION

PAUL DUNCAN

NO EXIT PRESS

THE THIRD DEGREE

CONTENTS

COPS

INVESTIGATORS

ROBBERS

THE THIRD DEGREE

ACKNOWLEDGEMENTS

Thanks to John Kennedy Melling for his profiles of John Coffin and Charmian Daniels, his bibliography of the work of Gwendoline Butler and sight of the *Medico-Legal Bulletin*.

Thanks to Peter Dillon-Parkin for his overview of the books of Patricia Cornwell and interview with Gwendoline Butler.

Thanks to Crow Dillon-Parkin for her interview with Elizabeth George.

Thanks to Peter Mann for his overview of the books of Walter Mosley.

Finally, thanks to my parents, without whom I would not have been possible.

IS IT SAFE?

THIS BOOK IS CALLED *The Third Degree.* As the name might suggest, this is a book of interviews with crime writers. Some of the writers are bestsellers, some are well-known as crime writers, others are lauded in the more literary newspapers and magazines. They all have a distinct view of the world.

Over the past year, Paul Duncan, Peter Dillon-Parkin and Crow Dillon-Parkin have been interviewing crime writers for Crime Time magazine, which they edit. Most of the interviews in this book are expanded versions of those interviews and some are new for this collection.

Our objective was to assemble a book which would give an overview of the state of crime writing today and to ask that age old question - is the purpose of writing to comfort, to educate or to make us face reality? Or is it all three?

Dr Elliott Leyton, in his interview, puts forward the opinion, when referring to interviews with serial killers, that 'the interview, as a data source, is a profoundly flawed instrument. When you interview a killer a long time after the event, he's got his whole act prepared and he'll tell you exactly what he wants you to understand.'

As far as I'm aware, the crime writers in this book are not serial killers. However, some of them are very adept at manipulating information, telling you what you want to hear and what they want to tell you. They may have been interviewed many times previously, developed anecdotes, catch-phrases, stock answers. This is all very entertaining and part of the promotion business but you have to look beyond that, to look at what has gone unsaid, at the way they phrase their answers, whether consciously or unconsciously.

If possible, if they allowed me, I wanted to find out what made them write the things they write? What makes them write crime-orientated literature? Is it an emotional thing? Is it an intellectual challenge? Is it work or an obsession?

How do you decode these interviews? Here are a few clues...

Forget the style of their answers - it can often disguise the content. For example, Patricia Cornwell, however mannered and precise, advocates the use of guns for self-defence, whereas tough, barking James Ellroy thinks there should be no guns whatsoever. Who would have believed it?

Always look for what they don't say. Michael Dibdin reviews literature but writes genre books. I couldn't really find out why he doesn't write literature. What do you think? Lawrence Block has written books about how to write books,

PAUL DUNCAN

yet says that he writes instinctively, from his subconscious. Is it one rule for others and another for him? Have I misunderstood him?

Make lists of similarities. Patricia Cornwell and James Ellroy live in guarded enclaves. Gwendoline Butler and Andrew Klavan believe in storytelling.

Make lists of differences. Derek Raymond lived his characters and was emotionally involved with them, whereas Lawrence Block is not emotionally touched by his characters at all. Edward Bunker's work is based on a life of crime whereas Paul Buck's isn't (as far as I know).

The clues are there. It's up to you to find the answers.

The criminal act is an act against society, an act against an individual and, ultimately, an act of self-destruction. What drives people to do this? What's going on in their minds?

These concerns are pondered in crime fiction. But not all crime fiction ponders these questions.

In crime fiction, the crime is almost always solved, the villain is vanquished, and all is put right in the world. No matter how hard writers try to dress it up with swearing, violence and a bit of the old in-out, this is the prevailing world-view of most crime writers. In fact, it's the world-view of most writers of popular fiction. It's popular because it reasserts the world as an orderly and comprehensible place, which we can control. This is valuable in some ways, mostly as a balm, to comfort us when we feel uncertain. It has a place. It makes the world seem like a safer place to live in.

In real life, crime isn't so easily vanquished. The world isn't so safe. Just turn on the TV and watch the news to see for yourself.

America and Great Britain have vastly different attitudes to law enforcement, which is reflected in their crime fiction.

In America, arguments are sorted out at the end of a gun - a legacy of the wild west. The cops wait until the dust settles then wade in and throw their weight around. For this reason, the private eye, the lone, honourable gunfighter who tumbles into town and sorts out the bad guys by fair means or foul, works well in an American setting.

In Great Britain, arguments are sorted using the law. People sit down, have civilised meetings and abide by the court's decision. The police have the powers to intervene before things go wrong and are more trusted. For this reason, the police procedural is better suited to British soil than other forms.

The police enforce the law, making the world safe. Investigators raise the alarm, telling us the world is unsafe. Criminals make the world unsafe.

The modern trend of crime novels/thrillers is to make the criminal a horrific character. Like horror fiction, they dehumanise the villain of the piece, make them a supernatural entity, something which is easy to be afraid of, to hate. The criminal is akin to the Indians in old westerns, a cheap way of manipulating plot, of writing without responsibility.

There are only a handful of serial killers world-wide, yet they are predominant in crime fiction. Everyone's a serial killer, meticulously planning a la Dr Hannibal Lecter or Professor Moriarty. In reality, murderers are usually opportunistic, almost random, impulsive, definitely occasional. Books give us a distorted view of the world, distorted to play on our fears and then placate them, not to solve them.

There are a few writers who think of the criminal as a human being, who write without judgement on the people, but perhaps judge society. (This is the way things are. How did it get this way? Can we change it for the better?) Perhaps they don't have the answers, but at least they raise the questions.

I believe that everything a writer says in their books is a part of them. Some writers may mask themselves by adopting a voice or style, or may be totally unaware of their revelations, but everything every character says is selected by the writer. This is an important point to remember.

Before I interview a writer, I read as many of their books as I can because I want to know what the writer thinks about. If the writer spends a year or so writing a book, a great many of their thoughts are going to make it into the book.

Obviously, whatever a writer has experienced in their life will be included in one form or another. More often than not writers consciously use their life. Edward Bunker was a criminal. Patricia Cornwell has met and worked with FBI agents, forensic scientists and police officers. So that's what they write about.

I think a writer's imagination is just as important, if not more important, as whatever life experiences they may have had. Creating outside of their own experiences, to push themselves into emotions they have not felt before, means that they can project themselves into other people. Knowing and empathising with our fellow human beings is an important skill. If this emotion can be communicated to the reader, then the writer can consider their job well done.

So, you're snuggled up in bed. It's cold and windy outside, a branch scraping along the wall. Are you comfortable? Good, then you can begin learning about the wonderful world of crime fiction - just turn the page and read on.

Is it safe? Only if you turn the TV off and leave the light on.

Paul Duncan
Coventry, 21 November 1996

INTRODUCTION

"The dead won't talk to you if you don't
know them as a person"
Patricia Cornwell

IN A WORLD OF DAZZLING IMAGES - *persuasive, erotic, frightening - it is sometimes easy to overlook the substance of things. Their true purpose.*

Walking down The Strand on a wet weekday, all the dirt and grime being washed away, the front-of-theatre picture and poster displays coming up as new. The neon lives, bright against the grey buildings and grey sky. The theatres inviting, more alive than real life.

The Waldorf Hotel, plush velvet greens and reds, tries to maintain a level but the more I look, the more I see through it. The formality, the ritual of presenting yourself to the staff, their servile attitude, the stiff back, the practised tones. All scripted. And what happens? These professional yes-people charge pounds for tea that costs pence.

That's the punchline. The neon, the servile attitude, is all for selling.

It is easy to forget yourself, to get wound up in a world designed to get things from you. You have to be strong enough to look beyond the facades of everyday life and search for its truth, its substance. To do this, you first find the evidence, both physical and emotional, then you test, extrapolate and deduce.

Easier said than done.

In 1990, Patricia Cornwell launched her crime writing career with Postmortem, *the first book to feature forensic pathologist Dr Kay Scarpetta. It won lots of awards and sold lots of copies. Since then there have been five more Scarpetta books. In each one, besides the solving of a hideous crime, the good doctor's personality has developed and evolved. Patricia's writing has also evolved. From Potter's Field heralded a new high-powered action thriller direction, and may form the basis of the first Scarpetta film - Peter Guber is producer and Patricia is screenwriter and executive producer - which has been optioned by a major studio.*

The seventh Scarpetta book, Cause Of Death, *had a first printing of one million in America. Number eight,* Unnatural Exposure, *is complete and ready to go in 1997, and Patricia signed a $24 million contract for Scarpetta books nine to eleven. March 1997 sees the launch of new characters, Police Detective Virginia West and news photographer Andy Brazil, in* The Hornet's Nest. *A light, satirical look at the police in Charlotte, North Carolina, it is hoped that, if successful, this will result in a new series.*

Paul Duncan met Patricia Cornwell at the Waldorf Hotel. Patricia's words were accompanied by the theme to Gone With The Wind endlessly repeating in the background.

Verbal Evidence

Dr Kay Scarpetta is not similar to anyone. It probably has something to do with the fact that I didn't have anyone in mind when I came up with her. Also, because I'm so rooted in reality - to the real professionals and the real cases - I tend to get somewhat removed from literary, TV or film characters. They, to me, are not reality, so they have no bearing on my work. This means I have a difficult time trying to explain my characters because people like to categorise them by comparing them to other characters.

However, having created this popular character - a female medical examiner who works for the FBI at Quantico - all sorts of variations of her have started to appear in the past five years. The most notable is probably Dana Scully in *The X-Files*, who has expressed some of the same ideas and thoughts as Kay Scarpetta.

This is one of the reasons why Peter Guber and I are not wasting any time in producing the first Scarpetta film. Unfortunately, my books are the inspiration for other people to come up with other strong female protagonists, particular in the FBI or medical fields. I won't even watch or read these other things that people tell me about because they'll probably just aggravate me.

Patricia knows what she's talking about. In 1979, after graduating with an English major from Davidson College in Davidson, North Carolina, she became an investigative crime reporter for the Charlotte Observer. It was here that she first became interested in crime and, as part of her job, she gained access to police departments, morgues, laboratories, and detective squad rooms - the people and places that would later turn up in her books. After her move to Richmond, Patricia became a volunteer police officer and was on the streets in uniform. In 1985, she joined the Virginia Chief Medical Examiner's Office as a computer analyst. Patricia wanted to write crime fiction and it was the perfect opportunity for her to do research AND get paid for it at the same time. Eventually, when her manuscripts went unpublished, she ended up needing the job. For six years Patricia witnessed hundreds of autopsies, attended medical school lectures, labs and trials. She researched in the morgue's medical library, wrote technical documents, helped edit the Medico-Legal Bulletin, contributing articles on DNA profiling to link serial killers, the relationship between the medical examiner and the press, drug-related homicides in Virginia and even the importance of accurate technical details in crime fiction. She left the Chief Medical Examiner's Office in 1991 but is now a consultant for them - an honourary title which allows her access for her research. Patricia first went to the FBI headquarters at Quantico to do research for the Chief Medical Examiner's Office, but now visits to do training and research. She teaches classes in media relations and other subjects to the FBI and other investigative agencies.

One of the reasons I've been fortunate enough to have access to a lot of places and information is because I have a platform of legitimacy from my profession and background. You also earn your credibility through word of mouth and by meeting people. I can't continue to enjoy the world these people live in unless they know they can trust me. They read the books, think I'm okay and the doors open.

You work to get the facts right?

It's an unforgiving world. If you get something wrong, people turn off you just like that. Besides that, I want to get it right for myself, keep it honest. It's very important to me personally, to get it right, to know what it feels like and to experience it as much as I can.

With access to all this information, and with her two years experience as an award-winning crime reporter for the Charlotte Observer, *I would have thought that Patricia would be writing fact, not fiction.*

Sometimes fiction is truer than fact. Actually, I do both, because the scaffolding of all my stories is fact, whether it is a procedure, or the type of case, or the kinds of individuals. It is all rooted in experience and research. That's the fact. The fiction of it is the way that I want the characters to work the cases.

People have asked me over the years why I don't write True Crime and I tell them that I could not bring myself to victimise people all over again. If you have a son or daughter murdered in what turns out to be a sensational crime about which books are written, and you have been on the side of the fence where I have been - seeing relatives sitting in the waiting rooms and the looks on their faces as they come to find out what's happened to their child - I don't want to write about things in gory detail that could upset those relatives all over again. There are cases where people find it cathartic to write about their experiences, and I don't bump the people who do it, it's just that I couldn't, and I don't want to.

The books have very little violence in them. All we see are the effects, both physical and emotional, of violence committed off-screen.

That's because that's all that Scarpetta sees. It's very rare that Scarpetta will witness a violent act unless she herself commits it, as she's had to do in several books when she's had to defend herself. I only show violence when the bad guys are getting it, not when the victim is getting it.

Is that planned, or is it just the way it's worked out?

That's the way I feel. Violence is a reality to me. I mean, I've had my hands on these dead bodies, I've been to the murder trials, I've been to the crime scenes. I've seen people roll through doors who've had their lives viciously ripped from them. I have no use for the people who commit those kinds of acts. My sympathy is for the victims. That's why I'm very comfortable with Scarpetta because she is their defender. That's the way I feel. I couldn't do it any other way.

Scarpetta is very single-minded. She's on a crusade.

I'd say she and I both have lives consumed by what we do and what we believe. It's that I express mine in a different way than she does. She actually works the cases and I tell the story of the cases. I have said many times that what I really consider myself to be is a scribe to the people out there doing the real work, whether it is the forensic pathologists, the FBI agents, the police, the scientists, the prosecutors... Someone needs to tell their stories, go in their labs and find out exactly what they're doing today. 'Well, I'm using a gas chromatograph to do this...', or '...the scanning electron microscope to determine which element this is...' They need someone like me to do that, and that's really what I consider my job.

She is so driven or obsessive about her job that it seems, perhaps, sad that she has so little life outside her job.

It's not so much obsessive or driven as it is being devoted. For one to say that Scarpetta is obsessive or driven is like saying that a priest is. It's like a calling. She has taken on a mantle to help people who have no power. She's like a missionary, or a minister, or priest to the people who can no longer speak in a language that other people can understand. That's the way I regard what I do too.

People can also say the same thing about me. I'm divorced, I haven't remarried, I have no kids, you never read in the papers about me dating someone, and so on. It's not that I don't have a private life, or friends, and attachments - I think I have a very rich life in that way - but I deal with people in snatches. I can't have weeks on end with people I like unless I happen to be working with them. It's for the same reason. I'm not driven to be the number one crime writer in the world - it's not an ambition of mine - it's just that I'm devoted to what I'm doing as she is to what she's doing.

In the same way, I have to be as devoted to her so that I can tell her story and always learn the latest advances in technology or medicine that would be applicable to what she does so that I'm knowledgable enough to deal with it in a book. And that takes a lot of time.

Certainly, the temptation is to compare Patricia and Kay.

We're the same, but we're different. Certainly, some things are the same - how could they not be because they're coming out of me? So we probably share the same genetic code, by and large, but we're not exactly the same people. Maybe she's another manifestation of what I would be like if I did what she did for a living? Certainly, there are parallels.

I think it would be difficult to write about somebody like her if you didn't share some of the same qualities. Like, for example, a devotion to justice, integrity and decency, fighting for people who can't fight for themselves, trying to make the world a little better.

You can't fake that. You either feel it or you don't. I couldn't make you feel what she feels if I didn't feel it.

Reading Cruel And Unusual, The Body Farm and From Potter's Field, which read as a trilogy, there is a purely good figure, Kay, who knows about evil, and knows that pure evil is irredeemable and must be destroyed. With her are her friends and acquaintances, who leave Kay and

experience evil in some form. Having learnt about and been touched by evil, these friends are eventually redeemed. They return to the purely good figure and help fight the irredeemable evil figure, Temple Brooks Gault. This very much like heroic fiction. Are you aware of this?

I've never broken it down into the literary description you just gave me.

When I write it's kinda like keeping an eye on the ball when playing tennis. The commentators will define all these things going on - what just happened and why it happened. I never see that. I just keep my eye on the ball and play.

For each book, I come up with a case I want her to work and then I go through the pilgrimage with her, and I simply put things down pretty much the way I see them, and the way I know them from reality. In reality, of course, nobody is pure good and nobody is pure bad, but there are certainly good and evil people. Without a doubt Temple Brooks Gault is evil. That doesn't mean that he doesn't have good qualities. I don't know what they are and I don't care what they are, and I'm sure Kay doesn't care what they are either.

If you work in these professions, when people do things which are this heinous, you're not interested in their good qualities. You just want to figure out enough about them so that you can catch them, or at least give them a name so you can find them.

As far as Kay is concerned, she is not perfect, but she is purely good in terms of her integrity and morality where justice is concerned. She is having an affair with a married man, Benton Wesley - that's not moral. That's not even smart. She knows it too and she has trouble with it. She's not always done the right thing with Lucy, and she knows it. And Lucy knows it too. But Kay tries.

I think it's on the personal front that it's more difficult which, I think, is true for most of us. You will never catch me being dishonest in the business world or even in my profession, but sometimes I might be dishonest in my personal life because I don't say something I should say because it's too hard for me to say it. That's where Kay's weaker.

In those three books, as a matter of fact, I was trying very hard to get Kay to loosen up a little bit. I think you see that because she has more emotional situations on her hands.

So there was no design for the three books?

No. I start each one with a case and I never know where each will go. For instance, *The Body Farm* was a really hard book for me to write because I set it in my own childhood, in the foothills of western North Carolina. In a way, it was almost like killing off myself as a little girl, by putting myself imaginatively in that environment.

If you're a little girl with no power, like Emily Steiner was, buried beneath the cold earth and people don't know the truth about your death, who would you want to find out who did it? You'd want Scarpetta.

She can't make the child alive again, but she can make her talk. Kay can do something for the living, to make it easy for them to cope with this evil which has occurred - that's really what she does in each of her books.

Maybe we see it more and more in subsequent ones because it becomes more defined to me what her mission is. After all, just like you, I get to know her better each time. I know her a whole lot better now than I did in *Postmortem* and, I suspect, three years from now I will know her even better than I do now.

Whilst at the Chief Medical Examiner's Office, Patricia wrote three unpublished crime fiction books - full of poisonings, buried treasure and wills - in which Dr Kay Scarpetta was a minor character. One of the editors who rejected her advised her to write about what she knows, and to let Scarpetta take centre stage. Patricia was looking for a story for Scarpetta. Around that time, a serial killer was raping and strangling professional women in Richmond - Patricia was separated from her husband, living alone, frightened and bought her first gun for her own protection - and this became the kernel for Postmortem *(1990). The book became an immediate worldwide success, winning all five major mystery awards.*

Where does the character of Dr Kay Scarpetta come from?

I have a suspicion that - and this may sound bizarre - one of her genetic coils is from my own relationship with Ruth Graham when I was growing up. She is a very powerful woman, very beautiful and very, very kind. She has a heart of gold and is a compassionate person but, in her own way, is reserved. She was certainly a heroic character to me at a period of time in my life when I had no power, when I was very young. That's the sort of person you want to come save you when something bad happens.

When she was five, Patricia's parents broke up. Two years later she moved with her mother and two brothers to Montreat, a small town in North Carolina, just two miles from the home of evangelist Billy Graham. Growing up, she heard many stories about the kind things Billy's wife, Ruth, did. One Christmas, Patricia's mother had a nervous breakdown and tried to give her children to Ruth. Ruth got the children accommodation with local missionaries for three months, until Patricia's mother was well again. Later, Patricia became friends with Ruth, who became a sort of surrogate mother and a great influence on a troubled teenager with low self-esteem. Patricia was encouraged by Ruth to write short stories and poems. In 1981, after winning an award for her crime reporting at the Charlotte Observer, *Patricia had to leave to move with her husband to Richmond, Virginia, where he studied for the ministry. It was here, after much deliberation, that she wrote a biography of Ruth Bell Graham called* A Time For Remembering *(1983).*

I, and many others, still view Ruth Graham as a heroic person. It plugs into some horrible, tremendous need on your part to have that kind of figure in your life. That's where Lucy's relationship with Kay comes from. I'm not saying that Lucy is me but, being aware of that situation has allowed me to explore the character of a powerful person and their relationship with someone with potential and who needs them around. It's been a lot of fun to bounce ideas around and see how they develop.

Kay's niece, Lucy, has grown up in the books. She's had problems, the most prominent being a disastrous gay relationship in *The Body Farm*. Kay seems afraid to tell Lucy how she feels about things?

Yes, she does. It would be no fun to read if Scarpetta did it all right at the beginning because there would be no development. In *The Body Farm*, Kay finds it difficult to talk to Lucy about being gay. In *From Potter's Field*, she deals with it by being more open minded with Lucy's friend Janet, and in the way she responds to Marino when he makes a abusive remark about 'queers.' In *Cause Of Death*, Kay actually begins to have conversations with Lucy about her being gay. In the book, Lucy cannot spend Christmas with her lover, Janet, because Janet's parents don't know about them being a couple, so Lucy feels sorry for herself and starts drinking. Kay finds Lucy drunk, at which point Lucy tells Kay that she doesn't know what it feels like to be discriminated against. Kay responds angrily that she does know about it and smacks some sense into Lucy. Eventually, they get to talk about the situation. That's something Kay would not have done a couple of books ago. She's blossoming.

It's probably true of a lot of professional women, and it's probably true of me as well, where you go through this transition. First you start off open, like children, then you go through a period of hardship, tragedy and even abuse of one form or another. As a result, you tighten up, retreat into an activity like intellectualism, sports or art, where you can be as open as you like in that activity but you're closed as a human being. You stay that way for a while, achieving in that activity.

When I started the series I was surrounded by professional women in their fifties and sixties who were like old battleships. There was a stiffness about them. I imagined that if you hugged them they would crackle like paper.

You write about and are involved in very male worlds.

That's another reason why women close up. It's hard to go into those worlds and not start to pull an armour around yourself. That's what Kay did and that's what I had to do. I grew up with brothers. I grew up around boys. I played on the men's tennis team all through High School. I know what it's like to have boys try to hit you with tennis balls because they don't want you there. I never lost a match, so they hated me even more. I went into my own little cocoon to protect myself which is partly why I ended up marrying one of my English professors in college because this nice, older man felt very safe.

The point is that I understand these things. I think that women need to learn that you do what you have to do to protect yourself if you're making a difficult transition in a world that doesn't really want you. But then there comes a point where you have to have a reckoning with yourself - where you say 'I can still be soft, I can still let people know about my feelings, and I can be strong.' I think Scarpetta is beginning to demonstrate that she is stronger than she has ever been

PATRICIA CORNWELL

and that she is also softer.

I used to be more uptight than I am now. Each day, I was going down to the office and seeing these unbelievable things in the autopsy room. It does something to you. You put up all these walls because it's so unbearable and draining.

I wouldn't be able to attend an autopsy. I would see the bodies as people and think of their past lives and emotions. I would find that too upsetting.

That is why you would probably be a good forensic pathologist. That's exactly what the good ones do. They don't look on the body they're cutting as a thing - the bad ones do because it's easier to divorce themselves from their humanity. The dead won't talk to you if you don't know them as a person.

If you really want to hear what they have to say you have to believe in their humanity. Yes, it Is a sacrifice because it takes a lot out of you, but I think it takes more out of you not to do that because I think a part of you dies by degrees if you refuse to give a person their humanity. Even if they are dead.

I think one of the reasons that people stay with Scarpetta for 400 pages is because she does give people their humanity - she gives them names. She went through the whole of *From Potter's Field* determined to give the dead woman her name. When the man was beating his horse, she went up to him and asked him the horse's name and then asked him *'Do you beat Snow White every day, or just on Christmas Day?'* She always gives a name to the victim, whether it's a horse or a bald lady found in Central Park. That's what a good forensic pathologist will do. So you might be surprised at yourself. You might do better with it than you think.

I mean, it's not fun, but quite honestly the only way to endure some of the most difficult cases is if you give them their humanity. For example, one day I was with my friend Dr Marcella Fierro, who's now the chief medical examiner - she's one of the best forensic pathologists in the world, and I've been very lucky to have her as a mentor. We were going down to the morgue in the elevator and there was this horrible smell from a body we had found in the river. It had been there for several weeks in the middle of summer. I had smelt bodies before but this was the worst. It was really, really wretched. I was going down to help, to scribe the labels. I looked at Marcella and said that sometimes I really didn't know how she could stand this. She looked at me and said that she just tried to remember who he was.

And when you think of that, suddenly you no longer see this bloated, hideous corpse but a man wearing a hat, T-shirt, shorts and tennis shoes, and he's out on the river fishing with his son. I saw him for the rest of the morning and I was a good trouper and I did my job. If you cannot give that much humanity back to that person why in the world would you want to spend that much time with what's left with him?

So, oddly enough, to survive the experience you must embrace your feelings for the dead person not divorce yourself from them.

Patricia told me that the comment most people make to her in interviews is that her books are all about death.

My reply is that my books are all about life. What books have they been reading? Everything Scarpetta does is about living. She wants to prevent further death, to give peace of mind to the families, justice for the death. She does everything for the living. She is driven by her humanity, by her outrage over people who have taken power from others. It's not about death, but about death coming to the aid of the living. It's like the motto over the chief medical examiner's office in New York, which is true by the way, which says that you would find little conversation or laughter in this place where death delights to help the living.

Patricia has followed the first book with a Scarpetta book every year, each of which tops the bestseller charts. As a result of this success Patricia has become a multi-million dollar business, employing eight people to look after her interests, to allow her to spend fourteen or so hours a day writing. She has also become more careful, living in a guarded residential area - much like Scarpetta herself - and registering in hotels under aliases. Patricia receives more than her share of letters from weirdos, has been stalked, and has had police protection for some of her book signings.

Reading the books, the threat comes mostly from a member of the family. The killer is the mother, father, brother or sister.

It's very painful, but the statistics show that for the majority of homicides both the victim and perpetrator knew each other. Only a small percentage are random killers like Ted Bundy, who just pick up strangers at shopping malls. Those are the ones you hear about most, but they really don't happen all that often. The most pervasive homicides are the husband killing the wife, the father or mother killing the child, a child killing another child, a friend killing a friend.

I have found in my own life - I have security concerns obviously because of the way things have gone - that almost every infraction committed against me or my company has always been by someone I know. It's the way it works. The person who steals from me is someone I know. The person who lies about me is someone I know. Even people who get obsessions end up being someone you've had contact with. But we don't like to think about it because the fabric of our existence feels quite threatened. We like to think we are safe with the people around us. All I can say is pick wisely.

Betrayal is a common theme in the books.

I doubt there isn't a person out there who hasn't been betrayed in one way or another. It's as common as weeds. I have to deal with it too. People betray me all the time. Especially being an employer now. It's tough because people get close to you then they try to blackmail you, they lie about you. They do all sorts of things to get money off you.

Really!?

Oh absolutely. You can't believe that this is happening to you when you have been nothing but kind to them. They see it as an opportunity to take advantage.

PATRICIA CORNWELL

This is not uncommon.

I think that if there is a moral lesson in my books, one could dwell on what a dark world it seems, but I would prefer to dwell on the light that goes through it. I think the challenge for any of us is to live in a world that isn't very nice and not let it drag you down regardless of the betrayals, the cruelty and the violence. Basically, Scarpetta, Lucy, Marino, and Benton Wesley may have their moments, but they pretty much keep sailing in a straight line.

This is what I was trying to explain earlier about heroic fiction. Each character is touched by evil, but they return to the heroic quest for good.

I don't dispute that. Each of the characters have their spills - Marino with the widow in *The Body Farm*, Lucy with the drink and so on - but they all come back to Scarpetta. Ultimately, she is the healer.

I guess that is the ironical thing that, even though her patients are dead, I think that above and beyond all else, I would say that Scarpetta is the healer. She heals these people, but they also make her life brighter too.

Psychokller ...Qu'est-Ce Que C'est?

THE 'KILLER ON THE LOOSE' book runs from Mary Roberts Rhinehart's *The Bat*, to films like *Dirty Harry*, and the oeuvre of Thomas Harris. Grisly crimes are committed by deranged person. Investigator investigates. More crimes. Investigator closes in. Investigator imperilled. Investigator triumphant.

There is a surge in the popularity of the serial killer novel. Structurally it's a fusion of the 'killer on the loose' sub-genre with the 'sequence crime' type of novel in which a series of crimes has, or appears to have a pattern - *The ABC Murders, There Was An Old Lady...* etc. Serial killer novels also use a series of crimes to set up a puzzle, but give us the additional frisson that has historically been provided by other forms of literature such as the horror novel. The serial killer, like the monstrous protagonist of horror fiction, has a motivation that is societally incomprehensible, being neither financial nor personal, and the serial killer is often portrayed as 'different' and 'inhuman'. We prefer to see the actions of the serial killer as different from our own, as opposed to an extreme version of activities we participate in, and opinions we hold. The actions of the killer/monster attack the accepted morality of the society within which they operate. This invites us to consider a world where the mores of white, middle class society have been disregarded in favour of a totally individualist, self-referential and unempathic world view. Most serial killers would sympathise with Margaret Thatcher's oft quoted *'there is no such thing as society'.*

The purpose of the heroes of these novels is to ensure normal service is resumed as soon as possible. Having taken a voyeuristic peek at chaos, we are pulled back from the brink. Most heroes are male - policemen, psychologists, profilers - white and middle class.

Patricia Cornwell's Kay Scarpetta novels are a variation on this theme. Scarpetta is the chief medical examiner of Richmond, Virginia, a woman in a man's world, doing an unpleasant job. Her position is representative of white middle class America, but as a woman she receives closer scrutiny than a man in the same position might. She combines elements of both the 'insider' hero and the 'outsider' villain of serial killer and horror novels.

Scarpetta is introduced to us in *Postmortem* (1990). The book's plot - about a psychopathic killer - is gripping but standard, her treatment of the characters is not. Her relationships with her friends and associates, cop Pete Marino, FBI man Mark Thomas, FBI profiler Benton Wesley, and her niece Lucy are well realised and convincing, and in the seven books that include *Postmortem* have evolved in many ways. *Postmortem* has a good puzzle, and an innovative perspective (the 'woman in peril' is also the hero) that would explain Cornwell's best-seller status in novelty terms.

By the time of *Body Of Evidence* (1991) her interest in the lives of her characters and their vulnerability begins to mark her out as an author to watch. The plot of *Body Of Evidence* is the most confused of the six, due to the attempt to shoehorn a love interest into Scarpetta's life. Unusually the violence is motivated, not by lust but by a more direct motive. *All That Remains* (1992) is a return to form, and the themes of betrayal and loss that have increasingly come to the fore in the previous two novels break surface with a vengeance. Everyone except Marino seems to be hiding something from Scarpetta, and even Abby, the sister of one of the victims from *Postmortem* is manipulating Scarpetta for her own ends.

The first three books have a strangely hazy quality in retrospect. Scarpetta and the cast are well realised, the villains less so. In this Cornwell demonstrates the differences between herself and the run-of-the-mill Thomas Harris impersonators whose novels litter the bookstands. They fail to understand that the attraction of Harris 's central character Hannibal Lecter is that he is educated and intelligent enough to perceive the problems his pyschopathology presents. Like Austin Nunne, the serial killer in Colin Wilson's *Ritual In The Dark*, his character is born out of a serious wish on the author's part to explore the nature of such men. In lesser hands the veneer of intelligence is used clumsily and the brilliant individual who is also a serial killer becomes the 'brilliant serial killer'. In real life serial killers are generally understimulated individuals who require bigger and bigger thrills to keep them interested in life, and tend to be dull individuals like Ted Bundy or the Wests. Cornwell's killers lack characterisation, because she is concerned not with an understanding of the killer's psychology, or the use of the killer as a Dracula substitute, but with the effects of evil on ordinary people.

From *Cruel And Unusual* (1993) onwards Cornwell dispenses with many of the

PATRICIA CORNWELL

traditions of this kind of book and is as much interested in the moral dimension of serial killings as in the puzzle aspect. Evil for her is a real and tangible thing, an almost physical contagion - the killers are corrupt, and will corrupt others. The question is: how far towards the nature of the killer can pursuit of them take you before you are touched by corruption? Her characters are tested, and occasionally fail, but it is Scarpetta's moral sense, and its testing, her rejection of moral pragmatism that is the centre of the novels.

Despite what might be considered a fundamentalist notion of justice, Cornwell deals with personal matters of choice in an adult, sensible and unhysterical manner. Adultery and sexuality are matters for the individual - the moral choice she is interested in affects society - the general rather than the particular. In this area she seems to stand for a libertarian view of mankind - what affects ourselves is our business, what affects others is everybody's.

In *Cruel and Unusual*, *The Body Farm* (1994) and *From Potters Field* (1995), Cornwell provides us with a central plot thread in the person of psychopath, killer and madman around town Temple Brooks Gault. Gault is, as Benton Wesley says in *Cruel and Unusual*, 'off the charts', not conforming to any of the standard profiles for a psychopath. Throughout the trilogy, changes to and expansion of Scarpetta's 'family' - Benton Wesley, Pete Marino, her niece Lucy - are as important to the reader as the main plot, and although this may sound like soap opera, in fact it has more of the characteristics of heroic fiction. Unusually in American fiction there is little of the 'cowboy factor' - the overriding concern for the individual - in Scarpetta. She is motivated as much for the general good as out of a specific sense of injury. In the course of the trilogy both Lucy and Marino will be compromised for personal reasons, but will be redeemed in a sequence structurally reminiscent of heroic fantasy. All three books concern Temple Brooks Gault, but the first two are skirmishes in which he is hardly glimpsed - only his actions, and his effect on others, are seen. The crimes investigated parallel to the Gault case seem almost to be outpourings of evil from the poisoned well of his soul. The strong moral tone that has always pervaded Cornwell's books is strengthened to a high degree through the trilogy. As Scarpetta and her band progress towards Gault we are reminded of similar journeys to Mordor, or Green Angel Tower, to face evil at its source.

In *Cruel and Unusual* Scarpetta and Marino are confronted by the possibility that a recently executed prisoner is in fact alive and committing a series of grotesque murders that extend to Scarpetta's own staff at the Medical Examiner's Office. Scarpetta is compromised personally and professionally in the media circus that follows and is suspended from her job, under heavy pressure to resign, and ends up in front of a Grand Jury investigation into whether or not she could be the murderer.

Technically the solution to these crimes and Scarpetta's vindication provide the main thrust of the novel, but there are two other strains that command our attention. From early on in the book we detect a hidden hand behind events, and at the denouement the murderer escapes. This robs us of the catharsis which is the stock in trade of the 'killer on the loose' novel and instead Scarpetta's vindication and her personal growth become the 'reward' at the end of the book. Scarpetta begins to understand the damage that her lover Mark's death has inflicted upon her life, and realises that she can be mistaken, as she has a rapprochement with her hated law school professor who ends the book as her attorney.

In *The Body Farm*, a killing with strong resemblances to the murders in *Cruel and Unusual* draws Scarpetta, Benton Wesley and Pete Marino into a case that will exacerbate both the divisions and attractions between the trio, with near fatal consequences in Marino's case. His (unstated) love for Scarpetta, and his feelings of rejection lead him into the arms of the victim's mother, with horrifying consequences. Scarpetta's niece Lucy has a larger role, having joined the FBI to develop CAIN, their offender profiling and tracking system, and her fall from grace is swift.

In *From Potter's Field*, with differences plastered over if not healed, the protagonists begin the final hunt for Temple Brooks Gault - a confrontation that will end in a terrifying game of cat and mouse in the New York Subway systems. Typically for Cornwell the mystery of Gault is not 'solved' in any meaningful sense; some of his past is recounted, but at the end Gault remains an enigma, as at the end of *Lord Of The Rings*, Sauron's evil cannot be explained by a bad childhood.

In her latest book *Cause Of Death* (1996), the plot is almost invisible. It bubbles, fairly satisfactorily beneath the surface, and shows that Cornwell is not prepared to stay in the 'writes well about psychokillers' ghetto. In common with the thrust of her last few books *Cause of Death* is a meditation on the nature of evil, and its effects on those who deal with it. The emotional temperature of Scarpetta's extended family in the aftermath of their 'war' against Temple Brooks Gault is the concern for much of the book, the tone melancholy, as if what they've seen distances the characters from ordinary life. Scarpetta shows an increasing pragmatism - when was the last time you remember the heroine being threatened and *having the sense to leg it?* - and finally addresses directly the issue of Lucy's homosexuality. The book contains some of Cornwell's most definite statements on the nature of evil:

"'These people are consorting with evil,' I said. 'And I respect that there is evil in the world and it is not to be taken lightly.'"

Exactly.

As much as James Ellroy wants us to find ourselves in the shoes of the monsters that inhabit his books and recognise our common lineage, Cornwell wants us to admit that some acts are beyond understanding and to reject their authors comprehensively. Who is right is another argument, but the debate is fascinating.

PDP

Derek Raymond

LONDON. SUNDAY, 23RD MAY 1993. *It was a gloriously sunny afternoon. I walked up Charing Cross Road, where secondhand bookshops proudly presented the latest expensive bargains, slightly foxed. Through Chinatown. Exotic fragrances wafted from all-day grocers. Dissent was also in the air - teenagers handed out militant newspapers typeset in Cantonese. Into the heart of London's Soho. The porn and peep shows were open for business as usual, all appetites catered. I was chafing at the bit, hungry for information, ready to devour every word uttered by that master of the Black Novel: Robin Cook. Who?*

In France, he is a revered writer, having received the Chevalier des Arts et des Lettres. His books have been adapted for French TV. The French police even offered him Georges Simenon's old room. At the time of our meeting, he had just come back from Niemes in the South of France where, for three months, he'd been running a two days a week course on his life and work. 40 students on the course. His first day, he stands up and says that it'd be much nicer if they retired to the bar and discussed his work there.

In England, mention Robin Cook, and people either think of some politician, or a writer of medical thrillers. This is why Robin has adopted the name Derek Raymond, after two late friends of his, for his recent series of Factory novels. Factory is what both fuzz and villains call a police station. In this case, the factory is in Poland Street, and the central character is a nameless detective working for Unexplained Deaths.

The detective, haunted by an insane wife who killed their child, is a moral man who wants to right the wrongs he sees. To him, being a policeman is a vocation, not a job. He ignores the conventions of policing and police procedurals, by investigating the emotions and backgrounds of the victims, both living and dead. He allows himself to feel for them, to be hurt by what happens to them. Raymond allows us to share these emotions through the use of tapes/diaries of the victims in He Died With His Eyes Open and I Was Dora Suarez. In the end, the Detective is so overwhelmed by the injustice of the world, that he takes the law into his own hands.

These are not nice or entertaining novels in the traditional sense. They incite you to feel things you'd rather forget. They put pictures into your mind that you'd rather not see. It's a vaccine. The intention is to give you a little pain, so that you learn from it. Perhaps, then, you can avoid/understand pain in the future, perhaps suffer a little less.

It is a physical, emotional, practical fiction, about the weak, sweet people - the flowers of our society who get trampled on. It is not a fiction of puzzles and abstract ideas. The people breathe, eat and shit. When they swear they say 'fuck,' not 'damn,' or 'oh my.' Of course, different people react in different ways, but to deny the obscene in the world is, in itself, an obscene act.

He Lived With His Eyes Open

So, I walk into the Coach & Horses on Greek Street, in the heart of Soho (assuming it's got one) and immediately see Robin at the bar. He's tall and very thin, gaunt, white faced. Like an older version of Munch's The Scream, but wearing a beret. He's very sociable, chatty. Playful, even. Talks with an upper class Etonian accent, but uses words an Etonian wouldn't. So, with the first Castlemaine 4X in front of Robin and a Gitane between his lips, and me with an orange juice, we decide to start talking for the tape.

I've got questions for you.

I thought you probably might have.

Being as it's an interview.

That's what I'm here for.

So, to you, what is and isn't a black novel?

It's really focused on a certain sector of society. Or, if you like, a certain sector of the human psyche, under certain kinds of social pressure. That's what I really mean by it. The results are bound to be black. You can see the kind of things I mean all over the place. People tend to pretend it doesn't exist, and I insist that it does. It's black because it's so depressing. It's black in the way that Emile Zola's novels are black.

Because they're about real life.

I think so. I try to make mine as realistic as I can. There are very, very few good writers who have never written anything black. You can pick any world-class writer and he's done something black. Shakespeare did Hamlet, King Lear. I don't believe in writers who just write cheerful, romantic, Mills & Boon books.

That's escapism. That's a completely different form of book.

Indeed. I'm not remotely interested in reading or writing that sort of book.

You never feel you need cheering up then?

No. I'm a remarkably cheerful person, as a matter of fact. Philosophical. Yeah. Until I get on a typewriter - then my mood changes.

Robin is a man with a history. A criminal history. You can read about a lot of it in his autobiography, The Hidden Files. Basically, he fronted a few dummy companies for well-known London gangsters. Eventually, there was a murder, had to say goodbye to England for a few years. So he knows what he's talking about.

You can't really write the kind of books I write unless you're at least partly bent. It's very important, that, because if you're not, you can't really ascribe to the villain his true value, or his lack of value. You've got to really mix in that world.

You stress this a lot in The Hidden Files.

I'm glad. It's a point well worth making.

Not everyone has access to that world.

Indeed. So they shouldn't be writing that kind of book. But they do. That's a mistake. They should be writing other kinds of books, I think.

There are people I know who have the capacity to be bent, but they're not.

I'm not saying that you have to be a psycho, but that you have to live in a bent sort of way and appreciate bent people, villains. I've been programmed to be the sort of person who can get into the bent world and get back out again, if I'm fucking lucky and don't get my head kicked in. I'm a novelist, and not a petty thief or something, because I can get back out again. All the research in the world won't replace experience. Can't.

Were there times when you were in danger?

Oh certainly. Very much so. I was in danger of losing my liberty for quite some considerable time. Need nerves of steel. Wouldn't do it again now. Too slow on the draw. I'll be 62 next month.

I read your first novel *The Crust On Its Uppers*, which features some wideboy characters.

That's right.

That's all about the villains as heroes, glorifying them. Whereas the Factory novels concentrate on the victims. It's almost as if you're paying back...

...for all the terrible things that I've done.

Do you feel that way?

... Yes. I think I do...I think I do. I think it's the difference between being 30 when I wrote *Crust*, and being 50 when I wrote *He Died With His Eyes Open*. In the intervening 20 years, you change your way of looking at things. It's increased experience. And growing older. Yep. You think *'hello, time's running out here'* and your viewpoint changes.

Were you irresponsible when you were younger?

I was very responsible to myself. I wasn't irresponsible - I was much more anarchic. It's very easy to get confused between those two, but they are different. Being anarchic is to explode, to get rid of what's bothering you. I said I didn't like any of this, so I just wanted to kill it.

I have a penetrating mind in a way, I suppose, because I cut through all the shit, as best I can, I suppose in a quasi-surgical way, and understand what is going on. Why are the wankers running this place and not us? There is nothing irresponsible about that. I call that healthy opposition, in a literary sense.

A couple of young women sit down next to us. Attractive. We look at them as we talk. Distracted. They chat on, occasionally embarrassed as the meaning of some of our words sink in.

The opening chapter of I Was Dora Suarez, *the fourth Factory novel, has a horrific description of a murder. In fact, when Robin submitted it, the editor got sick all over the manuscript. 'He made a frightful mess of it, actually.' He changed publishers.*

***I Was Dora Suarez* was very shocking.**

It was meant to be for Christ's sake. There's nothing pretty about murder.

I talked to some people about the book. They said they thought you just put in some of the scenes to shock. They thought it was obscene.

It is obscene. If you'd been at the scene of a murder that's the one word you'd use to describe it. You'd say it was obscene. It's reality. It's true, fuck it. I don't know why people think I shouldn't write this sort of stuff. It happens all the time. Just pick up a newspaper. I think it's obscene, so I bloody well say so.

Forgive me for getting hot under the collar.

People just deny that these sort of things go on.

Everything in the book is true. It's based on three different cases. What the killer does to his private parts happened. The stuff about the rats going up people's arseholes is true. It's obscene. It's true. That's all I've got to say to people who criticise on that level.

In *The Hidden Files*, I talked about people who like to read books about murders that are all prettied up. Hercule Poirot and all that...

The Laura Ashley school of crime writing.

Thank you. That's why I don't like novels by P D James and all that, either. The Americans have no such inhibitions. That's why they do the books so much better than we do. We have exactly the same material to work with, but we just end up with polite stains in the carpet.

I think the modern Americans writers generally write to shock.

I don't think so. *Homeboy* by Seth Morgan. This guy had done it all: hooking pussy; petty villainy; a life in jail. And it shows. It's shocking because the contents are shocking, not because he's written it in a particularly sensationalistic way. I mean, if I shot you now, it would be a sensational event. Your brains'd end up over the window. The top of your head all over the place. Running down the walls.

You paint such a pretty picture.

That's what happens when someone pulls the trigger of a 9mm at point blank range.

I had a gun pulled on me once. A little black hole staring at me. The psycho holding it said it wouldn't hurt. I wouldn't feel a thing. *'Not unless he misses,'* I thought. That's black, isn't it? Not exactly Mickey Mouse, is it?

But who's going to read about all this blood and violence?

An awful lot of people, actually. Not the middle classes, though, with rare exceptions. Let's face it: who wants to read a middle class crime novel, particularly? It's written by a middle class writer, living somewhere nice in Hampstead, who gets up every morning, has breakfast, then goes into his study to work, locked up in his ivory tower, before going out to his club. Never gets out. Never sees the world. That's not literature, that's hyped up pap. That's a blanket statement and not always true, but it's about 90% true for British and European writers. It's different in America.

Do you think so? I think there are Black Writers from the Fifties - Jim Thompson, David Goodis - but are there any writing now?

Certainly James Ellroy's early novels: *Blood On The Moon; Suicide Hill; Silent Terror; Brown's Requiem*. That's a good backlog. He knows what it's like. As a kid, came back home from a weekend at his father's to find his mother dead. That shook him up quite a lot, to put it mildly.

Do you see Black Novels as working class novels, or for the working class?

No. I see them as human novels. To me, the elements of human nature I described earlier are present in everybody, irrespective of social barriers.

Robin tells me about the time he was crossing the road in Soho, walked between two cars, over a bundle of rags, realised it was a dead man. It was so offhand. The dead man was so inconspicuous. It reminded me of Staniland, the man found dead at the beginning of He Died With His Eyes Open, *the first Factory novel. The young women sitting beside us look at their watches, shoulder their bags, and move on.*

I thought Staniland was more alive than any of the other characters in *He Died With His Eyes Open*.

Exactly.

The victim is usually an embarrassing stain on the floor.

I hate to see victims. I'm always on the side of the victim. Always. They piss on the little man, and I don't like that. Even if it's the little man's own fault. Still doesn't sit with me any better.

Reading Staniland's taped monologues in the book, I thought that Staniland was you.

They all are. All my characters are me. You can't separate the little blighters from me. Unless, you're writing documentary stuff - that's different. As soon as you're writing fiction... Fiction. I don't quite know what that word means. If you define it as invention, there's very little invention that goes into my books really. It's mostly concentration and transposition.

Fiction is the spirit of reality. It's trying to explain reality in a different way.

Indeed. That seems to be the purpose of novels, really. Not many of the novels I've read come up to that standard, but there you go...

Do you see yourself as a victim?

I have done. I don't any more, but I can transform myself, think of myself as a victim, in a flash. They both exist in me - the dominating individual, and the submissive one.

Do you recognise good and evil in yourself?

Certainly I do. Both sharply present. The evil usually outweighs the good, but it's too idle to do anything about it. But not on a typewriter. When you're writing, you forget yourself entirely. You transpose yourself into another situation, so you, as an individual, cease to count as far as the writing is concerned, and you become the person you are from the characters you create. I probably haven't explained that very well, have I?

I've done a little bit a writing, not much, but I've become afraid at certain points.

That's a good sign. Excellent. If it frightens you, go for it. If you don't take a risk, you won't get anywhere.

Do you feel more alive when you're writing?

Ah. Yes, I think I do. It's like a day at the races. It's more like the characters are alive in me, and I just let them run, let them do what they like. There's no point in having a dog and barking yourself - let them do the bloody work.

But they're you anyway.

As far as I'm the one wielding the typewriter, yes. But beyond that I'm not at all sure about that. You reach a misty point where you're not sure you're you, somebody else, or a lot of people all at the same time. All I can say is that it takes me a long time to come back to myself after I finish one of these books, a long time. It took me eighteen months to get over *I Was Dora Suarez*. Some people say I still haven't. It almost killed me, the bastard. Glad I did it though.

Do you learn anything about yourself?

Can't help it. 'Course, you forget it immediately. If you didn't, you'd go mad. That's just nature, that is. It's like women having babies. They think *'God, that was absolute hell.'* Then before you can say knife, they're all ready to have another one.

It's always been in your subconscious. It's just a matter of bringing it out. Once it's out, most people just let it slide. They'd rather not know. It takes an idiot like me to tell them *'No. No. This is the way it is.'* But you end up wishing you fucking hadn't.

Two young men enter, shake hands, sit down, with their own drinks. They met Derek before in a pub, or at a party. 'Sorry. We're interrupting,' *says Mark, thin, bleary-eyed. Was he on something, or just tired?* 'No, it's okay.' *Get talking, like you do. Turns out he lives nearby, grotty little room, overlooks an alleyway and yard.* 'We don't use the yard at night. The local villains use it. Get whoever. Give 'em a going over. Most nights. It's not nice. Nobody says anything.'

Steve, Mark's friend, stocky. 'I've got a job on today. Painting a butcher's. Should 'ave done it last week but I pissed off early. Need some white spirits. Do you think they'll have some here?' *Steve staggers to his feet and walks up to the bar, uphill all the way. Waits around, under a sign saying Wines & Spirits. We're watching him. Comes back empty handed.* 'They don't have any.'

Mark tells me about his dad. 'You know Jack Hawkins, the actor?' *I remembered him in* The Bridge On The River Kwai. *He was dubbed by someone else - Anthony Hopkins I think, or was it Richard Burton?* 'That's right. He had throat cancer. Had a hole in his throat. Learnt how to speak by burping. He taught the man who taught my dad how to do it. My dad never told me he had cancer. Wouldn't talk about it. Me and my sisters weren't supposed to know about it, but we knew something was wrong. I asked my mum and she told me. Every time I went home to visit, he'd act as if nothing was wrong. Had to ask my mum about him, to see how he was. He was too proud. Couldn't admit there was anything wrong with him. He was a miner.'

Steve said he'd get the drinks in. 'Give us some money, Mark - I haven't got enough.' *He stumbled up to the bar again, came back empty.* 'They've closed.' *It wasn't Steve's day.*

We nursed our drinks. There were a lot of police about. 'There's a gay event up the road, but no-one's turned up except the police. There's three or four people dancing to a DJ, and three or four hundred police watching them.' *He talked about AIDS, about the number of people who still think it's a gay disease. Then he spurted out:* 'I'm not gay, you know! I've got a girlfriend!' *He gave me an invite to Disco Scum -* 'A scandalous evening of sleazy glamour' *it says - and they left.*

I hope I've explained the black novel to your satisfaction. If not, keep on asking me until you get enough. Keep corkscrewing away. I like people asking me difficult questions, especially on a Sunday morning.

It's afternoon.

Not if you didn't get to bed until twenty to five like me. I always work at night. I find it easier. No interruptions, no disturbances. I can just get on with it. Then I sleep during the day, when I can.

Don't you get lonely working like that?

I feel lonely sometimes, but then I expect to - the way I live. I take it into account. You've got to. If you succumbed to loneliness then you wouldn't be able to do the work anyhow, because you have to do the work on your own. That's the kind of demand writing makes on you. Anyway, I'm not very family minded. I'm not a kids and carpet slippers sort of person - it doesn't fit me. That's why I've been married so often *[five times - he refers to them by their number]* and all my relationships have been run into the sand.

Some of your early books were satires. Those books remind me of a cross between absurd writers like Franz Kafka and Gerald Kersh...

Gerald Kersh! *Clean, Bright And Slightly Oiled? They Died With Their Boots Clean?* Excellent! Much underrated. Very seriously good writer that man.

Then why aren't his books in print?

Because he upset too many people. Definitely. He wrote mostly in the late Forties. Another good writer is Julian Maclaren-Ross. Wrote *Memoirs Of The Forties*, about Soho around the war. Out of print now. I came onto the Soho scene in 1951, when I came out of the army. I continued on from where he left off. You've got to read that book. The problem is getting hold of a copy. He's dead as well. Dreadful pisspot. Used to sit in a club I used to go to called The Canvas Arms in Dean Street. I'm going back to the Sixties now. Black floppy hat, big black coat, and a huge black cane with a silver knob on. Tongue like a whiplash. Didn't want to get anywhere near him. Particularly if you said *'you silly old poofter, what are you wearing that gear for?'* Whoever it was'd end up all over the floor, cut to ribbons by his tongue. Never had a pot to piss in. Always on the sauce.

You've got a reputation for the drink, haven't you?

My detractors say I'm an alcoholic, but that's quite untrue. Otherwise I'd be

DEREK RAYMOND

dead years ago, I should think. I certainly like a drink - I don't believe in writers who don't, actually. I don't mean to help write, but to learn anything. If you sit down with an orange juice in front of you, you can't really expect to learn anything exciting. I can't see it, really.

There I am, with an orange juice in front of me, thinking, 'I've done okay so far...'

It's that's old joke of waking up and not knowing where you are. Of course, you've got to be disciplined as well. When you wake up in a strange place like that, you don't have a pen and paper handy, so you've got to remember it all. Keep it locked up in here *[pointing at head]* until you get to a typewriter. So, even though I've got a rotten memory in some ways, I've got a very good one in others. Get back. Think. Head down. Write it word for word. It's the only way.

Would you still write, even if you couldn't get published?

'Course I would. In fact, it took me an awful long time before I did get published. I wrote eight or nine novels before my first one got published when I was 30. It was still difficult to sell my books after that. That's why I went abroad to sell myself. I'm 62, and spent about 30 years outside England.

Another thing I should say is that I don't write for money. That's a major point, that. I create markets, I don't pursue them. If I make money, then that's not bad. If I don't...then I'll still survive. I hate possessions. Mortgages, things like that. I just have the essentials - fire, table and chair, computer to write on, bed. As long as I have money to buy the next round, I'm okay. That gives me the freedom to write what I want, with no-one to pressure me, except myself. I refuse to be crammed into a category.

I'm not writing to get a good review in the Sunday Times, or to win the Booker prize, or the Golden Dagger award. In fact, if I had a machine gun, I'd mow down the whole blue rinse set. I write for myself, in the hope that there is one person out there who understands what I'm on about.

Why do people write books? The error has crept in that the reason is to tell a story, whereas anyone who has ever read real literature knows perfectly well that the reason is also to try as well as the author can to tell the truth.

Do you get emotional when you write?

'Course I do. Good God, yes. In the heat of it, I don't think about it at all. Just get it down. Clean it up afterwards.

I always know the beginning and the end, know the characters, and what it's about. I sometimes get secondary characters that I like, and I let them run because they're interesting. If they go off the plot, then I have to get them back on it.

Is the plot more important or the people?

People. The plot is just what people do. If you stick rigidly to a plot, then you're back to whodunits, which is the last thing I want.

Your plots are very simple, and it's all just people meeting, their interaction, and learning about them that way.

That's all I set out to do. The plot is just a frame.

It's not written as a crime book.

No. They're not thrillers. I just write them from beginning to end, Paul. Cut out the dull bits and leave the rest.

You mention God and the Devil quite a lot in *The Hidden Files*. I wondered if you had any leanings in that direction?

Didn't I make it clear?

I thought I'd ask, for the interview.

Well, I don't believe in them. I certainly believe in good and evil, but God and the Devil are just icons.

Are people a mixture of good and evil? Can there be a purely good person? Purely bad?

You can't generalise about this sort of thing. I can think of several killers I've met who haven't got anything but evil in them at all. They pretend to be good, but that's just fake. 95% of them is thoroughly evil, with everything that that entails. On the other hand, you have a handful of people like Mahatma Ghandi and Mother Theresa who are the reverse. The good people are getting thinner on the ground, whilst there are more and more bad.

Why is that?

Social conditions. Without a doubt. I don't know whether you've read a psychiatrist called Melanie Klein, who wrote *The Behaviour Of Children*. That's very interesting. It's too long to go into any detail, but basically she says that a child's character is formed for life by its experiences up until the age of four - five at the latest. After that, there's no more to be done. Bop. Set. Programmed. You can jump up and down until you're blue in the face but you can't change that person's character at all. Cowardice. Heroism. Multiple killers. Saints. Everything. I'm not insisting on it, but that's the theory I subscribe to.

You're saying there that people can't change and develop themselves.

No. I don't think so. Not significantly. No.

So even if someone feels something, and they know it's wrong intellectually, they can't change themselves, stop themselves?

No. The intellect, logic, is only a tool. The motivation, that's the emotions. The intellect just turns emotions into a plan, to achieve the results your emotions want, whether it's raising a loan or killing a few people. Whatever. Starting a church. Get a few punters interested. Nice bit of pony. Long serving.

That racket's been going on a while.

Couple of thousand years that we know of.

Notice how they don't like all these new guys coming onto their patch, taking their punters.

No. And look at how it ends up. Just look at Waco, Texas. Good God, that went up the spout in a massive way. Didn't surprise me at all.

A friend of mine had a large collection of True Crime books, then

picked up one about a victim. He realised that all the True Crime books glorified the killers and psychopaths, and ignored the people whose lives they ruined. He got rid of all his True Crime books.

I like the way your Factory series concentrates on the victims of crime.

Indeed. One or more people have to die to satisfy one person's egocentricity. I can't see any justification for that at all.

There seems to be a cult of the serial killer...

As soon as you have a cult of any kind, you've got an assortment of idiots.

Why are you so fascinated with crime?

Probably because I've been involved in it. Like madness, it interests me because I want to know why it is there, why it is present in society. I always look at the social reasons first. Most writers write about the haves and the have-nots, and the reasons for it. I think Dickens would find 1993 Britain a very familiar place, I should think. Thanks to this government we're leaving the 1990s and going back to the 1820s. We'll be going back to the 1770s soon if we carry on with this regressive government. I was coming in past Brixton this morning and you should have seen the people - crammed in like rats. If you're going to cram people in like rats, they're going to act like them.

Of course, London is a totally different experience to Paris, for example. In Paris, they push all the have-nots out to the suburbs, to keep the centre clean for the rich and the tourists. Don't want any of that rubbish here. I saw a marvellous bit of graffiti when I was driving through Paris. It read: You're driving us out to the suburbs - the suburbs surround you. I thought *'Very good. Sharp.'*

It's much more unpredictable in London. Though absolute hell to live in, of course. Much more interesting to observe. I've got the chameleon-like ability to blend in with the crowd. I don't just observe. That would be terrible. That wouldn't do at all.

We finish our drinks. Robin suggests Kettner's. Just round the corner. Posh tea-rooms fallen on hard times. Or perhaps our standards are higher now. Not as high as Kettner's prices though. Robin pegs the waitress as Polish. Polish-Italian, she tells us, but still a nice accent.

I read an enormous amount when I was young. I told myself to read everything then because I wouldn't have time when I got older - and I turned out to be dead right.

Having got all my grounding in language, and the way it's used in books, now I tend to do all my observation directly, from personal experience, from listening to people.

So who are your models?

I've always been heavily influenced by French literature: Camus, Sartre. Then there's Dostoyevsky, Kafka. The sort of people you'd normally consider as role models. When I started writing, I wrote ordinary novels, satirical, about people. I didn't write crime novels until I was about 50 because I'd read Chandler and thought he'd done it all.

In *The Hidden Files*, you mention some pulp writers, like Jim Thompson and David Goodis, but you don't seem to give them much of a look-in, as though you didn't think much of them.

I think a hell of a lot of them, but I didn't have the room to go into all that. I'd have never of finished. It was an enormous wodge as it was. It would need a volume two to get all that in. In fact, someone has proposed it, but I can't see myself getting around to it in the near future. It's good - it's better to have too much work than too little.

I'm not a well-read person, particularly not in crime fiction, because I can't write and read. If I read anything, it gets into whatever I'm writing, you see? That's just me. I love reading, but I never have the time. However, I read an occasional manuscript for publishers. I've just read what I think is a seriously good, Black Novel - *Dirty Weekend* by Helen Zahavi. Have you read it?

No.

I whacked that out in one. She really did her homework. She must have got seriously close to psychopaths.

Do you feel like an outsider, as though you're apart from everybody?

Certainly not. Except when I'm looking at people, yes. I often jump on the bus and go wherever it takes me, pop into the nearest pub. I don't know anyone, so I'm an outsider there, but only because I've done it deliberately. I'm a very gregarious person - except when I'm not. Like when I'm writing - I don't want to see anyone then. That's why all my relationships collapsed. *'Not now'* I'd say, *'It'll have to wait. It'll have to wait until tomorrow because I've got this writing to do.'* Of course, the other person gets fed up with this, understandably. Sorry about that. It has to be done that way, because otherwise I'd get nothing done at all. I've got a terribly one-tracked mind. I just go for it.

Robin carries on talking about the things he loves most. He's fascinated by war authors, which is why he's so familiar with Gerald Kersh, and adores the poetry of Wilfred Owen. 'There has to be poetry in a book before it is any good. You must love poetry.' His beliefs are absolute. Just as you can't write a book unless you experience things first hand, Robin insists that psycho killers are bores, without imagination.

You can't have a killer with a sense of humour. They're boring people. Egotists. Humourless. You're on the wrong track there, I'm afraid. Though there is a horribly funny side to murder, as a matter of fact - as long as it isn't your own - because, apart from Jack The Ripper, I have never heard of a killer with a single spark of humour. I've spent much of my life studying bores, and I've come to the conclusion that the bore bears a close relationship with the assassin. Study of the first forms a base for the study of the second. I don't see how any examination of the Black Novel could be complete unless the telltale dullness of the killer and the bore were not considered side by side. The bore and the killer are both engaged in the

DEREK RAYMOND

blind pursuit of power - power is the best shield that the disordered personality can conceive against being revealed as the laughing stock that he secretly suspects himself to be. The greatest danger the bore represents is that he makes a beeline for public life.

He talks about Niemes, where he lectured.

It's an open city. In France, if you commit a crime you can get thrown out of the city. Niemes is an open city - anyone can go there. It's an interesting mix, being a port as well.

Robin was offered the use of Georges Simenon's old room in the offices of the French CID.

Some prisoners in Angloueme were doing this literature course, and they were given the choice of a writer to invite for a talk. So they pick me and I go along. I'm locked in this cell with these prisoners - the guard is outside and can't hear. They're doing a lot of time for fraud, that sort of thing. I start talking about writing and they stop me. They start asking me about the last woman I'd been with. They've been locked up for so long, they'd worn out all their fantasies - they wanted some fresh ones from me...

Most of my major fans, as you might expect, are in jail doing porridge.

Because you're writing about things they know about.

'Course I am. Those are the people I want to get at, anyway.

You want to change them.

Yes. I can see how the whole thing works, you see, and I want to show them. Men get a buzz from crime. It's a high. I know it was a high for me. And women. They're as excited by crime as much as men, make no mistake. They know men's weak points better than men themselves. They play on them.

Do you see yourself as a moral writer then?

I don't like amoral novelists. I don't like the facade that that creates. I sometimes get books to read from publishers, to get comments for cover blurb. I got one recently by someone I've never heard of - so I've no personal axe to grind here - and it was well written, mind, but there was no counterpoint, no humanity, to offset the amoral acts of the central character. I don't like that at all. So in that sense, yes, I'm a moralist. I've got morals but I don't overtly stuff them down people's throat in my writing.

Have you seen the world change?

Yes. Enormously. For the worse. I've never believed the 'Golden Age' line - there's never been any such thing. Never. Got to remember that. Very important to nail that one down. People say they wished they'd lived in the 16th century. 'You fucking wouldn't' I'd tell them. If you had toothache, darling, you'd be in dead schtuck. If you started to go blind, there was no such thing as spectacles. You'd soon be in the shit.

Even in my lifetime, it's changed enormously. Britain has always been a country based on the phrase: you can't. Whatever it is you want to do, there's always a reason why you can't. 'I'm sorry, you can't do that here, no.' It was bad enough back in 1950, but now the restrictions are absolute legion in comparison. You can't even smoke on the top deck of a bus now. You can't do this. You can't do that. It all looks freer, but it's all an illusion. My God, the country must be run by wankers if they believe that the Maastricht treaty will make us freer. Why do you think I spent most of the last 30 years living on the continent and not in Britain? I think we should get rid of them. But we can't, they just won't resign.

I was in Maidstone last year.

Really? That's my home town. Terrible place.

This is the centre of Tory land, this is supposed to be prosperous, yet half the shops are closed and turned into charity shops.

We're going back to Dickens' time. Back to the 19th century. People have given up. They're apathetic. They're just going into their little corners and dying. They can't see a way out.

Don't you think that the sort of books being written now should be the equivalent of what Zola and Dickens wrote?

Definitely. Dickens is probably more relevant today than he ever was. The problem is, everyone thinks of his novels as cosy reads, something to read in front of a log fire over Christmas. Nice cosy novels about people suffering and uncomfortable. But of course, it all happened a long time ago, and nothing like that happens now, does it?

I argued with Robin about the number of pints he'd had so far, and he always ended up with a total which was less than mine. We walked down to The French House, a pub on the next road. It was here, fresh off the boat from New York in 1960, that he ran into a friend who got him a job managing five companies for con man Charles Da Silva and, when skint in 1965, ran into another friend who go him a job at a porno bookshop. Robin picked up his messages and packages from behind the bar. 'My office.' Chatted.

Ronnie sat between us.

Ronnie was a petite (Thai?) woman who Robin introduced as 'the most beautiful and intelligent woman I know. A deadly combination.' She looked young, but turned out to be divorced from a Scotsman, with boys in their late twenties. Impossible! But the details she mentioned were too natural to be lies. Weren't they?

Dressed in shorts and light top, Ronnie complained about feeling cold. She worked in a club, didn't state doing what, vague, but there were other girls there, gossip, did catering, up early to catch the markets. She was all touchy-feely, looking directly into your eyes, her fingers lightly resting, occasionally, on your arms and legs. Pleasant, serious, open.

Lighting up, she told us about a man - money, young, sure of himself, handsome - who'd come into the club, asked her out. She said he was nice, but she didn't fancy him, she had a boyfriend anyway. (Her boyfriend - there's another story.) He pestered her a little, but he was okay. The girls in the club, by the way, think he's nice and wouldn't mind going out with him. Ronnie could see that they'd like the sexy cars and glitzy lifestyle, but 'I didn't want to be another one of his possessions, y'know?'

Next, he comes in with flowers and chocolates and all lovey dovey, coaxing, charming. He's going on about her, as if he knew her, as if he'd had long talks with her before. *(Robin leans forward at this stage, 4X in one hand, fag in other, puts his face right up close to mine, gives me the long, slow, knowing wink and says 'Sure sign of a psycho, that. No doubt about it,' then leans back and nods that he knows he's right.)* She says no, that she's not interested. Thinks no more of it.

So anyway, a little time passes, she's leaving one night, and he's outside, waiting for her. Now, it's early in the morning, 2 - 3, and bear in mind Ronnie has to get up early for the markets, and this guy thinks the night is young and he's in with a chance. She decides it's best to sweet talk him away, and get away in her taxi - you never know what's going to happen. She gets in her taxi, goes home, tells the taxi to come back a little later to take her to the markets, and nods off.

Ring, ring. It's this guy again, on the phone. He's cancelled the taxi and he's going to escort her to the market. She's fucking furious. What gives this guy the right to interfere with her life like this? He's a fucking madman. *(Robin nods and winks again. He's right, you know.)*

So she had to accept his lift to the markets, to get the food. She got rid of him then, but he still comes to the club and pesters her. She doesn't know what to do to get rid of him for good. She doesn't know what's going to happen next. Robin just nods.

The Cook Report

BORN JUNE 12TH 1931 into a well-to-do family. Educated at Eton during and just after the Second World War. Walked out when he had enough. *"Only man who hated it as much as me was Orwell. Absolutely vile place. Hotbed of vice"*. Did his National Service digging latrines for a tank regiment. Popped off to Spain for a fortnight, ended up there four years. The smuggling of cars and tape recorders took place between several countries. Also spent time in America (as a waiter), Italy, Morocco and Turkey. Wrote about nine unpublished novels, the major one being *The Interns*, of which only extracts survive.

Early 1960s, back to swinging London. East End thugs, being known to the police, needed fronts, so who better than respectable West End 'morries' (everyone in the West End was Jewish and seemed to be called Maurice). Selling investments to banks and the public in new houses on the South coast that never got built, thousands of pounds were handed over to his 'fellow businessmen' at the Dorchester or Ritz. The names of Charles Da Silva and The Krays have 'leaked' on occasion. One time he was arrested and grilled by police for 17 hours about some missing paintings. Ended up as a pornographer in St Anne's Court, the sign behind the counter reading: The following MPs will not be served... Later minicab driver and abattoir assistant. All these experiences ended up in his books written as Robin Cook.

He spent most of his time in French vineyards during the 1970s and 1980s - in a tower in Aveyron, North of Montpellier. Started writing again, this time from the other side of crime, and became a celebrated author in France. Returned to north London in the 1990s, ensconced in Coach & Horses, extolling the virtues and vices of the Black Novel which, in a letter, he once described to me as something 'which you might compare to the feeling a man has in a downward express lift on the 33rd floor when he hears someone above him cutting the cables.' He died peacefully in his sleep, of cancer, on July 30 1994. John Williams, literary executor of Robin's estate, is presently assessing Robin's papers and hopes to publish a biography and arrange a short story collection as well as reprints of the older books.

Cook's Books

The Crust On Its Uppers (1962)
A couple of morries (Sixties Soho wise guys) from the upper crust get drunk, get high and end up stuffing a car full of drugs for a big score. Totally natural. Totally convincing. Totally involving. The scary thing is - the villains are the good guys.

Bombe Surprise (1963)
A light-hearted rib-tickler about those rather funny fascist chappies - BRITAIN STRONG, BRITAIN FREE. Mind where you put that bayonet, young man! Chance would be a fine thing.

The Legacy Of The Stiff Upper Lip (1966)
Semi-autobiographic, follow-on from The Crust On Its Uppers. George William Breakwater, in conversation with his psychiatrist, relives his life as public school outcast á la Lindsay Anderson's If...., and finding a conscience in a Spanish village stricken with typhoid.

Public Parts And Private Places (1967)
This kind of lowlife Evelyn Waugh black comedy features an autobiographical central character running a sex shop, his sister a femme fatale. A lowkey, sad book which ends hideously. In other words, a very good book which should be reprinted this instant.

A State Of Denmark (1970)
An ex-journo works the Italian vines whilst the life juice of England is crushed by the jackboots of fascism. But, the new dictator is an old enemy, and the journo is deported home where he must face the consequences of speaking his own mind. This book really gets under your skin - very tense.

DEREK RAYMOND

The Tenants Of Dirt Street (1971)

Everything you ever wanted to know about keeping a brothel but were too scared of catching something you couldn't explain to the wife. The life and crimes of Lord Eylau whose ambition is to run off with the vicar's blind daughter. A comedy of rudeness that amuses, but nothing more. Features some of the characters from *Public Parts And Private Places*.

Raymond's Revue

Le Soleil Qui S'etaint (1983)

Only published in France (in French, obviously), this is a so-so spy thriller about an anti-terrorist agency. Efforts are being made to track down the original manuscript written in English.

He Died With His Eyes Open (1984)

The first Factory Novel. Staniland, a nobody, is dead and forgotten by all but the Detective Sergeant. Listening to tapes of the dead man baring his soul, the DS eventually offers his life in exchange for justice. The change is more than in name - from Robin Cook to Derek Raymond - for Derek attempts to make reparation for his past. He shows us how the dead lived, and what we missed by not taking notice of them when they were alive.

Filmed in 1985 by French writer/director Jacques Deray, starring Michel Serrault, Charlotte Rampling and Elisabeth Depardieu.

The Devil's Home On Leave (1985)

The second Factory Novel. A horrific killer (ex-Army, chucked out of Belfast, boils his victims in a big vat) is on the loose with connections to a foreign intelligence agency. The case is in the hands of the Detective Sergeant, but he becomes more and more embroiled in events which are too hot to handle. A good but not great book. It has been filmed for French television.

How The Dead Live (1986)

The third Factory Novel. The Detective Sergeant goes to Wiltshire for a spot of detecting. All is not as cosy as one might first suspect. The voices and settings are brooding and mysterious, but it lacks sparkle. Another good but not great book. Claude Chabrol was supposed to turn this into a film at one stage, with Philippe Noiret as the nameless policeman.

Nightmare In The Street (1987)

"...*a failure as a book, and I am far from being to only person to think so.*" Only published in France, this police thriller is set is France and has been described as flawed, but good. Apparently, not as good as the Factory books.

I Was Dora Suarez (1990)

The fourth Factory Novel. Derek took the face of a dead, anonymous girl in a police photograph, christened her Dora and wrote this book. "*It was my atonement for fifty years' indifference to the miserable state of this world*".

The Detective Sergeant reads Dora's notebook, and comes to love her. The killer is totally out of control. This is one of the great books of noir fiction.

(Derek made an hour long recording of extracts from the book, with music by James Johnston and Terry Edwards (Gallon Drunk), which is available on Gorse CD.)

The Hidden Files (1992)

Autobiography. A frank mixture of reminiscence, chat and bile about black novels, childhood rebellion, metaphysics and gangsters. "*The title comes from the hidden files in a computer, which help the computer work. In the same way, for a writer, there's hidden work that doesn't come out in the writing. I took writing memoirs to mean that people wanted to see the files they normally didn't need to see when they read the books*".

Dead Man Upright (1993)

The fifth Factory Novel. The DS talks to an alcoholic ex-copper who thinks there's a sixty-year-old serial killer living on the top floor of his block of flats. When the DS stops laughing, he realises his mate may be right...

Not Till The Red Fog Rises (1994)

Originally titled *One More Chance*, Robin explained; "*The detective is now the villain, on the other side of the counter. It's the same character really, but it's not*".

Gust gets parole after serving ten for armed robbery, but is a little strapped for cash. He joins a hijacking scam, only to be leaned on from some pretty heavy people who can nip him back inside pronto. Now Gust is pretty heavy himself - he manages to impair the physical well-being of a couple of Soho club punters - but between the threat of going back in and his girlfriend getting cut up, he begins to see red...

DEREK RAYMOND

Gwendoline Butler

I HAVE BEEN A FAN OF THE *extraordinary crime fiction of Gwendoline Butler since I first discovered the Coffin series, at Pudsey library in Yorkshire. I have always loved the darker end of the classic British crime novel - Gladys Mitchell's* Rising Of The Moon, *Margery Allingham's* Tiger In The Smoke *and* More Work For The Undertaker *- but these are usually oddities in a career. Imagine my surprise on finding an author whose entire oeuvre is devoted to the blacker side of the British imagination. Her books are filled with Dickensian characters, bizarre crimes and a decidedly black sense of humour.*

Gwen writes under two names - her own and Jennie Melville. I shied away from the Melvilles for some time - they appeared to be more conventional police procedurals, albeit with a female as the central character (Gwen is in fact the originator of the female police procedural, Prime Suspect *fans.) I needn't have worried. The Butler flair for the macabre is there in all its glory.*

Extraordinarily, when we have to import writers of the traditional crime story (Ms' George and Grimes), Gwen, in many ways the last innovator of this line of crime fiction, is relatively uncelebrated. Despite being one of the top one hundred authors borrowed from libraries, you will search in vain for the serried ranks of Butler or Melville paperbacks in WH Smith's. Crime Time wanted to encourage booksellers to return those yellowing Rendells, and past their sell-by-date Jameses and stock the authentic voice of British crime fiction. I set out on Christmas Eve, limping due to a march fracture of my foot, to talk to Gwen. I followed up our meeting with a dinner at the Reform Club and many faxes and conversations.

The main body of the conversation is to the sound of me munching gorgeous mince pies made by Gwen's daughter Lucilla.

Peter Dillon-Parkin

Making Sentences

How did you get started, and what interested you about the genre?

I enjoyed reading detective stories. The first, one of the first books I remember reading was Gaston Leroux's *Murder in the Yellow Room*. I remember reading that, even before I read *Pickwick Papers*, which was the other big landmark in my reading life, and I think I must have been between eight and ten, so it was quite early on, and I loved the genre. Well, then I read History at Oxford and became a historian, but I decided I wanted to do some writing, so I wrote a children's history book, which I tried to sell, but as I knew quite a lot of history and not much about children, obviously no-one wanted to buy that. But it made me realise I liked making sentences. I also realised that I hadn't actually got a great theme, or a great story I wanted to investigate, so I thought well, I like reading detective stories, I know people who read one a day, there's got to be a market there. I wrote my first one, which I was lucky enough to get published...

That would be *Receipt for Murder*?

That was *Receipt for Murder*. I wrote it, my husband read it, and he thought it was all right - I think he was surprised actually, how well I could do it - and I sent it off to a young man I knew who worked at Gollancz - Hilary Rubenstein, actually - who was my contemporary at Oxford. And after a while he sent it back, but with a very praising letter, saying he'd wanted to publish it but a couple of others on the committee hadn't, so I accepted the praise, and then I remembered what Charlotte Bronte said to Mrs Gaskell - perhaps you know it yourself? - "Never trust praise from a publisher unless it comes with an offer to publish", so I rewrote the book a little bit, and I said to my husband "I think I need an agent. If he takes it on, I'll know there's a future for me, and if he doesn't, I'll know there's nothing doing", so he found me an agent! You can see that my husband was very helpful, and the agent took it on. It was actually George Greenfield, who was a very young agent then, who eventually became one of the most powerful ones in London, so I was lucky there. He took me on, and he got it published, and it got good reviews, one of which said 'I hope she writes another book' or 'We look forward to the next one'. Now, that's what you want, isn't it?

Absolutely!

And of course I did write another one, and I think after that, the first one was good, the second couple I was still learning what to do, but I was lucky to be able to learn while publishing. By that time we'd - am I going on a bit?

No, you carry on!

By that time we'd left Oxford, and had moved to St. Andrews in Scotland, and I had a young child (whom you've just seen!) and I decided I wanted to invent another persona. I felt I'd got a lot of writing energy and I felt I'd like to burst out a bit. And at that time I wanted to establish another persona that was male or neutral, I didn't want to be just another woman, reviewed as a woman. I wrote...I think it was... you know, I can't remember the title of that one - it was the first Melville...

Come Home and Be Killed.

That's it. I sent it off to George Greenfield, who sold it very quickly, within a fortnight. And I enjoyed writing that, it gave me a lot of fun, but Michael Joseph accepted it, and they said no, I couldn't have a neutral or male name, Mary Fitt had just died and they wanted another woman. That's how publishing works!

[laughing]

Isn't it extraordinary!? I've not told you this before?

No!

So I took my grandmother's name and became Jennie Melville, well, she was MacMelville actually, and that's the beginning of Melville and Butler, so I went on from there.

Then *Coffin for Pandora*, which was a bit of a sport, as you might say, inasmuch as it was called *Coffin for Pandora* but it was quite different, it was a Victorian Gothic.

Mm, that's one of the ones I haven't been able to get hold of.

Really? We must get you a copy. Anyway, it won a prize and got good reviews, but even more important it attracted the attention of the Americans, who had published me before, and it was the time when Gothic Romances were enormously popular, and um...

Mmm! [mince pie heaven]

Lucilla made those, she's a good cook.

So for a period of about four years I wrote - they had a suspense element, but they were more romantic suspense - under both Butler and Melville.

Then when my husband died, I simply couldn't do that sort of thing; it sort of killed it inside me. I suppose because I was miserable, really, and so for about eighteen months I didn't really write much at all. And I decided then that I'd go back to detective fiction, so I went back to straight Coffin, reinvented the chap really, had to fudge his age a bit, and I reinvented Charmian Daniels as a detective and placed her in Windsor. So that's the history of Butler and Melville.

There seems to be a very strong sense of place about...

Oh yes!

I've only been able to read the later novels...

You couldn't get the others.

...but there seems to be a really strong sense of place about both the Coffin and Daniels books.

Well that's a very valid point, and in fact one American magazine publisher has just asked me to write an article dwelling on that side of it, so I have been thinking about it. And it's perfectly true, I do have a very strong sense of place. When I wrote that first detective story I was really recreating part of London where I grew up, in a way.

Would this be when you started to rewrite the Coffin series, or the original?

No, the very first one of all. He wasn't in that, but it was about a part of south

London, Greenwich and Blackheath, that I'd grown up in. So I was certainly reinventing where I had been, and Charmian Daniels - well, that was different. I've now located her in Windsor, which is where I live. Yes, I do have a very strong sense of place. London, in particular, I'm drawn to, and I've really rebuilt it several times in my imagination, and when I relocated Coffin in the thing I call the second City of London - well, David Owen invented the word - I thought I could give him whatever I wanted there. Windsor, I've created two districts there, partly because it's easier to invent your own sub-district, so I've invented Cheasey, but the rest of Windsor I make fairly 'as it is'. I use proper names, like Peascod [pronounced Pezcod] street, which exists - Peas-cod street, I thought it was, when I first saw it. Does that help?

The Second City of London is Docklands?

Yes it is.

But obviously your interest is before Canary Wharf - does that exist in your version, or is that not part of it?

I don't dwell on that really.

That's what I thought...

It's much more south of that, but I do use the Docklands Light Railway a bit.

In the books often the motivating force for plot is something that has happened in the past - in fact the only other author I can think of who has plots that are so based on elements of the past is Ross MacDonald, who also has buried things coming to light.

Yes, yes, but I suppose that's because I've always been interested in the past, and that's why I became a historian. And that's reflected, I suppose, in the way that I write, it's been a constant interest to me, the past, and still is, actually.

In *Baby Drop* you say *'the past eats the present'*.

I suppose I believe that.

There's always an ambiguity about the past in your books, so things that seem to be settled are not necessarily settled, and that seems to combine very strongly with another element, which is the ambiguity about identity.

Yes.

Which seems to be quite a strong theme.

Yes, you're quite right about that. I hadn't noticed that myself, but now you point it out, yes, it is true. I suppose we are continually reinventing ourselves.

In *A Coffin From The Past* you use a strange framing sequence, in which every few chapters we get a section of the action leading up to and, eventually, depicting the murder. This is like something from one of Priestley's time plays.

I had read the time plays, but I wasn't thinking of them. I just thought it would be an amusing way of presenting a detective story; to rerun the death scene, adding a bit each time around. My editor rang up to ask if I'd made a mistake!

If I'm not mistaken there's an amount of black humour in your work.

Well, that idea amused me, especially as I have a kind of serious-joke ending. So yes there is humour. It is the humour of the creator who is watching her characters, and sees the joke they may not see for themselves. Irony I suppose you could call it. If there is a great creator in the skies, then I think he, or she , why not she, has that sense of humour. And yes, it can be black humour.

A familiar theme in the books is the mistaken corpse; that is, the corpse whose identity appears to be obvious, but isn't obvious.

Ye-e-es, it does intrigue me, that sort of thing.

In *A Dark Coffin*, Harry Trent, has a twin brother, and there's an ambiguity about whether he exists of not and what I really liked about it was the fact that in most detective fiction, when there's this kind of ambiguity about twins, which is one of the great clankers of detective fiction, the people in the book never notice what the reader notices, but in *A Dark Coffin*, the people in the book *say* what you think, which is "IS there a brother?", and it wrong-foots you permanently.

I've got twin brothers, by the way [both laugh], so the idea of twins is not fantastic. Indeed, I was a twin myself, and I suppose that perhaps accounts for something. My twin died, and I don't ever remember her, I was only a baby, but, um, it's interested me as I've got older, you know, what she would have been like, and what our relationship... My brothers are very close in many ways, and yet have grown apart, obviously as they've got older, and have had different careers. One became a politician and the other one's an academic. I just wonder what my sister would have been like...

My mother was a twin. I have a kind of half-brother, because my mother's sister had a son, and in some ways we're very much alike, and in some ways we're not at all.

It's interesting, that.

I just find it odd, the feeling of recognition you get, when you meet someone who's very like you. You make a whole set of assumptions based on that, your feeling towards them is dictated by that. I have a Scottish friend called Matt, who comes from the same village my mother comes from, and he looks more like a brother to me than I can possibly imagine; in fact his daughter, when she was little, would say 'daddy' at photos of me, and my children would at photos of him.

That's interesting, yes.

I've always had this automatic warmth towards him, because he just seems like, and of course he isn't, a member of my family. I think the ambiguity about what constitutes personality is interesting. One of the things I notice in your books is that very often we see people from the outside, by their actions, and you can't really ever make a judgement in any of your books about who's likely to be the hero or the villain...

No...

Because apart from Coffin's and Charmian Daniels' internal dialogues... your other characters are quite opaque. It's difficult to discern motives, shall we say?

Well, that's partly, you know, I do that on purpose, really; a cast of characters, any one of which might be guilty. But as far as character goes, I think one does change, and invent oneself every so often. I'm quite sure I am not the same person I was ten years ago, and certainly not the same person I was as an undergraduate at Oxford. It just happens. Interesting.

Are John Coffin and Charmian Daniels real to you?

Yes, yes they are. To some extent they're extensions of me, but yes. Coffin especially I have a sense of the physicality of.

Lawrence Block said he didn't feel that either of his characters really exist.

Oh yes, they exist for me. John Coffin I named after an American family I knew in Oxford. It is a fairly common name in the West Country. I placed him initially in the rather elegant South Thames area that I know well. I have promoted him, rather like Sir John Appleby and Sir John Meredith.

And Charmian Daniels?

She is based on a red-headed police woman I saw undergoing training in St. Andrews, Fife, and I was interested to hear from a member of the family that she has retired but still lives there. Charmian is not yet retiring!

You invented the womens' police procedural with Charmian...

Yes, I wanted to show that women detectives can get equally involved in routine, danger, and murder. Her private life is separate from her husband's, as was mine. So! Next - any more questions?

How do you write?

Oh. I just do it, sentence by sentence. I just plunge in, really, because you can always wipe out, especially now we've all got word processors. I just begin writing, and the first paragraph of the first book I know I will scrap, it doesn't matter, it oils the wheels. And I try and write regularly, well, I do, I write regularly every day, except on Christmas Days and things like that, although, if I was at home I probably would be writing; um, about a thousand words a day, I try to do. I just don't allow myself any blocks, I just push on, through the block, knowing I can edit it out.

Would you agree that you can sit there and write complete rubbish, as long as you write, because you're getting somewhere?

Yes, I'll write stuff that I know I'm going to cut out, just to get it going. On the whole, that works.

Sometimes I find myself writing almost to explain something about the story to myself. And often when I get to a certain point in a book I think, I'm going to have to build in another incident, another bit of dialogue, to explain what's going on. I go back and rewrite, and sometimes I've got quite a long way into the plot before

I realise that essential elements are missing and have got to be put there. And I may - is that one of the cats? You're not allergic to cats? I've got several.

No, I've got one of my own, that's where I got the march fracture from, looking for it.

Oh, did it get lost?

It went walkies for a long time. I got it back, but I had to walk round a lot of Edgbaston shouting out 'Tyger!', while onlookers hastily crossed the street away from the madman.

Glad you found it. My cat's gone into a cats' boarding house while I'm here, Bellmead, which is the country annexe of the Battersea Dogs' Home, near Windsor. I took her in on Wednesday, I hate doing it to her.

Ours is fifteen now, which is really pretty old.

One of my cats lived to be nearly twenty. Anyway, I think that's Daisy, I can't really tell the difference, you're Daisy, aren't you, yes, cos you're smaller, aren't you?

Smaller?! *[To gigantic cat]* Dearie me, you're *smaller*?

Sorry!

That's all right!

So, next question?

Inspiration!

Oh, I don't wait for *that!*

[both laugh]

You couldn't write the number of books I've written if you waited to be inspired. Sometimes it comes, that's what's so delightful; I start a book and I think to myself, 'I've got nothing to write about, what am I going to do?', and often, that's the book that, in the end, is a better one than one where I think to myself 'Oh I've had a good idea!' Can you understand that?

Yes.

Life's very kind.

I think sometimes you just have to work, don't you?

Yes it is work, it is work.

I mean you have to treat it as work.

Oh I do, I've never had any illusions, it absolutely is work, but it's work I greatly enjoy, I really do, and I think I'm lucky that the gods have allowed me to make it a career.

One of the other questions I wanted to ask you, and I don't want to be provocative here...

No, do be.

PD James's comments about the working class not having to deal with moral questions - I notice that you have a lot of working class characters and they do very definitely have moral choice..

Well, I come from a working class background. My family were lightermen and watermen along the river for generations and both my brothers were apprenticed to my father, although they never worked on the river, but he wanted them to keep up the family tradition. Allan still goes to Waterman's Hall, I think. That's the world I come from, really.

So you wouldn't agree that the working class don't have to deal with moral questions then, I take it?

That's mistaken, but my personae always have the character to pass moral judgement. I think she's been on the defensive a bit.

I don't think she intended to say that, I don't think she thought it out too well.

I wrote to her, I was rather saddened that so many people turned on her, I thought it was malicious in a kind of way.

It did fire an interesting debate, and gave a lot of publicity to a lot of people. I must admit I do think her books have become a tad, er, tedious.

What authors do you like in contemporary crime fiction? Who do you read by choice?

Reg Hill is very good.

Top man!

I agree with you there; he wasn't always but he's come on immensely, but I don't take to the Slough ones with the...

...Joe Sixsmith...

... because he doesn't understand - he's never been to Slough, to begin with.

He's from Yorkshire isn't he?

Yes.

He writes Luton as a Yorkshire town. I lived in Yorkshire for eight years and used to visit Luton, and it's nothing like the books.

I think he should have kept off that, but I think it was because he'd sold the Dalziel and Pascoe novels to TV, and he wanted to leave the field a bit clear for them to get on with it, and then it all fell through, but now they're being revived.

By someone decent this time, thank God!

Well I don't know how decent, now who did the first series? Oh they were *hopeless!*

Hale and Pace. Warren Clarke is Dalziel in the new series.

That's right! I think that's wrong too.

I think he can probably play it though.

He's a better actor. He's an actor, anyway. Let's put it like that. [Both laughing]

The worst thing about the first one was that everyone in it was OK, apart from Hale and Pace.

Yes.

Which was really embarrassing.

But anyway I do like Reg Hill, I like Peter Lovesey, I like Simon Brett - well he's always amusing, but as detective stories they're sometimes not much cop - but he's always witty. I like Marion Babson because I find her amusing, I just do. I like lot of Americans. Never liked Ellis Peters a whole lot, but my daughter loves her.

No, I can't read her.

So I always got them for her. I like Michael Pearce; again I don't think the plots are that good...

No, but they're very amusing.

He's got a very nice way of writing. I'm reading them now.

They're very droll. I think they're an entertainment, and I think Simon Brett's are an entertainment.

They are, yes. You don't read them for the detection, you read them for the dialogue. They fall within the genre. But we are entertained.

Do you like Patricia Cornwell?

We-e-ell, I've read them all. I found them very, very, interesting, but it's become apparent that all she's got is this scientific side, and the actual plots are getting more and more...

Have you read the last three?

Yes, I've read 'em all.

I've just written an overview of them and in the last three she's not really writing detective fiction, but heroic fiction. Really it's almost not like detective fiction at all.

She's got this interesting material, and at first we all loved it because it was fascinating. But you can have too much of it, and that's all she's got, really. I had this feeling with the last one that there'd been another hand actually shaping and rewriting the plot, and the solid material in it, and perhaps had an American editor wade in and do the rest. Mind you she creates some remarkably awful people.

She obviously believes that there are certain kinds of people who are just evil, and that's the end of the story. Do you have any feelings about that?

No I don't think there are. I think there must be some very wicked people around, as the West trial suggests, very strange people, living in a world I happily don't comprehend. Perhaps even the Wests were kind to their cats, you don't know, do you?

In your own books there are people who do the most horrific things, for the most trivial reasons...

Mm, well, I think that happens.

The people who kill the young girl in *Baby Drop*, are people whose sense of the world is completely off-kilter.

Yes, I suppose that is the way I feel it. I don't think I'm a very self-analytical writer, I just want to create, and I do it, I don't necessarily dig into myself too much.

Your books are, in a lot of ways, very traditional crime novels...

They are.

But some very untraditional things happen in them - I'm thinking of the double Grand Guignol climax to *Windsor Red*, the transvestite club in *A Coffin For Charley*...

[Laughs] I enjoyed creating that! But I do know some rather odd people, in the theatrical world, and academics are not necessarily straightforward. I've been surprised, as I've got older and odder how odd people are underneath.

Yes, the West case is almost a classic British murder, in that it's secretive and it's behind closed doors, and there's a sense of guilt and shame about it. Whereas in America, very probably Fred would be selling his life story, because there doesn't seem to be the sense of guilt or shame...

That's interesting.

... and a lot of your sense of the murder is to do with hidden things.

Yes, yes it certainly is that.

There's a sense of foreboding in your books, and a sense that people can be unfaithful, or are not necessarily to be relied on, that people reveal different aspects of themselves to different people.

Well I think that's true - I think the surface of life is unstable and does break up.

Mark Timlin has made reference to 'girly' crime fiction, by which I presume he was referring to classic crime fiction. Your books are far away from 'girly' stuff and deal with much harder-edged subjects.

Yes, indeed, I've never felt a 'girly' writer, in any way.

I was watching a trailer for Taggart with a Dungeons and Dragons theme, and you did Dungeons and Dragons in *Coffin Underground*, and rather better.

Yes, yes I did.

And there's a wonderful Coffin with an adolescent who's involved in a UFO society, and his internal monologue is one of the most convincing evocations of the social inadequate, club joining mentality, and I found that *most* interesting...

Well, thank you, I enjoyed doing that. Perhaps I spread myself too thin, really, but I do enjoy that sort of creation - rather odd people, sometimes they're good, sometimes they're wicked. They don't fit into any easy classification, I don't think.

No, I don't think the books do generally. The Melville titles have the most extraordinary cast and events, for an allegedly 'straightforward' police procedural - witches, severed heads, mannequins that move... the entirety of *Baby Drop* seems to be a discourse on mortality and the nature of it.

I suppose it's been preoccupying me a bit lately; it does as one gets older, I think.

WHEN MY GOOD FRIEND Gwendoline Butler asked me to contribute this biographical note for John Coffin, I was delighted because of my connections with London. John Coffin is a south of the River Thames man; his grandfather came from Oxford, and the blood of the medieval Whitechair family runs in his veins. Some years later he learnt his real mother was a famous musical comedy actress, who claimed to be a natural daughter of King Edward VII, although whether her name figures in the famous confidential register kept in a certain Royal Office may never be known. A child by a father unknown to *Debrett* or *The Stage Yearbook* can be inhibiting to a glamorous actress whose speciality is playing juveniles, so young John found himself being brought up by a relative of his father who had been his mother's dresser. She was probably a spinster cousin, glad of the money and company, who took the courtesy title of 'Mrs' like housekeepers. The paternal grandmother also took a hand in the boy's upbringing, which included attendance at Hook Road Senior Boys' School, which he obviously enjoyed as he called on his teacher later for help on a case. He first tried a spell in the Army, but that soon palled and he became a probationer policeman in his home area. In the plain clothes branch he became a Sergeant in 1958, and an Inspector a year later. In 1969 he was a Superintendent, and a Chief Superintendent nine years after. He

stayed in digs in the area, and twice bought himself a house, only to find previous occupants suitable subjects for his, and the pathologists', attention.

In 1961 he was sent to the Midlands to help solve a murder. At the theatre the leading lady was Venetia Stuart, who had acted with his mother, with a young ingenue named Patsy, short for Cleopatra (thank goodness my actor father wasn't playing in Lear at the time, was her only comment!) She was a suspect - Coffin cleared her, and like his fictional counterparts, married her - perhaps the theatre was in his blood, too. (Having been critic for *The Stage* newspaper for over thirty years, I do remember her.) I didn't watch television much then, but apart from her name in West End and touring casts, she had some nice parts in modern and period plays and comedies on the box. Sadly the rigours of his job and the two careers caused the marriage to founder. Patsy died together with their only child. After many years alone, apart from the occasional transitory girlfriend, he met again Stella Pinero, an actress he had known all his adult life. She is one of those very beautiful women, like two or three others I have known or could name, whose attractiveness never wears, sags or wrinkles. She appears regularly on television, in the West End and the occasional tour, and is the Artistic Director of the new St. Luke's Theatre and Workshop in the Second City of London, which is how they came together again.

John Coffin had always felt he was not an only child, so he was not unduly startled when Letitia Bingham wrote to him as his half- sister. She is a glamorous Atlantic jetsetter, and divorcee, whose face and wardrobe appear regularly in the English and American glossies, who stays in London either at the famous hotel just off Bond Street, or rents apartments off Knightsbridge. Coffin now knows he has also a half-brother William, a dour Writer to the Signet in Edinburgh, by yet another husband - yes, that makes three husbands - and she kept a diary. Coffin and Letty have to decide whether to publish. It was Letty who founded the Theatre, Workshop and Apartments in the former St. Luke's Church in the Second City of London, where John and Stella have flats.

So how has John crossed the river? The Second City of London was formed after the unprecedented creation of Docklands and the re-emergence of certain historic parts of East London, when boundaries were being re-drawn. When the position of the Chief Commander of the new Police Force was advertised (like the City of London, it is not part of the Met.) Coffin was among the many applicants - gossip says that half the ACPO applied. Coffin won, one of the youngest to hold such rank.

What of the future? He has received many Commissioner's recommendations for bravery, he has been wounded seriously twice - a bullet wound in 1968 that nearly finished him, and a stabbing by a murderer ten years later. He received the QPM, Queen's Police Medal, on his latest appointment; further honours seem in the offing. I have no doubt his Discharge Certificate will read "Exemplary". When he does retire, I wonder if the House of Lords and a literary career will beckon? Not a theatrical career - up till now he confines himself to amateur roles of the "My Lord, the carriage awaits" variety in Stella's Workshop productions. He is less aggressive, but still implacable in his ideals against crime; he has found, like I have, that a sensible, mature, discreet woman is an excellent sounding-board when talking problems out loud - even if they only echo!

We do have something else in common. When he was solving the case in which he was stabbed, it was on my own knowledge of fantasy games and their effects he called. If he is still speaking to me after this, he knows he can always call on me again!

Charmian Daniels

CHARMIAN DANIELS' POLICE CAREER has been marked by dedication, academic and administrative skills, and physical and psychological bravery. Born and educated in Dundee, the fourth child in a family of seven, she took a degree in Social Science at Glasgow University, and immediately joined the police. One year in Dundee, another in St. Andrews, then she applied to Deerham Hills, a new town about forty miles from London, and she was accepted into the detective branch, initially dealing with women and children. She became a walking computer of local villains and characters, at one point even infiltrating a gang of women bank robbers. She was soon made Sergeant, then Inspector. She transferred to the Met. for some years, her duties taking her as far as America. Finally, as a Chief Superintendent she headed the new Unit, acronymic SRADIC, with its own investigatory powers. She settled in Windsor, where she acquired property.

Academically, she studied at Midport University for a Diploma in Criminology later taking a sabbatical to write a thesis.

In her twenties, she was nearly killed in action, later was stabbed, and just avoided rape and murder by a killer in Windsor.

She married a Chief Inspector, a widower fifteen years her senior, with a son by his first marriage, but Rupert Ascham was killed on duty. Her other half-hearted

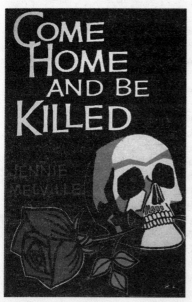

romances included two men later proved to be killers, perhaps fulfilling a job psychiatrist's evaluation of her tendency towards danger. Her present suitor is a titled intelligence chief, formerly a top policeman. She is tall, slim, extremely attractive, with brown eyes, and red hair, which as a young policewoman she tried dyeing blonde. She has excellent dress sense, buying expensive designer clothes, but on the job make-up, coiffure and clothes take second place. She still occasionally suffers from migraine and allergies. She has to cope with masculine jealousy, perhaps compounded by her tendency to actively lead her investigations, but she always keeps her sights firmly on her present and future role in police work.

GWENDOLINE BUTLER

Bibliography

NOVELS (SERIES: INSPECTOR JOHN COFFIN; INSPECTOR/SUPERINTENDENT WILLIAM WINTER)

Receipt for Murder, Bles, 1956
Dead in a Row (Coffin; Winter), Bles, 1957
The Dull Dead (Coffin; Winter), Bles, 1958
The Murdering Kind (Coffin; Winter), Bles, 1958
The Interloper, Bles, 1959
Death Lives Next Door (Coffin), Bles, 1960
Make Me a Murderer (Coffin), Bles, 1961
Coffin in Oxford, Bles, 1962
Coffin for Baby, Bles, 1963
Coffin Waiting, Bles, 1963
Coffin in Malta, Bles, 1964
A Nameless Coffin, Bles, 1966
Coffin Following, Bles, 1968
Coffin's Dark Number, Bles, 1969
A Coffin from the Past, Bles, 1970

"This has been a regular earner for me, running in to several editions. I used my background in historical research from Oxford. It is based on a tombstone found in an old city church by my husband in Clerkenwell. The beginning of my essays in the macabre affecting the ordinary man."

A Coffin for Pandora, Macmillan, 1973
A Coffin for the Canary, Macmillan, 1974
The Vesey Inheritance, Macmillan, 1976
The Brides of Friedberg, Macmillan, 1977
The Red Staircase, Collins, 1980
Coffin on the Water, Collins, 1986
Coffin in Fashion, Collins, 1987
Coffin Underground, Collins, 1988
Coffin in the Black Museum, Collins, 1989
Coffin and the Paper Man, Collins, 1990
Coffin on Murder Street, Collins, 1991
Cracking Open a Coffin, Collins, 1992
A Coffin for Charley, Collins, 1993
The Coffin Tree, Collins, 1994
A Dark Coffin, Collins, 1995

"A Dark Coffin *combines my love of the elegant world of the theatre with bloody murder. The Jeckyll and Hyde theme is central, but the victims are also not what they seem.*"

A Double Coffin, Collins, 1996

"*Can political memoirs result in murder? In* A Double Coffin *I wanted to consider the effects on children of the crimes of their parents, and how patient research can uncover the truth in two directions simultaneously, rather like digging the Channel Tunnel!*"

NOVELS AS JENNIE MELVILLE (SERIES: CHARMIAN DANIELS)

Come Home and Be Killed (Daniels), Joseph, 1962
Burning is a Substitute for Loving (Daniels), Joseph, 1963
Murderers' Houses (Daniels), Joseph, 1964
There Lies Your Love (Daniels), Joseph, 1965
Nell Alone (Daniels), Joseph, 1966
A Different Kind of Summer (Daniels), Joseph, 1967
The Hunter in the Shadows, Hodder and Stoughton, 1969
A New Kind of Killer, An Old Kind of Death (Daniels), Hodder, 1970
The Summer Assassin, Hodder and Stoughton, 1971
Ironwood, Hodder and Stoughton, 1972
Nun's Castle, Hodder and Stoughton, 1974
Raven's Forge, Macmillan, 1975
Dragon's Eye, Macmillan, 1977
Axwater, Macmillan, 1978
Murder has a Pretty Face (Daniels), Macmillan, 1981
The Painted Castle, Macmillan, 1982
The Hand of Glass, Macmillan, 1983
Listen to the Children, Macmillan, 1986
Death in the Garden, Macmillan, 1987
Windsor Red (Daniels), Macmillan, 1988
A Cure for Dying (Daniels), Macmillan, 1989
Witching Murder (Daniels), Macmillan, 1990
Footsteps in the Blood (Daniels), Macmillan, 1991
Dead Set (Daniels), Macmillan, 1992
Whoever Has the Heart (Daniels), Macmillan, 1993
Baby Drop (Daniels), Macmillan, 1994.
The Morbid Kitchen (Daniels), Macmillan, 1995
The Woman Who Was Not There (Daniels), Macmillan, 1996

"The Woman Who Was Not There *was based on my memories of a strange, small, dusty private museum of waxworks in Rome. I tried to show how the atmosphere can change both human and wax figures. I was bringing murder into Windsor and then taking it out again.*"

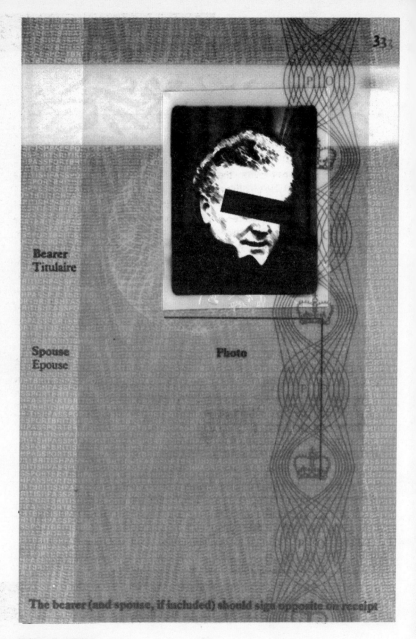

Bearer
Titulaire

Spouse
Epouse

Photo

The bearer (and spouse, if included) should sign opposite on receipt

PEOPLE DON'T HAVE TO BE A LONG WAY AWAY TO BE
DISTANT. *You can talk to them for hours and, at the end of it, not know them, not really. This is Zen's problem.*

Aurelio Zen is an Italian policeman who has to talk, to ask questions, to listen and, from this, discern the essence of the person he is interviewing. Even then, he can only guess as to their innocence or guilt, whether or not they are trustworthy, whose side they are on.

Ideally, Zen would prefer to be somewhere else. He is always the outsider, assigned to some distant town/city - Perugia, Sardinia, The Vatican - having to learn the ropes. Along the way, he leaves a trail of women, whether they be mother, wife, lover. And, when Zen does eventually return to his home city, Venice, in Dead Lagoon, *he wishes he hadn't - his dreams are shattered. The sombre mood of* Dead Lagoon *is replaced by farce in* Cosi Fan Tutti, *set in the seaport of Naples.*

Michael Dibdin is the author of five Aurelio Zen and six non-Zen crime novels. Born in Wolverhampton, he has lived around the world, has married twice and presently resides with crime writer Katherine Beck in Seattle, USA. Paul Duncan interviewed Michael Dibdin on the telephone, long-distance.

A Traveller's Guide

Are you more interested in the literary novel than the genre novel?

The books I review for the *Independent On Sunday* tend to be non-crime novels. There are two reasons for that. One, I like reading outside the genre. Two, reviewing inside the genre can be a bit sticky if you're also writing in it - if you put your boot into somebody, you're bound to end up on a panel with them. It just seems better to me to stay out of that, really.

I suppose the real answer you want from me is quite a complex one. I believe in the concept of the genre. I'm not one of these people who just wants to sweep away all the walls and compartments and say that, actually, it's all just fiction. One of the most interesting things about genre is that it IS a genre so, to use some post-modernistic terminology, we can be self-referential and do variations on things which anyone who has read at all widely in the genre will know has been done before.

For example, on the first page of my novel *Dirty Tricks*, the narrator says that he's been accused of murder, so you know that the book is a nod to books like Francis Iles' *Malice Aforethought*, where the criminal is the narrator. In a sense, all the big variations of what's doable in the genre have already been done. To me, that makes it more interesting, not less. Who wants to be the first person to write a novel about an Eskimo living at the North Pole, drinking whisky and trying to grow his toenails longer than anyone else? That kind of originality has it's place, I suppose, and if you're a really great writer you may be able to bring it off, but the failure rate is about 99.9%. It seems to me that there's much more to be done working within a genre.

Having said that, I don't see any absolute boundary between literature and genre. I see it as a spectrum, really. If you look at a writer like, for example, Patricia Highsmith, but there are others, she wrote the Ripley books, which clearly fit within certain aspects of the genre, but she also did other work which was on the edge of or outside the genre conventions.

She's a writer, full stop. She could write whatever she wanted, whether it was genre or not.

I interviewed her once, and she wasn't very forthcoming about questions about genre but I got the impression that she got an idea and ran with it. If it happened to run in a way that fed into the genre in some obvious way, that was fine. If it happened to be something that was more problematic, that was fine too. This, of course, was why she never made it big in America. The Americans, of course, are heavily into premarketing, prepackaging, targeting their audience. They want to reassure people that the new book is just the same as the old book only the name has changed. It's the supermarket concept - if you go into a Tesco's and buy a can of beans, you don't want the can you bought on Tuesday to be radically different from the tried and approved can you bought on Monday. Obviously, Highsmith was never going to fit into that kind of system in America. Interestingly, she did well in Europe.

Do you think you were, are or will be categorized?

I find the categorization question a bit of a bore, really. It's the kind of thing academics do to try and look as though they are earning a living. You're not an academic, are you?

...

Oh, you are. Sorry.

No, I'm not. I just thought I'd keep silent to add an edge to the conversation.

Right. Fine. In that case...

...fire away.

It just seem to me that there are people who go around, after the event, after people have done things, in much the same way as scientists classify species after the event. They didn't make the birds or butterflies or worms. They just say 'here they are' and try to sort them out. It seems to me that this may, or may not be useful, but I don't think it's a useful thing for writers to do. I think writers should be saying to themselves 'what do I want to write about?', 'is this a strong idea?' and 'what is the strongest way for me to develop it?' They should not have to worry about the way it fits into the market.

One of the things I've noticed since coming to America a couple of years ago is how much more attention writers over here pay to the marketability of their product and, therefore, they often write themselves into a corner when doing a series character.

Take, for example, Patricia Cornwell. She's number one in the bestseller lists here. At the moment, people have a great interest in forensic science, pathology, postmortem stuff but how far can you go with it? How many things can you do with it? I remember talking to Sara Paretsky about ten years ago about her V I Warshawski series and, even then, after three or four books, she felt the ideas were starting to dry up. Once you've got the characters set up, and you know how they think and feel, what their opinions are about everything on Earth, and you know the neighbours next door and the dog and so on, you lock yourself into a framework that is very reassuring from a marketing point of view but, it seems to me, to be sterile from a creative point of view.

If we take Patricia Cornwell as an example, she has changed her Dr. Kay Scarpetta books over the years and added soap opera and thriller elements. Also, she is beginning a new series, which diversifies her output, and stretches her creativity.

I'm not having a go at Patricia Cornwell. All I'm saying is that it's a trap you can fall into in the States and, increasingly, in the UK as well. I'm very lucky that my publishers, Faber & Faber, are generous enough or, if you like, old fashioned enough not to bother about this. They let me do what I want to do and, as long as it's not completely disastrous, will publish it.

Increasingly, in the States, publishers are looking for the new Sara Paretsky, the new Patricia Cornwell, the new Carl Hiaasen, or the new *Bridges Of Madison County*.

In genre writing, which is what we're talking about here, a lot of the issues are already prejudged because there are a lot of existing models for what you're trying to do. The whole thing becomes very Hollywood-ish - you've seen it all before, and it's all being run through committees who say what will and won't work. This won't work because it bombed last month, but this'll work this month because there's a film out this month just like it that's a smash and the public'll want another one. It just seems to me that this is not a good idea for anyone to follow, mainly because the predictions usually turn out to be completely wrong anyway.

You've written many non-Zen books. *The Last Sherlock Holmes Story* and *A Rich Full Death* are historical pastiches. *The Tryst* is a psychological thriller. *Dirty Tricks* is a black comedy from the criminal's point of view - a cross between Francis Iles and Nigel Williams. *The Dying Of The Light* is reminiscent of Agatha Christie's drawing room mysteries. *Dark Spectre* is a full-blooded American psycho-thriller. It's almost as though you've studiously avoided doing the same thing twice, and decided to sample each style and type of crime fiction.

That's a fair comment. That's pretty well what I have been doing.

Have you done this consciously?

Oh God no. I never do anything consciously, except pay bills and the like. What happens is first I get an idea which I get excited about - it's the only way I can start a book because I'm such a lazy person. If I consciously sat down and thought *'John Grisham has had tremendous success with a courtroom drama/lawyer type book so to make money I should write one,'* I couldn't do it. I probably couldn't do it technically anyway, because I don't know enough about that stuff. But I also couldn't bring myself to do it, because it would be too boring. So, what I tend to do is get an idea, and quite often that idea is an angle foreign to what other people are doing, but it's precisely that angle which seems, to me, to be so fascinating.

What angles are you usually concerned about? Is it in the characters? Is it a plot twist?

It varies with every book. Take *Dark Spectre*, for example, which was based on various things. Firstly, I spent five or six years in North America in the seventies. It felt like quite a big chunk of my life because five years when you're in your twenties feels a lot longer than five years when you're in your forties. I was exposed to American speech patterns and social behaviour, and wanted to use this knowledge in some way. Secondly, was the idea of a half-educated guy - not stupid by any means, and not ignorant, but someone who had a smattering of education and was trying to tackle all these huge questions. In the book it's the problem of evil, which has defeated the world's finest minds for the last three thousand years. This guy thought *'ah, I have the answer'* and I had a book.

For each book, the impulse is different, quite mysterious, personal even, although these impulses don't usually show up in the book itself.

The format of *Cosi Fan Tutti*, the fifth Aurelio Zen book, is much different than your other books. This one has shorter, snappier chapters. Why is that?

There are several reasons for that. The previous Zen book, *Dead Lagoon*, was a very dark book and, I think, the long chapters felt to me like a large 19th Century symphony with long movements, big melodies, and recurrent themes. It had that kind of rhythm to it. Although I'm happy with the book, it felt like a dead end - I couldn't see how I could continue with the series. To continue the genre discussion - considering that crime is one of the few areas where people still write series, the problem is how do I keep a series going? How do I go on making it interesting, useful, worthwhile to keep writing about this one person?

With *Dead Lagoon*, I'd come to the end of a way of doing it. Interestingly, while I was touring the book in the UK and US, a number of people said that they thought it was the end of the Zen series. They'd obviously read the book and thought that it represented some kind of closure. I didn't want that at all. I'd grown quite fond of Aurelio and wanted to keep the series going, and wanted to carry on writing about Italy. The question was: how was I going to be able to do it?

I had the idea of moving Zen down South to Naples. Initially, I was going to do a 'traditional' Zen book but, as soon as I went to Naples to do research for the book, I was very struck by the operatic quality of life there. Obviously, I'm not suggesting that it isn't perfectly real and, in many cases, horrible, for the people who live there. But, you cannot write about the place in a Northern, grim, dour way. It needed a different approach.

I happened to be listening to the Mozart opera *Cosi Fan Tutti* one evening and suddenly realised that it was set in Naples. Added to that, when you change the 'te' sound to 'ti', it becomes the saying the Italians use to explain why someone's ripped you off, or why someone's asked for a kickback on a deal you're putting together. *Cosi Fan Tutti* = 'that's life' or 'that's the way things are.' I thought that would be a nice way of changing the whole thing, to blend the operatic approach and lighten it up.

Each short chapter is based on the arias or numbers in the opera. The whole point of the 18th Century comic operas was that nothing lasted for very long - it's all brief, quick, light - so I continued that in the book.

MICHAEL DIBDIN

The ideas of duality, identity and duplicity in the book reminded me of Shakespeare's lighter plays.

I think I may have been slightly influenced here by a writer called Barbara Trapido who wrote *Temples Of Delight* and *Juggling*. *Temples Of Delight* uses a Mozart opera and *Juggling* uses Shakespeare comedy as reference points. All these ideas about doubles, duplicity, fake personalities, fake documents and fake people are in the books.

These were also Patricia Highsmith's themes.

She dealt with them in a much darker way.

I thought I could lighten the series and save it from a morass of doom and gloom. Now, the next Zen book, which I'm working on now, is going to be a halfway house between the dark and light of *Dead Lagoon* and *Cosi Fan Tutti*. Hopefully, I've set the series up for a new run of four or five books, without the dead weight of *Dead Lagoon* dragging it down.

For the first time, I've broken the rhythm of doing a non-Zen book between the Zen books. However, I do have ideas for more books, all of them with an American theme, but I have a feeling that they need a little more time in the oven before I write them. I don't want to rush into something which is half-baked.

Also, although all the comment I've had about *Cosi Fan Tutti* has been positive, I do think people will think the book a little odd and frivolous in comparison with the previous ones. I don't want to be predictable. I want to shake things up. I don't want people to think *'oh, there's a Michael Dibdin book'* and think it's just going to be the same as all the others.

The new Zen book, which is untitled as yet, is set in the Wine country, in Piedmont, Northern Italy.

Is Italy really as depressingly corrupt as you describe it?

It's not depressingly corrupt.

It's nicely corrupt then?

(Laughs) I would describe it as efficiently corrupt, or satisfactorily corrupt. I think corruption is depressing if there are other, perfectly good, ways of getting things done and then some asshole comes along and says, no, you can't do it that way, you've got to do it this way and pay me £500. The thing about Italy is that there's never been a perfectly good official way of getting things done. There are historical reasons, which would take too long to go into. Basically, the official structures, the Government structures, just haven't worked. So people have worked out alternative ways of getting things done which, at its mildest, is slipping a money envelope into the hands of a telephone guy so that you get pushed to the top of the list for telephone installations. At the worst, of course, you end up with the Mafia.

It's like VAT, then?

(Laughs)

Can you account for it, I wonder?

Well, no, you can't, which is how some of them have got caught. Al Capone, for example. Once the judges in Milan were allowed to seriously investigate the Mafia by the political powers that be, they started looking through their records and discovered huge discrepancies, money unaccounted for. The assumption was that the money had probably been handed over in a suitcase in some seedy motel room.

I can understand bribery and corruption in Third World countries because of the appalling economic and social conditions, where people are forced to do it to survive. However, in Italy, it seems to be a way of life.

It is a way of life, which is why it is so difficult to eradicate.

So corruption in Italy is not to be looked at as such a bad thing?

I'm not particularly interested in being judgmental about it. I'm just trying to understand how the Italians feel about it. In all the books, I describe the idea that everyone has some sort of power in Italy. Everyone, even someone insignificant like a doorman of a hotel or a building porter, has a measure of power. If you need him to do something for you, he's got you by the short and curlies. It extends all the way up from there to the large scale official corruptions going on.

There's no question that a huge amount of time and money is wasted. Essentially, it's anti-democratic because these are not things which are voted upon by people saying yes, we want a new power station or yes we want a new motorway. What happens is that people in the Government construct new power stations and motorways in order to reward people who've done favours for them politically, and paying them three times what the thing's worth in the process. They are basically public works projects designed to enrich the people who run the construction companies.

This is something which permeates the whole society in one way or another and so, to change it, is not just a question of changing the Government. That'd be a long, slow process, if it ever came about.

Has this corruption spread elsewhere? Do you see the same sort of thing in America, for instance?

I think corruption, like prostitution, exists everywhere because there is a demand. I don't think corruption is anywhere near as institutionalised in America as it is in Italy. The thing about the Italian way of doing things is that they don't see it as corruption. They see it as the way of getting things done. You're right, it's like VAT. It's the price you pay to get things done efficiently, or getting them done at all. That's their attitude.

The only way to beat them seems to be to join them, as Zen discovers in each book. The format, if there is a format to the books, is that in the first two thirds Zen tries to remain anonymous, as

nothing, out of the way. Then, when there is no other option, he acts, regrettably, and begins to play people off each other. But, of course, it works, but never in the way he expects it.

I think that's true. I've had a certain amount of criticism from people saying that he's too easy going and too corrupt, that they wanted someone stronger, less corrupt, more Anglo-Saxon.

I think the important thing about him is that he's a survivor.

Absolutely. He is. Italians like survivors. They respect that. When Margaret Thatcher was Prime Minister, she was known as The Iron Lady. In Italy, the title had a level of irony it didn't have elsewhere because calling someone iron means simply that they're inflexible, rigid and therefore ultimately fragile, because even iron can be broken if you apply enough force to it. Italian politicians, Aurelio Zen and everyone else each try to be rubber people, so that they bend with whatever prevailing wind is blowing, but don't break.

I don't think Zen sets out to do bad things, to corrupt people or to be corrupt himself, but he knows that the only way to get things done is by a measure of irregularity and cunning. That's how the people he's up against get things done, so there's no point in trying to playing the game with other rules because he'll lose.

In *Cosi Fan Tutti*, Zen changes location and identity. In each book he is the outsider. He's always from somewhere else. You've moved around a lot in your life. You've always been from somewhere else. Is there a connection?

Yes, I think there probably is a connection with my own experience but, originally, I made him that way in the first book of the series, *Ratking*, because I was writing about Perugia. I'd lived there for about four years when I wrote the book and I was very aware of the fact that I wasn't Perugian or Italian. I liked the idea of being the outsider. But, it's also a part of the genre to a certain extent. A lot of what Philip Marlowe does in the Raymond Chandler books involves hanging out with millionaires, rich playboys and spoilt brats.

He's the commentator.

But he's also the person who comes from the outside and is not fooled. I think he can only be a fictive commentator if all this is surprising to him. If he actually lived and moved among these people twenty-four hours a day, what they do wouldn't be remarkable to him. But when he visits them coming, as he does, from a different background, from a different part of LA, then you get his sense of 'oh, look at that gardener, and the marvellously chic lawn, and the old rich man in the glass house.' The fact that he's remarking on all this makes sense, in a way that wouldn't quite if he was already among them.

The first four Zen books definitely feel as though they are taken from Zen's point of view. You are not told anything he doesn't find out. In *Cosi Fan Tutti*, it is more of an ensemble piece and we see

multiple points of view.

That's partly because of the operatic conventions I was following.

Will this continue in the future?

I've gotten four or five chapters into the next book and, like *Dead Lagoon*, they are mostly from Zen's point of view. It's very much about him and how he feels about people. In comparison, *Cosi Fan Tutti* is pretty much a one-off. In it, I backed off and made Zen one character among many, many of whom are not quite who they appear to be. If I'd had the Zen point of view all the way through *Cosi Fan Tutti*, I would have sabotaged the duplicity. It had to come across as a dramatic spectacle, which is made very clear in the first chapter when the reader is introduced to the city as a stage upon which players act out the story. If you had a pipeline into Zen's mind and you're watching him going around, and know that you can trust him, then that sense would have been lost. In that case, you're no longer watching these things happening on the stage from the auditorium, you're actually there on stage with one of the characters. So I had to back off from him slightly to make things work.

In your non-Zen books, you've used the forms of different types of crime writing. Do you do this as a form of criticism or analysis or what?

It's certainly not criticism. The books that fit most into that idea are *The Last Sherlock Holmes Story* and *The Dying Of The Light*. *The Dying Of The Light* arose out of doing a television piece called *J'Accuse: Agatha Christie* for the *Without Walls* arts programme. I was being paid to be the devil's advocate and put the boot in.

I believe that the enormous success of Agatha Christie's books did create a problem for the genre in Britain. This, of course, was not her fault. What they wanted me to do was attack her personally and professionally. I said it wasn't possible because a) she was an extremely pleasant woman and I have no intention of going around hand-bagging old ladies, and b) far more to the point, there is no way you can fault Agatha Christie in terms of her doing what she set out to do. Her work was flawless, except maybe for the last four or five books. You can't attack people for achieving what they wanted to achieve, only for trying and failing. My actual line on that, or intended line, since the television people tried to get me to bend it to become more controversial, is that I thought it was bad news for the genre in Britain. That is, the genre was almost taken over by the enormous success of her books in most reader's minds. To give you an example of this, when I went to Paris to do promotion for the French edition of *Dirty Tricks* I did about ten interviews. Virtually every single interviewer asked me how I situated myself in relation to the tradition of Agatha Christie. There is simply no perceptible connection whatsoever between *Dirty Tricks* and Agatha Christie but, as far as they were concerned,

English Crime Writing = Agatha Christie. I was an English crime writer therefore I had to have a take.

If you had been an American, they would probably ask you how your book stood in relation to Raymond Chandler or Dashiell Hammett.

For the Agatha Christie programme, I could just as equally constructed a defence for her and her books. Her work has been enormously influential, not just massively popular. I've just been reviewing a biography of Samuel Beckett which is coming out in the Fall and can you guess who one of his favourite writers turns out to be? Lots of different people from lots of different backgrounds love to read her. They love the artificiality, the sense of the game, how it all fits together, the cleverness. There's nothing wrong with that.

Getting back to the original point. For the purposes of the film, we stayed in the hotel in Dorset, which is on an island and cut off at high tide, where Christie set *Ten Little Niggers* and one of her other books. It's an odd, creepy place which I saw as being like an old folks' home. I took that and combined it with the conventions of the Agatha Christie novels and the result was *The Dying Of The Light*, which was more of a homage than a criticism.

It was the same with the Sherlock Holmes book. It seems to me that he was much less cosy in the earlier books than the later ones, which is when, I guess, Sir Arthur Conan Doyle became pretty bored with him. In the early stories Holmes did these absolutely extraordinary things like going to Bath hospital and abusing corpses with a baseball bat to find out the postmortem effects. Or firing off a revolver in his room. Or snorting some cocaine. He's a much edgier and more interesting character in those stories. Also, because he's become such a household name, people think he's cosy. He's become transmogrified in some way, in much the same way as Quasimodo has become Disneyfied in *The Hunchback Of Notre Dame*.

It's like Charles Dickens. People regard him as some sort of safe, cosy, Christmas, children's author but he's anything but.

Good God, no. He's anything but. Exactly.

Somehow, people started ignoring some of the very, very odd stuff about Sherlock Holmes. Like his fanatical misogynism. Conan Doyle puts great stress on the fact that Sherlock loathes women and wants nothing to do with them, fears them, hates them. This has been consistently brushed over. Of course, in the later stories, he's much nicer to women, there's no more mention of his misogyny or his cocaine habit or his more extreme behaviour.

So, what I did was take the first two collections of short stories, and the first two novellas, and followed them out to their logical conclusion. I didn't expect my book to be definitive, but I thought it provided an interesting perspective on the character that may have been forgotten.

It's interesting - and you see this most noticeably on TV - that many

obnoxious or unpleasant central characters becomes more sympathetic the longer the series progresses. Is Zen going to go the same way?

I think the classic example of that is Morse, which is partly due to the TV adaptations. The Morse in the original books is much crustier, more curmudgeonly, less accommodating. He's not the sort of person you'd want to be stuck in a lift with for an hour. Whereas, the John Thaw character on TV was more urbane, erudite, clever, capable of being a bit rough sometimes, but basically a nice guy. I think that's because the TV people simply thought the book character wouldn't work on TV.

The books seemed to become nicer, as though the TV series was having an effect on the books.

I think that's true. I think you may have a point here, really, which is a little disturbing if, like me, you're trying to write a series character. If you look at the early V I Warshawski's by Sara Paretsky, Warshawski comes across as a straight cut-yer-balls-off feminist. Then by book four or five, she's suddenly got this dog and develops a friendship with the elderly neighbour next door. She doesn't have a family but she has this surrogate family. It's all sort of toned down a bit. What I liked about the early books was the rather provocative edginess that they had.

I think this may be just something that happens to series.

Often what happens, perhaps, is that writers begin to like their characters more and more, and the characters become nicer and nicer.

It's certainly true that, when I started what became the Zen series, I wasn't that particularly interested in Zen himself. When I wrote *Ratking*, I had no intentions or hopes to turn it into a series. I just wanted to write a book set in and about Italy because I felt I had something to say about the place that was potentially interesting. I needed a detective who came from the outside, very much like I had, and try the crack the code of the ways people did things in this very tight, inbred, closely related inward-looking country town. Zen was the result. I wasn't in love with Zen, or thought him particularly interesting. I was much more interested in the other characters in the book. The fact that he's there in every book I write about Italy now, means that obviously I'm writing more about him. Inevitably, what you describe is going to happen. I've tried to back off this as much as possible by leaving his character and lifestyle deliberately vague.

I think there are two other characters who are never ever mentioned as being characters in your books. The first is the city or place where the books are set. The second is the Ratking. ("A Ratking is something that happens when too many rats live in too small a place under too much pressure. Their tails become entwined and the more

they strain and stretch to free themselves the tighter grows the knot binding them, until at last it becomes a solid mass of embedded tissue. And the creature that's formed...is called a Ratking. ...The Ratking is self-regulating. It responds automatically and effectively to any threat. Each rat defends the interests of the others. The strength of each is the strength of all.") **Zen tries to destroy a different type of Ratking in each book. Do you see it like that?**

Yes, I suppose that's true in a way. It's a mystery. The mystery has to be solved. The mystery usually has to be involve connections between people which are not immediately apparent. Quite often these connections are family or, more often, politics, which in Italy usually amounts to the same thing.

Is your examination of Italian corruption based on personal experience and observation?

Yes. I started off as a language teacher at the International House in Perugia, then I was hired to do the same thing at Perugia University on a renewable one year contract. Like any other institution, I realised it wouldn't hurt to make a few contacts with the people at the top, which I duly did. Unfortunately, after three years, the person at the top got transferred to another university and the number two took over. The first thing he did, purely on principle, was to fire everyone he could fire who had been in the previous administration. These people were not his people. In other words, he thought all the people who'd worked for the previous guy were a Ratking. So a) he was suspicious of us and b) he wanted to bring in his own Ratking. This is when I realised that this was how it works. If you don't have the union behind you, or tenure, or if you don't have the Mafia or something...

If you don't have power.

Yes. If you don't have some little man in Rome whom you can ask to get people off your back, you are powerless.

This atmosphere of suspicion - you're either in my Ratking or someone else's. Is this what it's like in Italy?

It's more like the internet - it's networked. You can belong to more than one Ratking at the same time. That's one of the things which make it so fascinating - trying to find out who's allegiance is to what when the chips are down. The sure thing is that anyone who is powerless and on their own won't last for very long - they are going to get gobbled up.

Are these networks similar to the attitudes towards class in Britain and wealth in America?

Regarding class, I'll never forget an evening when I was teaching school in Perugia. There was a guy from an aristocratic family, very well off, big landowner, a spoilt brat basically. There was also a guy who worked at the local cement works, trying to upgrade his qualifications to get into a management position, a member of the Communist Party and extremely left wing. Politically, they were poles apart. They hardly said a word to each other from the beginning and I had them marked down as people who clearly never would because they were class enemies, to use an old phrase. One evening the aristocratic brat rolled up on a big Honda motorcycle he just bought and, it turned out that the guy from the cement works liked motorcycles. I went downstairs to have a smoke during a break from class and found both of them having an animated, enthusiastic discussion about this motorcycle and what it did and didn't do. I just stood there thinking that this would never happen in Britain. It would be an impossible scenario because there'd be too much resentment on one side and defensiveness on the other. The class issue doesn't function in Italy in quite the same way. It functions very much like it does in America - we all want the same thing, you've got it now, we hope to have it soon, and if we don't our children will have it. There isn't the same kind of feeling there is in Britain of being ground down, that things will never change, so fuck you.

There is a sense of continuity in Italy. People build Ratkings that outlast them.

The basic thing about the Ratkings, or Mafia, or any of the systems they build is that the model is always the family. Of course, the family, by definition, is something that continues. Each of the relatives may die, but the family persists. It's survival. You, as an individual, may or may not survive any given test, but the organisation carries on. There is a much more long term approach to things in Italy.

Another thing about Italy is that there are many instances of the whole country, more or less, doing the same thing. For example, at one o'clock all over the country, everyone is sitting down to a long, leisurely lunch. Not only that, but they're all basically eating the same thing. Obviously, some are paying £70-£80 a head in a swish restaurant and others have momma's homemade, but it's the same thing. If the people swapped around between say a company canteen and a top hotel in Milan or Rome, they wouldn't feel out of place. It seems to me that, in Britain, the rich and poor eat different things. Imagine swapping people between a fish & chip shop and an expensive London restaurant. They wouldn't know what to do. There is a better sense of cohesion and cultural unity in Italy.

Your books are set in different locations, at different times in history, and have different writing styles.

I'm not absolutely sure why this is. My parents were English but I was brought up in Northern Ireland from quite an early age, six or seven, so I grew up almost as an ex-patriot. I was very aware of the fact that I was different from the rest of the class at school. I didn't move back to England until I was eighteen - I went to Sussex University for three years, then went to Canada and then

America. That's part of it. I've never felt that warm, secure glow of 'now I'm home and everything else is abroad.'

Also, I like the idea that people in different places do things slightly differently even though we're all ultimately, more or less, doing the same thing. The Zen books are about Italy, certainly, but they're also about life I hope. They've been translated into 15 or 16 languages so, to some extent, that must be true otherwise people in Japan, Finland or Bulgaria are not going to care.

It's a bit like what we were talking about the crime genre. Many crime novels are different, yet they have the same underlying themes, which is why I think they are a very good way of writing about human life. On the whole, we're all both awfully similar and slightly different, and the tension between these makes it interesting.

I think crime fiction is very good at showing people at points of stress that normally wouldn't occur. The people reveal their true nature.

That's true. I think a lot of writers are becoming obsessed with either extreme inwardness or weird nightmarish surrealistic possibilities. The reassuring thing about crime fiction is they're all ultimately objective. A crime has been committed, usually a murder. There is a body. You can't deny that - it's there, on the floor, someone did it. You have to find out who did it. The only way you can find out is by working backwards, find out what happened before the body hit the floor, who was there, who did he know, who do they know and what was going on. Structurally, before you start writing, the nature of crime fiction means that it's about stuff that actually happens in the real world. I think it's a useful way of keeping writer's feet on the ground when quite a few writers have become quite hysterical. The very nature of crime fiction means that you have to deal in real stuff. There have been a few oddball takes on the genre thing - you go in, there's a body there, then ten minutes later there's no body there. In normal crime fiction, the body disappeared because someone moved it, or the witness was unreliable, or the body wasn't dead. Those are in the realm of the real. As soon as you get into the body disappearing at will, for no reason, it's not crime and you're getting into a different genre altogether.

The crime genre, and other genres, are plot based and involve physical movement. In literary fiction, on the other hand, the development of the characters and their emotions is the plot. Before you wrote _The Last Sherlock Holmes Story_, you wrote several literary novels which went unpublished. Do you have any ambition to write literary novels?

Not so far. If I have an idea for an absolutely smashing book which doesn't have to involve any crime elements then I would have a go. But that hasn't happened so far. At the moment, I'm very happy to work within the constraints of the genre, such as they are.

As you say, genre involves plotting, and I like plotting. I enjoy trying to be devious, to surprise the reader and confound their expectations. I like that and feel that, if I tried to do something else, it wouldn't work.

You feel uncomfortable without a plot.

I take your point. Obviously plot is important to crime novels but, as with all these things, there is a spectrum rather than purely black and white. For example, character is terribly important in Patricia Highsmith's Ripley books. Everything that happens in that book is a result of character, Ripley's relationship with these people who may or may not be gay. The way he operates the various scams depends upon his complete understanding of their character and their only partial understanding of his. Those are character-driven books.

I think that's one of the reasons why Patricia Highsmith, particularly in Europe, was regarded as a literary author.

I think this is true of the best crime fiction. If you look at James M Cain's *The Postman Always Rings Twice*, the book is about three characters: the old Greek husband, the young randy wife and the drifter. They have to be those characters for there to be a story. *Double Indemnity* as well - a classic, and the movie (Raymond Chandler screenplay, Billy Wilder direction) was probably better than the book. Fred MacMurray, the insurance guy, had to be just the right sort of intelligent sap to go for Barbara Stanwyck's plan, but not so intelligent that he'd be able to see all her plan. Life is like that sometimes.

Looking back on my own life, I have my own character and personality and I've met a lot of other people with their own characters and personalities and, on the basis of that, various things have happened. A lot of the time, what happened turned out to be different to what I thought would happen. Look at my marriages, for instance...

To an extent, it depends on character but, also, to an extent it has a life of its own because of two things. First, none of us as people really understand, fully, the other people we come into contact with and, for that matter, they probably don't understand themselves either. Secondly, stuff happens or, as the American bumper sticker has it: Shit happens. Babies are born. People get or lose inheritances and/or religion. Unpredictable things happen to people. So, even if you have the characters 100% sorted out in an existing situation, that doesn't mean that five minutes down the line, the situation can't completely change.

There's a chaos to the world. We try to control the world, but it won't let us.

That's right. The crime genre is about control, really, in its classical form. It's about Sherlock Holmes or Hercule Poirot or Philip Marlowe coming in sorting out the mess and putting everything back to rights. Now, in this later stage of crime fiction, and it's certainly in my books, there is a sense that you can't put things back to rights. Zen manages to find out a few things, clarifies part of the mystery, maybe even rights, in a legal sense, some of the wrongs that have been committed, but there are still things he doesn't understand and can't control at the end of the book. At the end of *Dead Lagoon*, for example, Zen discovers who killed the American but he can't do a damn thing about it. However, he gets some things completely wrong. Zen tries to pressure his friend into testifying and his friend has a break down as a result. It's a way of saying that we do our best, we get some of it right, some of it works out and some of it doesn't. Life's not neat and tidy.

The best we seem to be able to hope for is survival, to live to fight another day. This seems to be Zen's philosophy.

Yes, survival and to do his best to do the decent thing, however we may perceive that.

BORN MARCH 21, 1947 in Wolverhampton, Michael Dibdin's parents were Frederick John (a Physics teacher) and Peggy (a state-registered nurse). His father moved around a lot as part of his job but, in 1954, they settled in Lisburn, Northern Ireland. It was a rural upbringing, full of classical music and reading.

In 1965, aged 18, Michael travelled to Sussex University in England and, in 1968, received his degree in English Literature. He returned to Northern Ireland, to Belfast, where he worked as a part-time teacher for an industrial day-release course at the College Of Technology. Michael also worked in a friend's antique shop, called Nunn's Antiques, on the Shankhill Road - not the ideal place to be after Bloody Sunday.

Michael got his Masters degree in English Literature from the University of Alberta, Canada, in 1969. It was here that he first experienced the Hippie lifestyle and, for his troubles, was thrown off his PhD course. He married Benita Mitbrodt in 1971, who bore him a child, Moselle Benita. A variety of jobs throughout Western Canada followed, including painting and decorating. Michael was writing all the time, trying to write 'the great novel.'

To help get himself into print he moved to London in 1975 with his family, where he wrote three, long, unpublished novels whilst his wife worked as a waitress. Eventually, Michael forgot about literature and wrote a novel about Sherlock Holmes and Jack The Ripper called *The Last Sherlock Holmes Story*, which was very successful. His writing career was on its way. In 1979, his wife left him and went back to Canada with their child.

1980 saw Michael move to Perugia, Italy, where he was an English teacher at International House for a year. He spent three further years as a language assistant at the University of Perugia before moving to Oxford in 1984. It was in this period that he began using his experiences in Perugia to write the first of the Zen books, *Ratking*. Michael married Sybil Sheringham in 1986 and they had a child, Emma Yvette.

Ratking won the 1988 Gold Dagger Award, presented by the Crime Writer's Association, for best crime novel of the year. The Zen series continued, as well as a diverse number of non-Zen crime novels. After Michael's second marriage broke up in 1994, he moved to Seattle, where he now lives with Katherine Beck, a crime writer he met at a Barcelona crime writers' conference, and her three children. He's friends with ex-pat travel writer Jonathan Raban, with whom he sails in Puget Sound. Michael continues writing book reviews for the *Independent On Sunday*.

Bibliography

The Last Sherlock Holmes Story (1978)
At last, it can be told, Sherlock Holmes' staggering investigation of the Whitechapel Murders. Will he find out the secret identity of Jack The Ripper? You bet your boots.

A Rich Full Death (1986)
Poet Robert Browning investigates a murder in 19th century Florence.

Ratking (1988)
After accidentally solving the kidnapping of Prime Minister Moro - his own intelligence men kidnapped him - Aurelio Zen is made into an inspector of inspectors. He travels the country's police stations ensuring every bin, eraser and pencil is accounted for. By accident, he finds himself transferred from Rome to Perugia, heading the kidnapping of the head of a prominent family, where things go from bad to worse. Zen is trying to hide, to remain a nobody, but events conspire to place him in the public eye.

The Tryst (1989)
A psychological thriller and ghost story.

Vendetta (1990)
The second Aurelio Zen novel. In full view of the closed circuit cameras, a man is murdered. It's a family affair. Zen must go to Sardinia and investigate.

Dirty Tricks (1991)
An Oxford full of businessmen's lunches, meetings and dinner parties where the only topic of conversation is money, how much they've got, spent, will have.

Cabal (1992)
Set in the Vatican. Before he can do his job and solve the mystery, Zen must fight the bureaucracy of church and state.

The Dying Of The Light (1993)
Christie pastiche - a death, a country house, multiple suspects and a plodding policeman. Only the suspects are old people, the country house an old folks' home, and what's so mysterious about old people dying anyway?

Dead Lagoon (1994)

Zen returns to Venice, his home town, to investigate the death of a wealthy American. Reminiscing about his past, he solves the crime, but is let down by virtually everyone he used to know. The past is not so rosy when confronted with the present.

Dark Spectre (1995)

A cult based on the writings of William Blake believe that some people are more important than others, and the important ones declare themselves by killing the unimportant. *Dark Spectre* is about movement - at any one time millions of people in America are travelling from one place to another - they are rootless.

Cosi Fan Tutti (1996)

The fifth Aurelio Zen novel. A farce of duality and mistaken identity, set in Naples. A damn fine and funny read.

MICHAEL DIBDIN

Elizabeth George

I TALKED TO ELIZABETH GEORGE *at her Kensington pied à terre on Valentine's Day, and I still regret not taking a bunch of red roses. She and her publicist arrived late, thanks to a previous engagement running over, putting me into a major panic, this being my first big interview, but more than made up for it by stretching my allotted hour into almost two. I had set out in my best (Vivienne Westwood) suit feeling like Lois Lane (played by Terri Hatcher), but rapidly metamorphosed into Barbara Havers (played by Jo Brand) when faced with the small but perfectly formed Ms George. Much better looking than her photograph, dressed 'casually' in an antique rose sweater, black leggings and aerobic boots, the word soignée could have been coined for her. She made (very good) tea, and served shortbread, so it was amidst the tinkling of tea cups and the crunching of biscuits that I switched on my tape recorder.*

Crow Dillon-Parkin

A Class Double Act

Elizabeth is the author of eight novels featuring Detective Inspector Thomas Lynley and Sergeant Barbara Havers of New Scotland Yard. Lynley happens also to be the Eighth Earl of Asherton, and Havers is a working class ex-grammar school girl with a massive chip on her shoulder. My perceptive spellcheck program prefers to call them Lightly and Haters. At first sight this pairing is a recipe for disaster. "I will not work with that sodding little fop!" *rages Havers:*

"Was there **anyone** in all of Scotland Yard whom she hated more than she hated Lynley? He was a miraculous combination of every single thing she despised...He was the handsomest man she had ever seen. She loathed him."

Havers herself is not liked by anyone except Webberley, her commanding officer: "she seemed so entirely unpleasant with her tiny shifting eyes and her grim little mouth" *and is referred to as* "a truculent pigheaded little bitch" *by Chief Superintendent Hillier. But by the end of* A Great Deliverance, *they have developed a working relationship that is expanded upon in the subsequent novels, and eventually they become friends.*

The series features a cast of continuing characters who are gradually introduced, and who slip in and out of the lives of Lynley and Havers in an admirably natural way. These books are tightly plotted, evocatively located, and beautifully written; incidental characters are as fully realised as the main protagonists, and no matter how much the plots may twist and intertwine, the thread is never broken. The most recent, In the Presence of the Enemy, *deals with the kidnapping of a child whose mother is a Tory MP, and whose unacknowledged father is the editor of a tabloid newspaper. The kidnapper wants Dennis Luxford to tell the truth about his first-born, but the MP thinks he set it up himself to wreck her career and bring down the government. Lynley and Havers have a very difficult case to crack, as all the evidence points to Luxford being the villain, even when his own son goes missing. Havers gets a big chunk of the action to herself, though perhaps not in the way that most Havers fans would like!*

The first question I'd like to ask is: why crime fiction, and why England?

Because when I first began writing I wasn't sure if I could carry off a novel from its beginning to its end and crime fiction had a natural structure that pulled me through, a linear structure with an established through line, and that appealed to me. Additionally, I taught a class called 'The Mystery Story', and the more I taught, the more I began to think 'I think I could write one of these myself', so it's those two reasons that got me involved in writing crime fiction.

'Why England' is more difficult to explain. When I first started answering that question, I thought well, I taught English literature, I travelled here a lot; in the Sixties when the British influence was very dominant in American culture,

I was a teenager, and I was profoundly affected by that, and I developed a real fondness for England based upon that. That's how I used to answer the question but now I've realised that part of writing (this is going to sound as though I'm wearing a pyramid on my head!) involves the psychic connection, the spiritual soul connection between the artist and the material, if you're going to write well. I have a very strong emotional, psychic soul connection to England that I don't have to the United States. I can't explain why that's the case, but when I see certain locations in England, I feel immediately touched by them, and it's that feeling of being touched in a deep way that allows me to write about the place. I can't write about just any place in England; I can't just get in my car, drive some place and say 'Oh, OK, I'm going to set my story here'.

For the book I'm working on now, *Deception on His Mind*, I was looking for a sea-side town that had seen better days. I was going to go to Devon, to Ilfracombe because I'd been there a long time ago and I thought it had what I needed, but Tony, my editor said 'No, you need to go in the other direction, you need to go to Essex', and he recommended Clacton. So I went to Clacton, I spent a day there, and I did all my usual stuff of taking pictures, and speaking to people, and taking notes, speaking into my tape recorder, but the place didn't speak back to me. So I had a real bad feeling about it because I'd come to England to do the research, but I knew that if I tried to write a book about this place, I'd be faking it. I was staying in Frinton which is just up the road from Clacton, but I knew I couldn't use Frinton, it was too upscale, too upmarket, is that the term you guys use? Then I took a drive a few miles further north and ended up in Walton-on-the-Naze, and as soon as I saw it, I knew. I thought 'This is it'; it spoke to me, the energy was there. It's different from Clacton, it's got a different topography, slightly different architecture, its much smaller, it has the basic ingredients that I was looking for, the pleasure pier, the arcade, the sort of dying architecture that could be renovated and brought back to life if somebody was willing to invest the money in it, so it had all of that same stuff, and it had the additional things that made it more interesting. It had the old fossil-rich promontory the Naze itself and this area called the Twizzle, a section of land/water mass where the tide comes in and then all of the land masses then become islands, that are isolated, so it had all kinds of interesting plot-worthy aspects to it that Clacton didn't.

So you don't go with a plot, you go for a place?

I go with the plot kernel, but for the plot kernel to germinate into a story, the place has to do it.

Because your sense of place is just stunning.

Well see, what I do is keep working at it until I find a place that's stunning to me, because not everything works for me. A certain amount of what I do is what we in the United States call a real crap shoot, where I've decided that I'm going to go to a particular section of the country for one reason or another and I single out a number of different towns, villages, great houses, places of historical or natural significance, and look at them in the hope that somewhere along the line one of them will work as a location in a book.

That's a very English thing, that places speak to you, rather than you imposing something on them.

Well, yeah, I don't think of it's being particularly English in nature, that's what works for me.

You write well about the English class system, is that another attraction?

I find it interesting, because it's not analogous to anything in the United States, so it gives me an avenue to explore things. It makes the writing more difficult, because there are elements of the class system that would mean nothing to an American reader, but everything to an English reader; the type of cigarette somebody smokes, the type of car they drive, the type of simple vocabulary that's used - whether they call what I'm sitting on a sofa or a couch, or the room we're in a sitting room or a lounge - or what is the dread word you use for the bathroom, the toilet, lavatory... In the United States if you were to say, 'I need to use the toilet' - well, nobody would say that anyway, 'cause we have all kinds of euphemisms for it [laughs], but not class-oriented euphemisms. I do remember one night, sitting at dinner with a headmaster from Christ's Hospital, and we were talking about this whole idea, and he said [adopts English accent] 'Well, I know that in America you say *john*' and I almost fell off my chair laughing and he said 'My God, what did I say?' and I said, 'I can't even tell you why that's so funny, but you would never, ever, say that, in America.' And when I tell my American friends that story, they howl, because they understand it too, but nobody can explain why it's so funny.

It seems to be the middle classes who cause the most trouble.

In the books you mean?

In the books! The middle classes who think they know best. There's Lynley and his peer group and there's Havers putting her four penn'orth in when she thinks Lynley's got it wrong, but it's always these people who think that they're better...

Mmm, I never thought about that. I suppose it's because I thought it was too much of a cliché to have anybody from either of the two ends of the spectrum be the ones that were committing the crimes... That seemed much more of a cliché to me, to have Lynley wading in because some peer of the realm has strangled his wife, or something. It doesn't mean that I won't do that some day, that has a lot of scope for plenty of fun between Lynley and Havers, but I hadn't considered it this far.

Are there things, the relationships between classes, and the relationships between the sexes, that are different in England, that might be more interesting to you?

There's certainly vast differences in the way we look at class. Class in the United States is based almost entirely on money and education. So it's economics, it's not how old your blood is, I mean, people could care less how long your family has been in the country. If you're a success at what you're doing, that's what's admired in the United States. So, this British idea of [adopts horrified English accent] 'Oh my God, he's in trade!', well, everybody in the United States has been in trade at one time or another, that's how the country grew. So that's very, very different. I think we're a little bit more advanced with women's rights, than you are in England. Women are still an oppressed minority in the United States, but it's not nearly as bad as it used to be.

Most of the relationships between men and women in your books are troubled to some extent; Lynley seems to have been becoming more of a feminist as he's got older. Do you think that men and women can have honest relationships, the way he's trying desperately to have?

I think they can if they try desperately to have them!

He's really struggling, isn't he?

I don't think it's particularly natural; I wouldn't say an *equal* relationship isn't natural, but an *untroubled* male-female relationship *is* unnatural. I mean, I don't know anybody who has an untroubled relationship with their spouse or boyfriend or whatever - I don't even know same-sex couples who have untroubled relationships!

It almost seems to become more problematic for Lynley, the more he tries to be a reasonable person. He's just digging himself in deeper, exploring 'being a man'.

Well, you know what it is? He's discovering more about Helen. The less he takes her for granted as a female (and thereby the natural extension of his own desires) the more he's gonna discover what's going on with her, what's troubling her, and *why* it is that she didn't immediately accept him and want to rush off and marry him, and that for me has also been an interesting process of discovery as well. Because I knew that Helen didn't want to immediately marry him, but it took *me* a while to figure out why.

Because more or less anybody *would* jump at the chance to marry Lynley. Have you fallen in love with him, as Dorothy L Sayers was accused of doing with Lord Peter Wimsey?

Well, I remember a distinguished English crime writer giving a talk in which she was pooh-poohing Dorothy Sayers for being in love with Peter Wimsey, but my feeling is, if you're going to write a series, you could end up being with these characters for thirty-some years, and you're in much better shape if you love them, than if you end up thinking 'Why in God's name did I create this *creature* that I now have to work with?' So I'm not *in* love with any of the characters, but *loving* them? Absolutely!

You don't think you'll get tired of them?

Why sure! I may; we may have to get a divorce! I may get tired of them, but I'm not right now. I think one of the reasons is that I've given them pretty rich backgrounds, so that gives me a lot of scope. For example, in *In the Presence of the Enemy*, you see David St James, Simon St James's oldest brother; he's been mentioned in other books, but you finally get to meet him. You've never met Judith, Lynley's older sister, but she's been mentioned, and I know she's there.

How much of this back story do you have?

Oh, I know a *lot* about these people! Some of it I know from the very first novel that I wrote, that was never published, and would never *be* published - it would be like, 'Behave, or we'll publish this novel!' It's really, really [laughing] awful! But it has the back story on Lynley and his sister, and the death of her husband, Edward Davenport. So that's why I know about Judith and her predilection for slipping between the wrong sets of sheets.

Are you going to let Lynley and Helen get married? Are you going to let them live happily ever after? Will Debs and Simon ever have a baby? And will they be happy if they do?

Well, I'll say there are some yeses and some noes in all of that!

Will Havers EVER have a boyfriend?

[EG laughs]

Can she go out with that nice new neighbour of hers?

There are yeses and noes in all of this stuff!

These are all the sorts of questions I shouldn't be asking.

What's nice for me about this, is that I've created a situation that gives me some moving room, and growing room. And I don't like books that have continuing characters, with obligatory scenes; for example, the obligatory scene where the detective's neighbour toddles in, yet again, and blah-de-blah-de-blah. I don't like that, it's really boring. So for my books, sometimes you'll see someone, sometimes you won't; I refuse to put in an obligatory scene if it's not natural to the plot. For me it's important that the characters I create for an individual novel are fully realised, and I don't want to give them short shrift to bring in some little sub-plot about Havers and her neighbour. Having said that, I will say that Havers and her neighbour have a *huge* role to play in the book I'm writing right now! Because I thought 'I'd like to explore this a little bit'; now, how far I'm gonna get in that exploration, I generally don't know, when I begin a book. Sometimes I'll know what I want to happen between Lynley and Helen in a book, sometimes it happens, and sometimes Helen says, 'No, I don't think so, not this time'!

That's very like real life.

Yeah, there's an element of, you have plans, and they don't always work out, that's that kind of thing.

And sometimes they do and it's a complete surprise, like in *Well-Schooled In Murder*, where Helen agrees to go and try a new sherry

with Lynley.

But she says that's all she's going to do, and she asks 'Will that be enough?' and he lies, and says yes, that it will be enough.

There's an awful bit in _For the Sake of Elena_ where Lynley is talking with an adulterous lecturer, who's going on about how he just wanted to feel some young flesh again, he was tired of his wife and all her stretchmarks...

Mm, yeah, yes...

...and Lynley's thinking 'Oh no, this is what we're really like. Men are terrible. I'll end up doing this to Helen.'

What he's realised is that he wants what _he_ wants, and he's never really thought about what _she_ wants. He wanted this woman because he's ready to get married, he wants to have children, he wants her to have the children, and he never thinks, 'Wait a minute, what impact is this going to have on her life?'

Because presumably he, like so many other men, is used to having things completely his own way, just assuming that other people will go along with it.

Yeah, especially assuming, in Lynley's particular position, why wouldn't he think that some woman would be just mad to marry him and have his baby.

What an awful fate [both laughing] to have to marry him and have his children!

To have his children, and all that money, and two houses, and this and that. There's a section in _In the Presence of the Enemy_ where Helen's reflecting on the fact that she's long been able to resist all these things about Lynley - that he was handsome, that he was rich, and he's intelligent, and all these other things, but that the one thing that she could never resist is when he would make himself vulnerable. and that was just devastating to her, when she had to respond to his vulnerability. And I think that in some respects he knows that, too, that's the weapon he has to use against her.

Do you think it's fair to say that your books are more driven by character than by plot?

Oh, yeah! Absolutely.

There's an article in _Writers News_ that suggests that your plot style has shifted somewhat, with the last three books, in that the death that needs investigating isn't always the first thing that happens, and that gives you more space for exploring character.

Yes, that's always been the important thing to me. Sometimes I move the murder up front to sort of get the ball rolling, but the creation and exploration of character was where my commitment was from the very beginning. I think I've gotten better at doing it, with each successive book, but that's always what I wanted to do. I begin with the plot kernel (the killer, the victim and the motive) then the setting, and then I create the characters. That's a long process, designing them from the ground up, as if I were some sort of god, creating someone, not only physically and mentally but spiritually and psychologically, and historically. By the time I start writing about that character, I have a voice for them, an agenda, a through line, a pathology, and the person can emerge, much more realistically than if I were just putting a name on the page and saying 'Now what?'.

Mm, yes, this is a 'bad person's name' so... because it isn't always bad people, is it, who do these bad things?

No. *Missing Joseph* in particular was a book in which I wanted to write about a perfectly good person who has killed another perfectly good person, and the question was, why? Why did this happen, why did this person commit this horrible crime? I had to go back and think, well, what was it, and I looked for the circumstance that had the most creative energy. At first I thought it was that this woman and her husband had this child who wasn't theirs, and that had a little bit of energy. And I thought, OK, well, maybe not, maybe she's not married. So the fact that she wasn't married, had a little bit more energy. And I thought, she's not married, and somebody comes to this village, where she's hidden. Who could it be? Could it be somebody maybe transferred there, who would be transferred to a village...how about a vicar? OK so it's a vicar, how did the vicar know her? Well, maybe she was the vicar's housekeeper, maybe she's the vicar's cousin, maybe she's a woman who lived in the village and the vicar knew she could never have kids. And then I thought, wait a minute, what if she's the vicar's *wife*? And as soon as I said that, it was like, the energy just went, foom, foom, *voom!*

...because it's a real shock!

Oh yeah! And I knew that was the story, right then!

It's almost the purest motive, killing to protect your child.

Exactly. And that whole book was about that, you know, that there's no black, there's no white, there's just these terrific shades of grey. I think that some people, in writing a crime novel, want to do two things. First of all they want to kill someone who deserves to be killed, or they want the killer to be really evil and horrible. I generally don't set out to do that. I generally set out to kill someone who doesn't at all deserve it, because in real life, when people are murdered, they're usually really innocent people, who are either in the wrong place at the wrong time, or the victim of someone's obsession, or someone's jealousy, or someone's need for revenge. They get murdered for all kinds of strange and horrible reasons, and that to me is much more realistic. Now, does the reader get upset? Well, yeah... but real people get upset when members of their family are murdered! I mean, that's the whole point, to try to look at what a crime of grave enormity does to an individual, an institution, a society, or to a family.

Everything has consequences. That's always played out in your work.

I like to have everything in the book causally related. Now that may not mean causally related to the main plot, but I like it to be causally related to it's individual subplot. If you were to take all of the subplots, let's say all the Rodney Aronson stories out of *In The Presence of The Enemy*, and read his scenes one after another, then you should see the complete story, about him, and his relationship with Dennis Luxford.

So you've got several chains of events that go on together, with various consequences?

Yeah.

I was amazed that you killed Charlotte Bowen! I thought it was an incredibly brave thing to do...

Mmm, so, you thought it was going to be a kidnapping novel?

Well, I suspected that somebody would have to die, but I wasn't prepared for it to be her.

People say, in crime fiction you're not supposed to kill children or animals...as if children and animals are not killed, in real life. The genesis of this story is the kidnapping of a girl called Polly Klaus, in Northern California, a horrendous crime that happened just before I started to write *In The Presence Of The Enemy*, when I didn't know what I was going to write about at all, and I knew I was under contract to write a book... and I could not think of the plot... and this story broke, about a twelve year old girl who had been having a slumber party, with two other girls at her house. The mother was there, asleep in the other room and this man broke into the house, said to the girls, 'Which one of you lives here?' She said, 'I do', he tied up the other two, put gags on them, took her out, and murdered her.

It was horrible, and they didn't find her body for months and months, he'd hidden the body very cleverly, and people wanted to believe she was alive...and then they finally found the body. Well, that was my first idea, because I thought, it was such a bizarre kidnapping, that it had to have been an inside job, but it turned out that it was one of these random nutcases that had done it; but that's where it began, with the idea of kidnapping a child. At the same time as I was beginning it, Sue Grafton was writing *K is for Kidnap*. I had dinner with her, and I said to her, 'Are you doing *K is for Kidnap*?' and she said, 'God knows I tried! I got 400 pages into it and I had to throw it away.'

It's *K is for Killer*, isn't it?

Yeah, she couldn't do 'kidnap', she said, 'I'd tried so hard, and it just didn't work', and I thought, 'Well, that's a nice challenge, let me see if I can do it and make a kidnapping novel work.' Of course it ended up to be kidnappings and killing, well, it sort of went, kidnapping, killing, kidnapping! I wanted to take up the gauntlet, even though Sue Grafton didn't know that she had thrown it down [laughs].

I think kidnapping is one of those crimes that is very hard to resolve, fictionally, because you've got so much tension...

Plus how do you keep it going? You keep it going with getting phone calls from the kidnapper, and threatening notes, and this and that - it's pretty tough to keep it going.

It had an excellent twist, with the kidnapper turning out to be a policeman...

What I wanted to do is, you see, in America, Sergeant Havers is a very popular character, she's like, the favourite character of everyone, and people are always saying to me, 'Oh, can't Sergeant Havers have someone?' So I thought, what if the reader thinks 'Thank God! Elizabeth George has finally given Sergeant Havers a boyfriend!' [laughs]

I fell for it!

One of my girlfriends, it was so cute, when she was at the point where Havers had met Robin, and it had gone on for a couple of chapters, she said to me, 'Ohh, I like Robin Payne so much! This is so neat,' and I didn't say anything, and then afterwards she called me up and said 'You must think I'm really stupid!' [laughs] And I said 'No, that was what you were supposed to think', you were supposed to like him, you were supposed to think Sergeant Havers has finally got a boyfriend.

And she even almost got some sex, didn't she?

What I loved about it is when Lynley says to her, after he calls her on the phone and says *"Payne's our man"*, and then he says, *"Go back to what you were doing"*! [laughs]

You were so cruel to her!

And Havers is thinking, *"How the hell am I going to do that?!"*

I had this inkling that it was going to end in tears, but I thought maybe he would get killed in the line of duty or something, not that he'd be the murderer.

I also wanted to challenge myself with a physical fight, because I'd never really done a fight before. I'd had minor fights, at the end of *Payment in Blood* there's maybe one exchange of fisticuffs, and I wanted to see if I could do it. And I thought, wait a minute, how do I put the spin on this fight, *everybody* does fights, so I thought, well, how about if it's Sergeant Havers who has the fight, instead of Lynley, the 'manly man'.

I dunno, Havers is probably a better fighter than Lynley.

Yeah! So that was a lot of fun, to figure out exactly how to write that, and how this altercation was gonna take place, in this little castle.

I was worried you were going to kill Leo Luxford as well, by this point.

No, you see, because it came full circle, with Dennis Luxford's realisation of - what I like about Dennis Luxford, and I didn't expect to like him, as a character, and I really *did* like him, as he went along; he was supposed to be this scurrilous tabloid sleazeball, but I really started liking him, because to me, his struggles about his son were honest. Because I do think that any father, faced with an artistic, eccentric child, there's going to be a little niggle inside, where he starts thinking, 'Oh no, is this child gonna be gay?' and I think that's a worry for parents, I think it's an honest worry.

He really reminded me of my own son, I was really worried for him. But I think that kind of little boy would do what Leo did, in extremis. Dennis realised that it was OK for him to be a wimp, but then Leo turned out to be quite tough.

And in the end it didn't really matter. Leo was who he was, and Luxford was going to try to accept him, and do his best, from that point, to keep from quashing the kid down.

A lot of your characters - not just your main characters, but characters peculiar to each book - do end up changing and growing throughout the book; and it's the ones who don't, generally, who either are the villains or who end up being hurt...

...Mhm hm...

...like the wretched Eve Bowen, who in the end, did deserve, I think, to lose that poor child.

With *In The Presence Of The Enemy* I wanted to explore the flipside of what I'd been exploring in a lot of books, the whole issue of motherhood. The apogee of my exploration of motherhood was *Missing Joseph*, which was a long meditation on motherhood, so I thought, I really have, 'been there, done that', so I thought, what if I take a character who has had a child, but is just totally unsuited, because some people think just because you're a woman, you're suited to be a mother...I mean, 'You've got the right equipment, so, be a mother!' And I just don't believe that that is the natural state of every woman; so here's this woman who finds herself pregnant, and for political reasons, political expediency, knowing how everything is subject to scrutiny by the tabloids, finding herself pregnant, realises 'Well, I'm going to have to have this kid, and project myself as well as I can as a mother, champion of the family', and so on. And I wanted to explore the idea of a woman who doesn't feel maternal at all, who's driven by her career, who has a tremendous need for perfection, and who when this need is threatened, becomes a paranoid personality.

She has this one idea in her head, that Luxford is behind it, it's a real Tory mindset.

Well, she knows *she* hasn't told anybody, he's the only one who knows, this is her major secret. Whatever the source, it has to be Luxford, she can't see it any other way.

It seemed you suddenly got very topical, dealing with the tabloids,

and parliamentary sleaze...

Yeah, it was purely by chance that on the plane coming over to do this research, I opened up the British newspaper, and here was Tim Ye? - Yo? - and uh, a love child, and I couldn't believe my eyes - I was coming over here to do research about this MP with a love child, and it was playing out in the newspapers, even as I was doing the research! So it couldn't have been a luckier circumstance for me, because the tabloids did everything that I assumed that they would do, and my *God*! they were digging into his past, and I mean, good God! it was amazing!

Most of us don't need to know that stuff, but when you've got politicians telling us how we ought to live our lives...that hypocrisy...

Yes, well, that was what was so much fun, that's why I created the Recommitment to Basic British Values, in my book, and that was right when John Major was doing Back to Basics [laughs], and it was, I mean, it was funny, it was sort of ironic, but at the same time you just had to laugh at what hypocrites they were!

You had the Animal Rights movement in *Playing for the Ashes*, and I think it was just coming into paperback at the time we had all the veal calf protests, was that another piece of serendipity?

That was another coincidence. When I came to England to do the research for that book, I was doing a book on cricket, I knew that's what it was going to be. I always look in the papers to see what's going on, and I saw that they were having a big Animal Rights meeting at Earl's Court Exhibition Centre, so I went to that, and gathered a lot of information, and decided, yeah, I think I can use this in the book as well, so it was pure serendipity. I want the books to be able to stand the test of time so obviously they can't be too topical; not that I think I'm writing the world's greatest literature, but I'd like somebody to be able to pick them up ten years from now and read them and them still have some sort of impact on the reader, and still have some common reference points. I obviously have to be careful now not making any references to royal marriages, considering how fast and furiously they're falling by the wayside! I mean, time was, they were always gonna to be there, just like there will always be an England, but uh...

...I think *that's* looking doubtful now!

Ye-e-s, [laughs], but that's not the case any more, so I have to be pretty careful with those references. I think that Parliament will always have sleaze, and the tabloids, unless they put some controls on the press, which I know they've tried to do periodically, I'm pretty safe in having the tabloids used in the books too.

The British attitude to sex is just *so* peculiar...

Oh *yeah*!

It would take hundreds of years before people's attitudes shift.

It is the most interesting sort of attitude. I can remember reading about the whole Profumo scandal, I mean now, I certainly don't think it would bring down the government, but back then, it was in all the newspapers and magazines in the United States, and I never forgot any of those people. It's interesting the kind of knock-on effect that sort of press had.

Yes, culturally, it's just accepted now that if anybody does anything that's the slightest bit out of line in their private life, that's it, they're fair game for the tabloids, and can end up losing their career over what's essentially their private life, whereas in France, you're not allowed to say anything about people's private lives.

Yeah, well it's the same thing in the United States, too, that your private life is public game, and everybody goes after it, not only the tabloids, but what we would call the legitimate press, and then the tabloid television and news.

Do you think it's worse over there?

Well, shoot, I don't know. Because of the way your politicians are elected, I think it's probably worse in the United States. Because your governmental leader comes from within his party, but in the United States, the President's elected directly by the people, so he's probably more scrutinised, than the leaders are here, 'cause they'd be having to - God, there are over six hundred? people in Parliament. I don't imagine there's enough time, or energy to go through their pasts. In our country once the presidential candidates are established then, *hah*!

In America, the press can just kill somebody's campaign, in a way that they can't here, because here you've got the party machine behind you.

Absolutely. That's what happened to Ed Muskie, when Richard Nixon was trying to set things up so that he was running against George McGovern, he had the dirty tricks campaign going, and he ended up running against McGovern, who he wanted to run against. What a slimeball he was! But that's another story!

D'you think you'd ever write something set in America?

I've written one short story set in America, that's going to be published in an anthology this year. I was very pleased to come up with the idea for a short story, because I'm not a short story writer, at all. My philosophy has always been, why say it in a thousand words when you can say it in six hundred pages... It's hard for me to paint with broad enough brush strokes to be concise, it's real tough. In this instance I had an invitation to write something for an anthology at the precise moment that I had an idea for a short story, so I wrote it, and it takes place in Southern California, in Newport Beach, close to where I live. I used a quirky little place on Balboa Peninsula where I have my detective have his office up above a place I used to get my hair cut, JJ's Natural Haircutting. I really did have to look for quirky places, there's not much quirkiness in that particular part of Southern California. One thing that's helpful for me when I'm writing about England is that I notice the details, because it's a foreign country, but in the United States I don't notice the details because I see them every day, and details are an important part of setting, character, and plot.

How long do you have to spend somewhere, to get that feel?

It depends on the kind of research I'm doing. For location research, hmm, it's about a week...

As little as that?!

...to get the feeling for the place, yeah, about a week, and then I might go back a second time, to kind of fine tune it, and then I might go back a third time after I've got the rough draft done, just to make sure I've got everything correct. The harder things for me are the things that I can use for character details, because then you get into the kind of stores people shop in, the kinds of products that they buy, and what those products would say about them. In America, these are things I would just *know*, naturally, because I've lived there all my life. One of my students was writing a story, and she completely understood the idea of telling detail of character, because she said that the man and his wife were sitting at the kitchen table, wearing matching bowling shirts. That was it [clicks fingers] everybody in my writing group knew what the entire kitchen looked like. All she had to say was they were wearing matching bowling shirts, because it says everything about a class, a culture, everything, but that kind of stuff is ach! it's really, really difficult for me to know, so that's when I have to get on the phone, and call my friends, and say 'OK, here's the situation, this is the character, what would they be eating, what would they be smoking', and my friends in England are very, very wonderful, very supportive, and really, really help.

Playing for the Ashes **hinges on the kind of cigarette that...**

Yeah, and I was really proud, I did that all on my own and only got one pack of cigarettes wrong. I wrote a description of the characters, and then put down, this person smokes such-and-such, and then John Blake at the publishing company told me whether I was right or wrong.

Do you mind saying which one you got wrong?

I had the sixteen year old boy smoking Camel cigarettes.

Ooh no!

Yeah, see!

Not with his background!

So did you have an idea for an arson that wouldn't work the way the person who set it wanted it to work, or did you investigate arson first?

I investigated arson, because I knew that it was going to be called *Playing For*

The Ashes, so I knew it had to have something to do with a fire. I began by talking to the arson investigators. And it was interesting for me to find out how arson works, that if you were to set a fire this way, that the cigarette wouldn't burn, even if the entire house burnt down, it would still be there for the arson investigators to find.

I told them that I wanted a woman to start the fire. And they said, 'OK, if a woman starts the fire here are the ways women start fires, versus the way men start fires.' We went through all these different ways, and they suggested some pretty bizarre things. And I kept saying, 'that's not going to work with the plot', and then we finally came up with the cigarette and the arm chair, and how the whole fuse device would work. They actually gave me one of their books on arson, which was very helpful.

It's very technical, you don't just have 'an arson'.

Yeah, a convenient little arson. Originally I thought she was going to torch the whole place, but then I decided it was much nicer - and originally she wasn't going to kill Kenneth Fleming...in my mind, she was killing Gabriella Patten, but then I thought, wait a minute, what if?...she accidentally kills Kenneth Fleming? And then I felt all that energy all over again. And then that's when I knew she had to kill Kenneth Fleming and not Gabriella Patten, which wouldn't have been nearly as interesting.

It's a much more interesting puzzle, because you always assume that the person who has been killed *is* the intended victim.

It was a much more interesting story, I mean, the irony, the horror, here she is, she *loves* this man, and she's actually trying to save him from the heartbreak that Gabrielle is causing him, only to discover that she's killed the man she loves.

It is really tragic, isn't it? There's a lot of that tragedy of errors in your work, things go horribly wrong.

Hmm, yeah, people make dumb mistakes...

Either they have the Classical tragedy thing, the fatal character flaw, like Eve Bowen's awful pride, or they do the wrong thing, although they're trying to do the right thing. Like poor old Robin Payne, who's trying to help his dreadful, dreadful mother...

Only to find out, when she says 'There's been a dreadful misunderstanding'...

You also deal a lot with the family, the problems in the family.

Yeah, my books are about the family, and the dysfunctioning family, and I use the crime novel as a device to explore that. See, I used to read crime novels where no-one was related to anybody, including the victim, and I thought it was strange that someone would die, and nobody was ever sad or came forward to claim the body. I thought this is sort of interesting, people die and no-one's related to them. I didn't want to do that, I wanted to explore situations in which killer and victim had significant others, as well as the detectives. If a

ELIZABETH GEORGE

killing arises from a familial relationship, then obviously you're talking about a troubled family...

...murder doesn't happen in a family where everybody's getting on alright...

...and besides, if everyone's getting along alright and communicating, it'd be a boring book, a white bread story where everyone's really nice and everybody gets along. You don't have any drama, you don't have any tension, you have no conflict so that would be pretty tedious.

You wouldn't write about that, would you?

No, but you could probably do a comic novel based on that kind of thing!

Yeah [laughing]. You won't do a comic novel based on a dysfunctional family?

No, you could though. I mean, there are certainly a lot of comedies on television based on dysfunctional families.

Would you move to television?

You mean as a screenwriter?

Would you like to see...

...these things on TV?

They would be wonderful, I think.

Well, they've been optioned by Blue Heaven productions, ITV has given us three hours of TV time, and we were ready to roll on *A Great Deliverance*, in the Spring, for a Fall showing, and the screenwriter could not do an adaptation that the producer liked. So we have to find a new screenwriter, and we began that process in December, and I'm not quite sure where we are now, but it's looking better and better as far as getting it on television eventually.

Would you be doing the whole series?

Yeah, they were looking at doing the whole series.

Have they got anybody in mind, acting wise?

No, because they can't really even do that until they have a script to show somebody.

Because Lynley is going to be difficult.

Everybody says that! That's the one thing everyone says, 'Oh my God.'

Havers, well, there are some wonderful women about. *[During the interview I was racking my brain to remember the name of the actress I had thought would make a brilliant Havers, and it was only on the train home that 'Mossie Smith' sprang to mind. I sent Elizabeth George a note to this effect, and in her reply she said that Mossie was her first choice too, as long as the whole process didn't take so long that Mossie got too old for the part.]*

Havers is simple, Havers'll be the easiest of the roles to cast, Lynley will be the toughest.

He's almost too perfect physically, and Britain isn't terribly good

at that kind of actor.

You've got some pretty good looking guys running around.

It's whether you can get them to do the upper class thing.

Yes! That's really true. Well, we'll see.

Do you get to say whether you like someone for a part?

I get to participate; now, who knows what that means? I think if they find someone that they think is really, really perfect, and I'm down on my knees pleading them 'No!', I don't imagine that I will carry the day.

Like Anne Rice and *Interview with the Vampire*?

Yeah, exactly; but I don't think I'd go the Anne Rice route of screaming and yelling about it.

She did have to recant of course, when she saw it.

Yeah I know. That made me think the whole thing was a big publicity ploy, which I wouldn't doubt, you know, because it got everybody really interested in the film. I must have been the only person in America who always believed Tom Cruise could play that role.

I didn't believe it, because he's too short.

I had no problems, you know what, I thought he was so utterly wrong for the role he's gonna have to go in there and just, as we say, kick butt!

I wanted Rutger Hauer, like she did, because I think he's brilliant.

I thought she wanted Daniel Day Lewis - oh, she must have wanted him for the Brad Pitt part.

Originally, years and years ago, she wanted Rutger Hauer for Lestat, when he was younger, and less chubby, when he was in his *Bladerunner* days.

Yeah, he would have to be a lot thinner.

Or wear a big cloak. All the time.

Yeah [laughs].

I think Sean Bean would be a good Lynley if you could get him to do the voice.

That's *exactly* who I think would be a wonderful Lynley. But he's doing something right now on television [*Sharpe*], so I don't imagine he could do another show right now, could he? But he is *pre*-cisely who I'd like to see do it. But he'd have to be able to do the voice, that's what Tony Mott, my editor, always says.

It is quite a hard one to do.

But, he's an actor, he can do everything else. I think he'd be great.

What about anyone else?

I don't know that much about British television actors, I only really see what we get on *Masterpiece Theatre*. The reason I know who Sean Bean is, is he's been in several movies. He played the terrorist, who I called the terrorist with access to Concorde, in *Patriot Games*. He kept popping up in places;

ELIZABETH GEORGE

three hours after he had left Africa he was in America, you know, that kind of thing. And I remembered who that was when people pointed him out to me later on. I have seen the person who I would like to do Helen, and that's the woman who played Dorothea in *Middlemarch*, who is just perfect for Helen. Now, whether she could be that frivolous kind of, frivolous, but with frivolity as her defence, I don't know. But physically, she's perfect. Helen has this veneer of frivolity that really isn't who she is, but that's how she defends herself. My producer agrees, so she's the one that we would seek.

And this would be, hopefully, the back end of 1997?

I hope, if we can just get the script.

It's a long timescale, isn't it, will you get fed up waiting?

Well, this has been going on for years, this is the second group to option the books, so the last thing I worry about is whether these books are ever going to be made into a TV series.

You're more interested in writing the books?

Yeah, and not only that, but it takes forever, so why ever get your hopes up about something so risky, chancy and unlikely to occur!

Your books are whydunnits, not whodunnits?

Yeah, it's more why than who.

You write to find out things, rather than to say things?

Somewhat, certainly. Part of writing is to make it clear to me, and to the reader, why this was done, so that, if I'm successful, the reader understands the crime completely, rather than just have, 'she was killed because of the inheritance...' To have a psychological motivation, that I'm able to explain adequately, in the story, is important to me. You want your book to pass the refrigerator test. Alfred Hitchcock used to say that if the people who saw his movies didn't have any questions about the movies until they got home and opened the refrigerator, then it was a successful film. But, if they're saying 'Hang on...' while the credits are rolling, then you've got a problem. I think with books you want to do more than that, you want it to linger, give the reader something to think about as well as being entertainment.

I read *Missing Joseph* just after I had my daughter, and being postnatal, I found it a very difficult book, emotionally.

Yeah, I bet that would stay with ya...

Because there's a real rawness that carries on, makes you think. I assume this was your intention, to make people think things other than just, 'Let's get this crime sorted out'.

Exactly! [In *Missing Joseph*] I wanted the reader to be on the horns of the same dilemma that Lynley and Robin Sage were on, because their dilemma was 'what do you do?' There's this woman in London, who isn't a bad mother, not in an ideal situation, but she clearly loves this little cast of boys that have all had different fathers, so doesn't she *deserve* to get her daughter back? She hasn't really done anything wrong, so does she deserve to lose that child? And then, Juliet Spence is only trying to protect a child that she thinks needs protecting, so it's kind of an interesting kind of dilemma that everybody's facing, and I wanted the reader to have that same feeling. What do you do? What *do* you do?

In *Playing for the Ashes* Olivia gives her journals to Lynley, leaving him with another dilemma. He says to Helen right at the end of the book "I want things to be cut and dried", which is why he's become a detective in the first place. I think people who read detective fiction like to have everything sorted out by the end of the book, but life isn't like that, and, although so far you've always had the villain apprehended, you don't always leave things cut and dried. Lynley's left with a load of information about the Animal Rights movement that by rights he should be turning over, because these people are terrorists, no matter where your sympathies lie....and he's stuck with the dilemma, because he's a straight down the line guy.

Exactly, a lot of people didn't understand the ending, people said to me, 'Well I don't understand, why does Olivia write all this about the Animal Rights thing?' Well, because she wants him to face the same dilemma that he's asking her to face - how does it feel to betray somebody?

You mention the Kenneth Fleming murder trial in the new book, *In the Presence of the Enemy*. You had some feedback from a previous book, it's an ongoing thing, with consequences...

...But it should still stand alone, so that if you're reading it, it's not like 'Oh my God, I don't understand what this is all about', it doesn't need a little footnote, naming the book and its price [laughs].

How far in advance do you work?

Well, now I'm just writing the next one, the one that follows *In the Presence of the Enemy*. I'm about three hundred and fifty pages into that.

So you work quite fast? Well, it seems fast to me!

I do five pages a day, so on the one hand that doesn't seem very fast, but then at the end of the week you have twenty-five pages. So I've written about a third of the book, well, maybe a little more than that, I'd like to bring it in at about eight hundred and fifty pages, if I can.

Do you do much in the way of re-writing, or do you write it 'in best' first time?

Um, the first draft is the most difficult draft, 'cause subsequent drafts are generally polishing, they're generally not altering anything big in the story. So I take a lo-o-ot of time over my first draft, I'm pretty meticulous, I don't just sort of go, I'll slam it down on paper and then let my editor figure it out, or slam it down and hope that I can rewrite it later on. I try to get it as well done the first time through as I can, so that my work in second and third draft is fun, rather than agonising!

Yeah, because although it's the hardest it's probably the most interesting, the first draft?

Yeah, and it's also the scariest, it's the superlative of all of that stuff, you know, the most fun, but the most difficult, and all that. Because I don't know if it's gonna work or not, in the particular format I've chosen, with this particular set of characters. For example, right now, three hundred and fifty pages into this book, I know that I have to change something about one of the main characters. I can see it's not working, he's over the top, I need to rein him back in, which means I'm gonna have to go back through and really evaluate him, but I won't do that till the second draft. I'll just start reining him in more now, and see if I can bring it all into line later on.

That must be quite difficult, changing a character?

He'll still have the same core need, the same agenda, and the same pathology, but it's just his performance will be reined in. I had to do that with *For the Sake of Elena*; the murder victim's mother was running on such a high note she had no place to go! What I did was, I took all her scenes out, when I was done with the book, and then just reconstructed them. The same stuff happens, but her approach is a little bit different.

That's very meticulous!

Well, yeah, but I like it all to hang together, I really want the books to be good, to be worth someone's time, I want the reader to feel as if they're in the hands of an author who has really put forward a big effort and not just slammed something down and turned it into the publisher and collected their cheque and moved on.

Is your background in Literature a big help here?

I think my background in *writing* has been a tremendous help. Literature, yes, but my background as a writing instructor has really helped, because you can't teach what you don't learn yourself, and so the fact that I've had to spend so much time examining the art and craft of writing has been extremely helpful.

You don't teach any more, presumably?

I teach at the college level now, but I only teach every couple of semesters. I really don't have the time to teach a full load, or even one course every semester. Teaching is a big time commitment, more than anything else; I really like it, I really like interacting with my students, but what I want to do now is shorter seminars. I can't be there for the full eighteen weeks any more, because there are too many other obligations right now.

Does the machinery of being an established writer carry you along

with it?

Yeah.

...it's not just sitting in your work room writing...

Exactly...

...it's *being* 'Elizabeth George'.

Yeah, it's doing publicity stuff, book tours, public appearances, and things like that, so there's a lot more stuff that goes along with it. I work with a group of writers too, individually, in my home and we have a seminar that has been going on for about five years. We meet every week that I'm home, and when I go away sometimes they meet on their own, and sometimes they go, ah, 'Phew! she's gone, I don't have to write', and sometimes they use the time to write furiously, but I really, really, enjoy that continuing contact with other writers.

Do they get to see your work in progress?

Sometimes, but only if we don't have enough readers on a particular night, because I'm there to help them, it seems sort of ridiculous for me to be [laughing] taking their money and then having them critique my work, it doesn't seem very fair! But I do read to them occasionally.

Whose work do you like to read?

We-e-ell, let's see; I just finished Amy Tan's new book, I enjoy her stuff. I don't read much in crime literature, at all.

A bit too close to work?

Yeah, it's too close to it, I really actually never have read a lot of it. I do read PD James when she brings out a new book; I do occasionally read Ruth Rendell. I have read the 'oldies', you know, Dorothy L Sayers, Margery Allingham, Ngaio Marsh and Sir Arthur Conan Doyle. I've read some Colin Dexter, and some Minette Walters, but beyond that, the people whose work I really admire the most are John Fowles, who's probably had the largest impact on my writing, and John Le Carré, whose career I really admire the most, just because of the way he's grown as a writer. It's just amazing when you look at his first book and you look at how he's writing right now, I think he's just a magnificent writer. I'm trying to think of the people whose books I used to have here and grab off the shelves, modern writers. Alice Hoffman, I adore. She's an American who writes Magical Realism, and she's just, oh I love her books, she's just a wonderful writer, she writes with a great deal of *heart*. And I dip into the classics, I re-read Jane Austen periodically, and Thomas Hardy. I'm real eclectic, you know, I read the back of cereal boxes too!

A compulsive reader! How many more books do you have in the pipeline?

Just the one I'm writing right now. I used to know maybe one or two books ahead, but now it's just the one I'm working on right now.

Your titles are always very apt; do you get your titles early on?

ELIZABETH GEORGE

This time I didn't, this time I just got the title last week, after three hundred and fifty-some pages, and I realised what I wanted to call it. Sometimes I have it before, *Playing for the Ashes* I had about three years before, and sometimes I change. *Missing Joseph* was originally called the *Cipher in the Snow*, and as soon as I wrote the first scene in the National Gallery, and the guy said something about the painting was missing Joseph, I knew that was what it had to be called. Because then I could see how it was really double-edged, and I especially love it when I can come up with a double-edged title.

Yes, you did that right from the first one, *A Great Deliverance*. That was a really harrowing start to a series. Is there anything you're afraid of dealing with, anything you wouldn't do - having started off with child abuse and infanticide!?

If I was afraid of anything, it would mostly be, I would concerned about whether I would have the adequate resources to research it, that would be the only thing that would stop me from writing something. Or something that I felt was really boring, I mean, frankly, the nuclear power industry that PD James wrote about in that one book just doesn't interest me at all. It's the personal that interests me, so I would probably shy away from things that were impersonal or scientific, or financial, or beyond the scope of my interest. I would like to stick with things that I find interesting, because I'm the person who's going to have to spend a year or more writing about it! and if I'm not interested, then I don't feel I can deal with it with any degree of passion.

Will we see more of the latest member of Lynley's team, Nkata?

Ultimately, but not in this next book; so far, the only continuing character that you'll see is Havers. The other ones are there at the beginning but then it becomes Havers' book, and right now, that's the way I'll keep it but if it doesn't work out, I'll toss the whole thing out and begin again, and make it a regulation Lynley-Havers book.

Would that be a wrench, to do that?

Well, it'd be a disappointment sure, I'd be real disappointed in myself if I wasn't able to carry it off, but if it doesn't work, it doesn't work. I'm not gonna force something that's unworkable, because if you do that I think it's not gonna be a good book. But I'd love to be able to prove to myself that Barbara Havers can carry a book on her own, and she does have such great attitude, which I love [laughs]. and plus this is the first book I'm writing during a heatwave, too, which is great fun, it's just wonderful...

...mm, how's she going to dress, in a heatwave?!

Ohh, just wait! She has some pretty interesting things that she's wearing[laughs].

I bet[laughs]. But we shouldn't be laughing at her, her heart's in the right place.

Hmm.

Are you going to kill her mother off?
I've no plans to do that in the immediate future [laughs]
Poor Barbara, never mind. All the same, it is rather a burden for her.
Yeah. but see, I think everyone has some sort of burden, in one way or another.

Biography

ELIZABETH GEORGE was born in Warren, Ohio, on the 26th of February 1949. She attended the University of California, Riverside, gaining a BA in English. At the California State University, Fullerton, she later gained a MS. in counselling. She married Ira Tobin in 1971, and worked as an English teacher at Mater Dei High School in Santa Anna and at El Toro High School, both in California.

Since 1988 she has written and worked as a creative writing teacher at Coastline College in Costa Mesa, Irvine Valley College and the University of California, Irvine, all in California.

She received the Anthony and Agatha Best First Novel awards in 1989 for *A Great Deliverance* and received the Grand Prix de Litterature Policiere in 1990 for the same novel

Well Schooled In Murder was awarded the prestigious German prize for international mystery fiction, the MIMI in 1990.

Elizabeth lives in Huntington Beach, California, and is currently working on her ninth novel.

Bibliography

(Inspector Thomas Lynley and Sergeant Barbara Havers in all books)

A Great Deliverance (1988)

"I did it, and I'm not sorry" says Roberta Teys, sat with the decapitated corpse of her father. The village priest enlists Scotland Yard's help in proving her innocence, and for this case, Inspector Lynley is saddled with Sergeant Havers, who has been unable to get on with anyone, but who has an excellent brain concealed by a bad attitude. The investigation is made more difficult by Roberta's inability to speak after her initial confession. In finding the truth about William Teys murder, Lynley and Havers uncover more than they bargained for about the lives of the locals, and reveal a lot more about themselves than they might have wanted to. They end the novel as almost-friends, and as colleagues with a degree of professional respect for the other's abilities, but it is not an easy ride.

Payment in Blood (1989)

Almost a country house mystery; a theatre company is reading a new play at a large Scottish mansion, and the playwright is murdered that evening. Lynley loses his usual detachment, wanting desperately to pin the murder on the new lover of Lady Helen Clyde, an old friend with whom he has fallen in love. Havers believes they have been assigned the case because one of the suspects is a peer of the realm, so she is somewhat blinkered by her own views on class. She works hard to bring Lynley to his senses, and equally hard to obtain justice for the second murder victim , an innocent bystander. Lynley's jealousy almost destroys any chance he has of developing his relationship with Helen.

Well-Schooled in Murder (1990)

An old school friend of Lynley's seeks his help in finding a missing schoolboy. The boy turns up dead in a churchyard some distance away, and he has been tortured before being killed. Memories of Lynley's own school days surface when he and Havers go to Bredgar Chambers, an old public school with some very nasty things going on under the veneer of civilisation. The old school tie helps to open some doors, and Havers' natural mistrust of the upper classes and their motives proves very useful. The resolution of the murder does not lead to the *"black satisfaction of a murder avenged and a killer sent on his way to the bar of justice",* because too many lives have been shattered. Lynley finally meets Havers' mother, after eighteen months of Havers hiding the truth about her home life, and Lynley allowing her to do so. The book ends with the return of Lady Helen Clyde, and an agreement to taste some sherry.

A Suitable Vengeance (1991)

This novel is a prequel to the series so far, so does not feature Barbara Havers. George's exhaustive back story on her characters really comes into its own in this book. Lynley takes his girlfriend, hopefully soon to be wife, home to the ancestral seat in Cornwall. The rural peace is disrupted when a local journalist is savagely murdered, and Lynley's brother turns out to be involved somehow. Family secrets are painfully uncovered, and friendships and loyalties are tested to the limit. Although the crimes are eventually cleared up, it all ends very badly for Lynley, especially when he learns (very publicly) that his intended really loves another.

For the Sake of Elena (1992)

Bright, sexy, Elena Weaver gets her face bashed in on her early morning run - why? Cambridge CID have been turned away by Elena's college because they made a mess of investigating a suicide earlier that year, hence Scotland Yard's involvement. Lynley volunteers to take this case when he learns that it is in Cambridge - where Lady Helen Clyde just happens to be looking after her postnatally depressed sister. Havers is glad to get away from her senile mother, although she finally has to come to terms with the reality of the situation. As well as a neatly constructed mystery, this book examines the debt owed to parents by children, and vice versa, and the effects that motherhood, and obsessional love, has on women.

Missing Joseph (1993)

Deborah St James meets a vicar at the National Gallery, and confesses her troubles to him. Later, she and her husband go to his village to see him, only to find that he is dead. However, it soon looks as thought the accidental poisoning was not so accidental, but who would kill a vicar, and why? This "long meditation on motherhood" asks awkward questions about parental love, and about who deserves to be called a parent. Lynley investigates while ostensibly on leave, with Havers helping out from London.

Playing for the Ashes (1994)

Cricket and arson; not an obviously winning combination, but handled very well in this case. England batsman Kenneth Fleming has died in a smoke-stained cottage, but how did the fire start? When it becomes clear that this is a murder investigation, there are no end of suspects for Lynley and Havers to wade through. Interspersed with the main narrative is the journal of Olivia Whitelaw, for reasons which become clear only at the end of the book. The main theme here is betrayal, in the guise of love, and genuine tragedy.

In the Presence of the Enemy (1996)

This one starts with the reader saying 'Don't do it!' when Simon St James is asked by his brother to investigate a kidnapping without involving the police. By the time the police, in the form of Lynley and Havers are involved, it is too late. And then another child is kidnapped...

Short Stories

'The Evidence Exposed', in Sisters in Crime 2, edited by Marilyn Wallace
(1990)
'The Surprise of His Life', in Women on the Case, edited by Sara Paretsky
(1996)

ELIZABETH GEORGE

INVESTIGATORS

"The last time a crime was solved by a
private investigator was never."
James Ellroy

THE FIRST THING THAT HITS YOU ABOUT BLOCK'S WORK is the vast range of style and content. Cops, spies, private eyes. Pastiches, thrillers, serial killers. However, there are two recent series which have captivated readers all over the world. In the Burglar series he writes books that cross the boundary of funny into the territory of wit. In the Matt Scudder series he transforms what could have been a static, repetitive guilt-ridden ex-cop-turns-to-drink series into a trip through a morality maze where all the exits have been bricked up. Block breathes on his word processor and people leap out of his laser printer.

Even though he has been writing for almost forty years, his talent has only been recently recognised in the UK. In a way, this is good news because there are lots and lots of other characters and series ready and waiting to be reprinted. They are all fast, exciting, entertaining page-turners.

Quiet, soft-spoken, laid back, nothing to prove. That was Lawrence Block when Paul Duncan caught up with him.

Stolen Moments

Reading the Burglar series is a pleasure because Block makes it read so effortlessly. It is a quality he admires in other writers. Which other living writers he won't say because he doesn't like to offend friends or enemies alike. So what research and background information does Block do before he begins writing about Bernie G (for Grimes) Rhodenbarr, the burglar of the series?

I sometimes walk around to familiarise myself with the parts of the city that might be featured in the book. I read a variety of literature about True Crime but not much - my books don't usually depend upon untraceable poisons and exotic killing methods. I have to know less than meets the eye. For example, just because Bernie knows how to pick locks, it doesn't mean that I have to know as well.

So you're not a real-life burglar?

Sorry. No. However, I remember a fellow writer and former private investigator, Joe Gores, sent me a set of lockpicks for my wedding present. He said that since I write about Bernie, I should at least have a set. But, he said, I should probably know that possession of them is either a high misdemeanour or a low-grade felony depending on which state I'm in at the time.

Block didn't indicate whether or not he'd ever made use of them.

Also, I know a bunch of cops, ex-cops mostly, and a fair number of ex-criminals. Burglars are a different type of criminal. They don't do smash and grabs with all that violence - burglars are more elaborate.

Bernie is reminiscent of old-style gentleman villains, like Raffles, but these anti-heroes have a twisted sort of morality.

Bernie knows that what he does is reprehensible, but he just feels he's not able to deal with it. The books do have an ambiguous morality.

As do the Matt Scudder books.

That's right. We often hear that the archetypal private detective is a man with code, but I don't know too many people in the real world who fit that description in a significant way. My feeling with Scudder is that if he has a code, he's long since lost the decoding formula. What keeps him interesting for me is that he has to make it up as he goes along. He doesn't have an automatic keyed-in response to any given situation and he has to figure his way out of it.

In the same way, Bernie has to figure his way out of many sticky situations. He usually breaks into an apartment or house that, unfortunately, contains one very dead body. Then, he must escape, evade capture for the murder, and solve the puzzle before the happy handcuffers find him. The Burglar books are unlocked-door mysteries like the classical stories of John Dickson Carr and Rex Stout, but with the wit and style of Dashiell Hammett's The Thin Man.

I usually have a scene in the Burglar books where all the suspects are gathered in the one room and their alibis are exposed one by one. I like to do that - it's fun.

The Burglar books are easier in one respect because they're light, essentially fluff, and the reader is supposed to have a good time. However, the plot needs to be fairly convoluted. On the other hand, the Scudder books are more realistic and have more direct plots - you don't get many locked-door mysteries in real life.

I imagined that Block spent hours in deep thought planning intricate puzzles for the Burglar books, then he told me about his experience writing The Burglar Who Traded Ted Williams, *which he completed in twenty-five days.*

I had been thinking about the book for a few years - the previous Burglar book had been written nine years before - and I wanted to write a book with a baseball card background. I wrote a few draft chapters, to see if I could write the book, and found I liked the characters and the way the scenes were setting up. It was exhilarating writing in that voice again. It was also quite frightening because it was all going well, but I didn't know where it was going - there were lots of stray threads going off in all directions. It wasn't making sense, and I had no solution. Right up until the end I didn't know that I was going to be able to pull the threads together. Then it all fell into place. It was as if some part of my mind was making sense of it as I was going along, even though, on a conscious level, I didn't know the story. It scared me half to death, though, when I was writing it. Luckily, I've never completely painted myself into a corner that way.

The Matt Scudder series was conceived as a series character and Block was contracted to write the first three novels before any were published. In these three books, Scudder drank heavily and didn't think about much else. It is known that Block used to have a drink problem which, understandably, he doesn't like talking about. Block was also living alone in the same neighbourhood as Scudder. In contrast to the Burglar series, Scudder learns and evolves with each book.

Writing them at the time, I never expected Scudder to stop drinking. I thought that, as long as the series went on, he would continue living the same kind of life, as most series characters have always done. Then he began to change on me, and I saw that I had to allow that to happen. After he gave up drinking, he continued to change as his life changed and he aged.

Having one successful series is good, but having two is even more of a strain on a writer.

The past couple of years I've been doing one of each series a year, which is an impossible pace, so now I'll be doing one book a year and alternating the two characters. I'm committed, contractually, to more Scudders and Burglars.

I think that any series has a fixed life span, whatever length that is. When Sue Grafton said that she'd be doing twenty-six Kinsey Millhone books, I remember thinking how could she know that she would be able to write twenty-six books for that character. More power to her, that's great, and I'm sure she'll do it, but I know I couldn't write twenty-six books about Matthew Scudder or Bernie Rhodenbarr. On the other hand, there is no need to stop formally. I'll simply write a book then find out I can't write another. I hope not, because I like both characters, but I also feel ready for a break.

I have a couple of other things in preparation. I have written half a dozen short stories about a character named Keller. He's a wistful hitman - a professional killer. They're quite long short stories. All but one have run in *Playboy*. When I have enough, probably another three or so, they'll all be published in a book.

There may also be a collection of the Ehrengraf short stories, which were mostly published in Ellery Queen's Mystery Magazine *in the late seventies. Ehrengraf is a lawyer who doesn't mind committing the occasional crime to get his clients off.*

A lot of the time writing is just hard work interrupted by doubt. Often I'm writing and it's not working at all, but I've learned to press on because my judgment at that time may be completely off and, if I just carry on, it may indeed turn out to be just fine. Usually, the odds are that it's all right.

It's not always a joyous experience sitting at the keyboard.

I wondered whether Block gave the books to someone else to read?

No. I learned a long time ago not to let anybody read any of my work in progress. That's just an excuse for me to stop work and wait for a reaction, so I might as well press on and get it over with. When I'm done, my wife is the first to read it, and I know I can count on her to like it. Then I pass it around to my daughters, and they read it and give it their unqualified approval. Then I give it to the publishers for them to have a crack at it.

Go to the yes-women first.

That's right. The last thing a person wants at a moment like that is objective criticism. What use is that to me? Approval - that's what I want.

Perhaps someone should start up a reading service for authors that gives unqualified approval to every manuscript submitted.

That'd be good. A non-criticism service. You could make a mint from that idea. I know a lot of authors who'd use ya.

I'd better keep it under my hat, then.

In recent years, Block has gotten into the habit of going away to write. He visits secluded writers' colonies and hotel rooms to give himself the space and time to write uninterrupted. It sounds as if he sometimes had difficulty writing. It may be an awful pun, but I asked him if he ever got writer's block?

Sure. It happens occasionally.

Do you have any techniques for getting over it?

Not particularly. Actually, there's a fellow in New York called Jerrold Mundis who has a method of breaking writer's block. He does one-on-one sessions with blocked writers which are very effective. He's a friend of mine, so he's occasionally given me hints on what to do, but it's not a problem I have often.

Also, usually when I have a stretch when I don't feel like writing, I don't write. I take that time off, which is nice.

The books read effortlessly. They appear fully formed. Where is the work done? Thinking beforehand, or at the keyboard, or where?

I rarely feel ready to write the book. I usually feel I ought to know more about the book before I'm actually ready to write it.

The greater portion of my work as a writer takes place in the unconscious, where I can't see it and be aware of it. Something goes on there. This takes place during the substantial amount of time off between books. During this time, I occasionally think about the book but not that much happens on a conscious level. After that, however, the real work happens at the desk, at the keyboard, in the writing of it. Sometimes it goes quickly, without enormous effort, and sometimes it's reminiscent of trench warfare. However, those scenes which are the most trouble often seem to read as though they were no trouble to write.

The tone of the Burglar and Scudder books are completely different - one light, the other dark. Is that a problem?

Once I get into the particular mindset of whichever character I'm writing, it's not difficult for me to stay there. Also, there's less difference in writing the two series than there may be in reading them. Either way, just because a character I'm writing is in a light or a dark mood, it doesn't mean that I'm in that mood as well. Also, the difficulty in getting the sentences, paragraphs and scenes right, figuring out what's going to happen next, doesn't differ greatly from one sort of book to the next. So the experience of writing them is not as different as you may think.

Do you get emotional when you write?

Not often. I read about people that do, but I don't very often. The characters feel the emotion. I don't feel it myself.

I don't think that Bernie or Matt really exist. I don't become these characters. They exist in another universe entirely. The only reality they have for me is the places where they do things. For example, I can be walking down the street and remember that Bernie had a scene on this corner, or in that building.

Blockheads - that's what most film and TV people are. Okay, so they make money, but so what? Anyone can do that. Can they make a good film out of Block's books? Of course they could. But do they? Like heck.

First to hit the silver screen, in 1973, was the unpleasant Nightmare Honeymoon, *based on the novel* Deadly Honeymoon. *Next was the Matt Scudder book* Eight Million Ways To Die, *made into a 1986 film starring Jeff Bridges, Rosanna Arquette and Andy Garcia.*

I never thought the movie of *Eight Million Ways To Die* was very good. I thought Jeff Bridges was good as Scudder. Andy Garcia was good as well. In a television interview, Jeff Bridges said that it was a character he would like to play again if it was done right. I gather the people making the film had a bad time making it - there was a lot of interference. I know for a fact that they were making up areas of the script as they were going along, improvising scenes because they weren't written.

There is still interest in Scudder movies periodically, but I find that I sometimes don't want films made of characters I want to continue writing about, because the finished films put me off writing about the characters.

Next was Burglar *in 1987, with Whoopi Goldberg in the title role.*

The *Burglar* film was set in San Francisco instead of New York, which wasn't important to the script, and Bernie was changed from a white man to a black woman. It still could have been good - Whoopi Goldberg is a good actress - but the film had problems beyond the casting. It wasn't very good.

The problem with the films, and this applies to many adaptations, is that the filmmakers don't seem interested in keeping the spirit of the source material.

Ideally, the writer of the screenplay should refer to the book. But, if they don't want the book, but just one aspect of the book, then you're never going to have the book adapted properly.

Also, if one draft is done of the screenplay, and a rewrite is called, the writer only refers back to the first draft, not to the book. This means each draft can get further and further away from the novel.

Over the years, Block has written occasional screenplays - The Thief Who Couldn't Sleep *didn't sell and the third Paul Kavanagh book,* Not Comin' Home To You, *began life as a film treatment.*

Donald Westlake has done a great deal of movie work - that's where a large portion of his income has been coming from in recent years - and he enjoys that process very much. He likes working with others very much. I don't at all. I like going into a room and coming out with a book. I don't like being part of a collaborative venture. It's not fun for me, and I don't work well in that context.

In 1994 Block did several drafts of a TV show before they put someone else onto it to make some changes. So many changes, that Block probably won't recognise his own work if it gets done. Joe Early *is a two hour movie based on Block's award-winning Scudder short story* By The Dawn's Early Light *but it's set in a different time with different characters. Block said it'd be okay with him if it vanished without a trace. He's not interested in further scriptwriting.*

I write books for people to read, and it's nice to know that people actually read and enjoy what I write. Compare that to a friend who spent thirty years out in California making a good living writing TV pilots that never got made. He did well but now he has nothing to show for thirty years of work, only an empty shelf of books he might have written if he'd stayed with books. So I've never envied TV and film writers. I'm much happier as a novelist.

Some writers start from a great need to tell a particular story and, when they've told it, they've run out of energy and ideas. I started off with a great need to write, but no particular story to tell, so I'm always finding and developing stories. I think it's perfectly natural to grow until such time as the infirmities of age start eating up brain cells.

Block has started a memoir of his early days as a writer. As well as the crime short stories and novels throughout the sixties and seventies, Block wrote a lot of, say we say, salacious books. Are these covered in the memoirs?

Yes. There are whole areas that I have not been willing to be specific about in interviews over the years. It's all going in the manuscript.

This isn't a tease is it? I know of people who've been trying to put together complete bibliographies for years. You could write the manuscript, say it's all there, then burn it.

That's an idea. I could, couldn't I? Hmm...

Don't worry, I plan to get this one published. How many writers do you know who, with a finished manuscript in their hands, don't then go out and try to get it published?

I've never read any of these old books. Do they have any value?

No, no value at all. One of the things that pleases me no end is that, for the most part, they were not printed on acid-free paper. Let them dissolve! They had value in that they taught me how to write, and it was a paid apprenticeship. Not very well paid, but I made a living.

Block was one of a group of writers, which included Donald E Westlake, Hal Dresner, Marion Zimmer Bradley and Robert Silverberg, who knew each other and wrote the same kind of softcore porn books. The books are fairly innocuous compared to the sex scenes written in today's novels. Block's titles were written under various pen-names - Dr Benjamin Morse, Ben Christopher, Jill Emerson, Liz Crowley, John Dexter, Lesley Evans, Don Holliday, Andrew Shaw and Sheldon Lord - but you have to be careful when attributing books to him. Block taught other writers how to write these books, and they sometimes ghosted his pen-names. Not only that, but the publishers weren't the most reliable of people and it wasn't unknown for them to accidentally swap or drop pseudonyms.

Nevertheless, Block wrote some good books from the 60s and 70s which are gradually being reprinted.

It becomes difficult for me to look at early work but, at the same time, I'm delighted to have it republished. I try not to judge it. I think the reason I have trouble reading it, and tend to judge it harshly, is that I'm probably seeing the callow young man who wrote it. Also, when the early stuff is reprinted, I resist the impulse to make changes. I figure it should be all of its piece and of its time, and it should stand or fall on its own merits.

Biography

LAWRENCE BLOCK was born June 24 1938 in Buffalo, New York. Block likes to travel and, in recent years, he and his wife, Lynne, have obsessively tracked down and visited sixty-six towns and hamlets named Buffalo - a world record. They are finding more all the time and plan to add to their tally. In July 1995 they were filmed chasing polar bears just below the Artic Circle for the adventure travel show *Pathfinders*.

Encouraged by a school teacher, Block was about 15 when he realised he wanted to write. Block worked as a mailboy for Pines Publications, who published pulps and the Popular Library paperback imprint. In 1957 he began work for the Scott

Meredith Agency while at college. This involved reading manuscripts for a fee, saying it was good but finding faults which prevent publication, so writers would try again soon and enclose another fee.

"I dropped out of college to keep the job because I thought it was interesting. It was also around that time that I made my first sales, so it was a constructive place for me to be at that time."

Unbeknownst to a lot of people, Scott Meredith actually edited *Manhunt* magazine under various nom de plumes, and used this cover to pump the mag full of his own writers. Block had already had his first story accepted by *Manhunt - You Can't Lose*, February 1958 issue - but his knowledge of this 'situation' certainly didn't hinder his career.

"I stayed at the agency for 8 or 9 months and learnt everything I could from the job before I left and went back to college for a while. By this time I was writing professionally, making my living, and didn't have the right motivation for academic work any more, so I dropped out again. I wasn't making very much money from the writing, but I was doing what I wanted to do with my life."

After a falling out with Scott Meredith, and therefore the closure of some of his markets, Block expanded into writing articles about coin collecting, his chief extracurricular activity at that point. This led to a post as editor at the *Whitman Numistic Journal* from around 1964 to 1966. You'll often find a non-fiction book, *Guide Book To Australian Coins*, listed in Block's bibliography, but he never wrote it, if it exists. It was one of those books that was listed in catalogues as pending publication and has been erroneously listed ever since.

The next big thing for Block was his Evan Tanner series, published by Gold Medal from 1966, which he regards as the first character that was wholly his own creation. On the strength of it, he left Whitman.

The early seventies were filled with many sex-related titles by John Warren Wells and the like. Somehow, and don't ask me how, an entry for the fictitious John Warren Wells appeared in *Contemporary Authors* - the only pseudonym in this prestigious reference book - with a completely fake biography. Who wrote it and who got it in is as big a mystery as any in Block's books. Block's own entry in *Contemporary Authors* listed his hobby as 'collecting old subway cars.' I wonder where he keeps them all?

One non-mystery novel, *Ronald Rabbit Is A Dirty Old Man* (1971), was described by Isaac Asimov as either the funniest dirty book or the dirtiest funny book he'd ever read. It is also reputed to be the scarcest Block book.

The Scudder novels began in 1976, and the Burglars in 1977. This was also the year Block began writing a column about writing in the *Writer's Digest*, a column he continued for 14 years and used as the basis for several books on writing. Ever since, he's been going from strength to strength, picking up awards from all over the world, selling more copies, and writing better books.

Crime Bibliography

BURGLAR NOVELS
Burglars Can't Be Choosers (1977)
The first Burglar book actually started life as the fourth Scudder book. The idea was that a burglar was on the lam for a murder he discovered whilst on the job, and drafted Scudder to help out. The novel didn't work, but the burglar idea stuck and, when developed, he became Bernie G Rhodenbarr. The other mainstay of the series is Ray Kirschmann, the cop for whom no bribe is too large.

The Burglar In The Closet (1978)
Bernie is locked in the clothes cupboard of a smart New York apartment and he can see, just across the room, some even smarter jewels. Lovely. However, by the time he picks his way out of the cupboard, the jewels were gone and in their place their owner, Crystal Sheldrake. She was dead. Poor Bernie.

The Burglar Who Liked To Quote Kipling (1979)
This novel introduces Bernie's bookstore and his lesbian poodle-groomer friend Carolyn Kaiser. A long lost Rudyard Kipling poem is locked inside a millionaire's high security library so, purely in the interest of art you understand, Bernie decides to liberate it. Unfortunately, someone has also liberated a redhead from her life, and guess who the police want to book for murder one?

The Burglar Who Studied Spinoza (1981)
Bernie really enjoys breaking into houses and stealing expensive collections. So when Carolyn gives him the inside info on the Colcannon's house, Bernie pops along to relieve them of their coin collection. That's one coin. Worth a quarter of a million dollars. Only there's another burglar after it as well. And anyway, even if he does get it, who can he sell it to?

The Burglar Who Painted Like Mondrian (1983)
Imagine being framed for stealing a painting. Oh, and killing two people. Bernie doesn't have to imagine, because he's in the frame.

The Burglar Who Traded Ted Williams (1994)
Baseball cards - just pieces of printed cardboard that smell of chewing gum. Used to have them as a kid. They get chucked out with all the other juvenile rubbish. Wait a few years and 'They're worth HOW MUCH!!??' Yep, Bernie steals some. Or, more precisely, he HAS to steal some because the rent for his bookstore has been hiked up by the new landlord. Not only that, but Bernie is rusty - he hasn't stolen anything in ages. Does he still have the touch? Meanwhile, Carolyn gets Bernie a cat called Raffles.

The Burglar Who Thought He Was Bogart (1995)
Bernie is spending his nights watching Bogart movies, sharing his popcorn with Ilona (she's in the stealing business, too - hearts, that is). Meanwhile, Hugo

Candlemas asks Bernie to steal a portfolio. Okey dokey. But Hugo goes missing, a body turns up, Bernie is accused of murder, for once Ray believes Bernie didn't do it, Carolyn searches for the next Sue Grafton mystery and Raffles searches for clues.

MATTHEW SCUDDER NOVELS

Scudder is an ex-cop who killed an innocent bystander whilst on duty; guilt forces him to resign, leave his family, turn to alcohol. Perversely, he works behind a bar, and only takes cases which interest him personally. When he does take on a case, ten percent goes to the nearest church or, later, to needy people on the street - his way of trying to make some sort of reparation for his mistake. It is usually best to read this kind of series in order but I recommend you check out *When The Sacred Ginmill Closes* first. If you like that, you'll like the rest.

Sins Of The Fathers (1976)

A woman is slashed to death and the murderer found near the scene of the crime, hands still bloody. Hours later, the murderer kills himself in jail. Case closed. The woman's father asks Scudder to take the case. Easy money, thinks Scudder. Yeah. Sure.

In The Midst Of Death (1976)

Jerry Broadfield thinks he's a good cop but he's been charged with extortion and his former buddies in the NYPD would like to see him laid out on the morgue slab for squealing to a committee on police corruption. When a dead hooker turns up in his apartment, he's saddled with a murder rap as well. Broadfield screams frame-up and nobody believes him except ex-cop Scudder, but finding a killer among the stoolie cop's sleazebag connections is going to be as difficult as finding a cold beer in Hell, which is where Scudder is headed if he sticks his nose in too deep.

Time To Murder And Create (1977)

Spinner Jablon was dead and he knows who did it - well, he knows it was one of three people he was blackmailing. Spinner leaves a letter and money for Matt, telling him who these three people are. It's not often that Matt accepts cases from dead men.

A Stab In The Dark (1981)

Scudder believes that one victim of a mass-murderer is actually the victim of a different killer, and has to prove it. The change in Scudder begins with this book. At the end, he goes so far as to walk into an AA meeting, then walks right out and heads for the nearest bar.

Eight Million Days To Die (1982)

A prostitute wants out but before she makes it, she's killed. Her pimp, the prime suspect, hires Scudder to find out who did it. This is the book where Scudder comes to terms with his alcoholism and changes.

When The Sacred Ginmill Closes (1986)

After writing and incinerating several attempts at a new Scudder, Block won Edgar and Shamus awards for his Scudder short story *By Dawn's Early Light*, and then used the story as the basis for *When The Sacred Ginmill Closes*. The novel is very much a mood piece, about characters and places, about the past and betrayal. Most Scudder fans rate this as one of, if not the best, in the series.

Out On The Cutting Edge (1989)
Off the booze, and deep in Hell's Kitchen, Scudder searches for a lost girl, a would-be actress, and as the city heats up to boiling point, her trail gets colder and colder.

A Ticket To The Boneyard (1990)
As a cop, Scudder lied to a jury and psychopath James Leo Motley was sent down. Twelve years later, he's out, and a little miffed. He starts killing Scudder's friends, old lovers, even people with the same name. It's only a matter of time until he finds the right Scudder.

A Dance At The Slaughterhouse (1991)
A pregnant woman is raped, tortured and murdered by socialite Richard Thurman. The police can't prove it. The dead woman's brother thinks Matt can. His hunt for clues involves a guided tour of the snuff film world of sleazy New York city. This one won an Edgar award.

A Walk Among The Tombstones (1992)
Francine is kidnapped and a ransom is demanded. Her husband is a major dope-dealer, and he pays up. He gets his wife back - in little pieces. Matt gets involved and finds himself on the trail of a pair of psychopaths.

The Devil Knows You're Dead (1993)
A man is gunned down in the street. Just another senseless killing in New York city. A street crazy has the casings from the fatal bullets. An open and shut case. But not for Scudder, because the more he finds out about the victim, the more he finds out about himself.

A Long Line Of Dead Men (1994)
A secret club consisting of 31 men begin to die, one by one. Scudder is hired to investigate before the club runs out of members.

Even The Wicked (1996)
It's official. Scudder has his private eye licence and he knows how to use it. His first job is to protect Criminal Defence Attorney Adrian Whitfield from the Will Of The People - a killer who sends his hit-list to a tabloid newspaper columnist.

EVAN TANNER NOVELS
The Thief Who Couldn't Sleep (1966) - The Cancelled Czech (1966)
Tanner's Twelve Swingers (1967) - Two For Tanner (1967)
Here Come's A Hero (1968) - Tanner's Tiger (1968)
Me Tanner, You Jane (1970)

"From around 1963 or 1964, I had the character of Evan Tanner in my mind. He was a supporter of lost causes who couldn't sleep because of an impaired sleep centre in the brain. I never did anything with him because I couldn't find a story to put him in. Then, a friend told me the background of the Armenian gold cache in Balakesir in Turkey, and about how a couple of people who tried to get it but were beaten to the treasure, probably by several years. That gave me something for Tanner to do. I wrote the book, The Thief Who Couldn't Sleep, had a wonderful time writing it and before I had finished it, decided he was going to have more adventures."

The packaging and marketing of the character gives people the impression that Tanner is some sort of international spy. In fact, he is more of an offbeat adventurer, always on the run from someone in exotic locations around the world.

"He invariably went to places I had never been. Of course, I did little research on any of these places so I'm sure there are great, gaping errors in the novels. As you can imagine, this keeps me up nights.

"The books were light, fast, designed to be fun, so a strict adherence to reality was not really necessary. If you can believe that this guy can speak all the languages and never sleeps, you shouldn't really worry too much whether the river really goes through that town.

"Although I never received any complaints from the readers, I felt that I was beginning to repeat myself, so I stopped writing the Tanner series. Periodically, people ask me if I'm going to bring Tanner back, but I can't see it - it'd be difficult for me to get back into character again after all these years. Besides, it sort of belongs to the sixties. When people ask me whatever happened to Tanner, I point them to a map of Europe and ask them to listen to the radio and say that he's been busy."

LEO HAIG NOVELS (AS Chip Harrison).
Make Out With Murder (1974), reprinted as Five Little Rich Girls (1986)
The Topless Tulip Caper (1975)

"The first two Chip Harrison novels, No Score (1970) and Chip Harrison Scores Again (1971), were non-mystery books written from the point of view of a young man and were about his erotic adventures as he entered manhood. I liked the character and wanted to write about him some more but I couldn't work out how to continue. Then I decided to have him work for a detective. I was always a big fan of Rex Stout and the Nero Wolfe books, so the detective, Leo Haig, turned into a homage to Wolfe. They were great fun to write, but I could only sustain the idea for two stories."

OTHER CRIME NOVELS
Babe In The Woods by William Ard (ghost written by Block, 1960)

William Ard died quite young of cancer and left an unfinished manuscript for *Babe In The Woods*. He'd written the first two chapters and an outline. Block was asked to finish it, and he did - over a weekend.

"I haven't looked at it since then, but the beginning is awful, so I'm sure the rest of it is just as bad. I can only think that he wrote the outline secure in the knowledge that he would never have to finish the book. It was dopey. It was work-for-hire and that was that." When asked if he'd even met William Ard, Block replied, *"The only way I could have met him was through a Ouija board."*

Mona (1961)

Joe Martin, grifter, nipped and tucked money off anyone he met on his travels. Then he met Mona, and she clipped him, for murder...

Death Pulls A Double Cross (1961), reprinted as Coward's Kiss (1987)

This was originally a TV tie-in book about Markham, played by Ray Milland, but Block thought it turned into a good story, so he renamed the central character and sold it for more money. But he was still contracted to write the TV tie-in book, hence...

The Case Of The Pornographic Photos (1961)
reprinted as You Would Call It Murder (1987)
The Girl With The Long Green Heart (1965)

John Hayden had everything set up to get his money, lots of it. And he had fellow con-man, Doug Rance to help him out. Then he met Evelyn Stone and his life changed. He was in love with her, and she was in love with his money. Who said the course of true love ran smooth?

Deadly Honeymoon (1967)

Dave and Jill Wade are victims of rape and abuse on their honeymoon. They decide to take revenge by making their way, step by bloody step, up the rungs of the Organisation, to the Godfather...

After The First Death (1969)
The Specialists (1969)

A call girl has a bad time with a sadistic hood and ran to Eddie, who called his friends. Six of them, ex-soldiers, each with a unique talent, ready to prey on vermin the law never seemed able to touch. But the hood has specialists of his own...

Such Men Are Dangerous (as Paul Kavanagh, 1969)

Paul Kavanagh, an ex-Green Beret with nothing better to do, and his deadly partner, George Dattner, get an offer to steal a shipment of tactical nuclear weapons from the US Army worth more than two million dollars. They take up the offer.

This reads as though it is written by Kavanagh, which is why the pseudonym is used. It's also a little darker. The name was kept for two other books for marketing reasons.

The Triumph Of Evil (as Paul Kavanagh, 1971)
Not Comin' Home To You (as Paul Kavanagh, 1974)
Ariel (1980)

A dark psychological suspense novel with kids. Not a normal Block book.

Into The Night (by Cornell Woolrich, completed by Block, 1987)

When Cornell Woolrich died in 1968, he left an uncompleted manuscript of *Into The Night*. The first fourteen pages of this edition were trashed by Woolrich and the last twenty-four pages were missing. Block stepped into the breach and emulated the words of the master of dark suspense fiction in these and other places - writing about a fifth of the book. This is Woolrich's book, not Block's, following the woman-seeking-vengeance motif of his earlier *The Bride Wore Black* (1940) and *The Black Angel* (1943).

Random Walk (1988)

A serial killer story with two plots. Not a normal Block book.

SHORT STORY COLLECTIONS
Sometimes They Bite (1983)

Includes stories featuring Scudder and Ehrengraf.

Like A Lamb To The Slaughter (1984)

Includes stories featuring Ehrengraf, Bernie Rhodenbarr and Chip Harrison.

Some Days You Get The Bear (1993)

Includes stories featuring Scudder, Bernie Rhodenbarr, Keller and Ehrengraf.

TRUE CRIME WAS THE BREAK THROUGH BOOK *for Andrew Klavan, an American thriller writer who's been living in London since 1992. It is a novel written as a non-fiction book by reporter Stephen Everett, who tells of his race against time to save Frank Beachum, on Death Row and just hours away from a lethal injection. Whether or not Everett succeeds is always in doubt because there is no moralistic tone in Klavan's writing - this is an amoral world, and the bad stuff is just as likely to happen as the good stuff.*

Paul Duncan raced via bus and train to meet Andrew Klavan, and ended up arriving early and having a nice cup of tea as he waited.

Relaxing, I looked over my notes: Andrew's father had been a DJ for a major New York radio station. After dropping out of Berkeley college, Andrew worked as a radio journalist (he covered the Patty Hearst kidnapping), then for a small newspaper in Putnam County, New York State (involved in car chases, had life threatened, loved every moment). He contributed regularly to Village Voice and was a freelance news-writer for the WOR and ABC TV news departments. This all implies an inquisitive nature, looking for a story - would he be a media manipulator, or just blend facelessly into the crowd? Looking up, Andrew walked in, open, cheerful. God knows I'd be cheerful if I sold a book for a million dollars. Feeling ever-so-slightly jealous, I wondered how you sell a book for a million dollars?

Thrill Singer

Besides a good agent and good luck, the following happened: I finished the *True Crime* manuscript and went out to Hollywood, where it caused a lot of noise because people liked it. So they were all 'playing' for it, as they say out there.

The night of the auction was just absolute hell, waiting to see what was going to happen. I sat there with a bottle of brandy, watching it get lower, and lower, and stayed *stone cold sober*. It made a good sale, $1.2 million to Twentieth Century Fox.

There was a nagging doubt in my head. Something was not quite right. No-one just walks in and makes that kind of bread - there has to be a backstory, right? Yes. Andrew has been in Hollywood before. For two years he read novels for Columbia, to find out what properties they should consider. So an eye for what sells, what makes a movie, has been cultivated. Then there're film scripts...more on them later.

So, on the back of the film deal, *True Crime* went to New York and caused a lot of excitement there as well. We approached about 25 publishers, and everybody loved it. The auction started and the big companies put up the bids to get everyone else out of the running. And once someone comes in and mentions *that number*, it's very easy to say, '*OK, I'll take that.*' I had been out to a play with my wife and found out about the offer standing in a phone box in Piccadilly Circus.

How romantic! So the second million wasn't as exciting as the first one?
It was still pretty exciting.
I'll bet.

The idea of being on Death Row has been a nightmare of mine since I was a little kid. I find the precise, processional and ritualistic manner of being killed - which I always compare to human sacrifice - terrifying.

Because of this, I've always read huge amounts of articles, interviews, accounts on the subject. So, by the time I sat down to write *True Crime*, besides a couple of phone calls, it was all in my mind. I had everything in my mind to create the verisimilitude that all the most horrible nightmares have.

It has worked so well that an attorney in America wrote me a letter saying that he was about to address the American Bar Association but he couldn't find any articles about the case. He couldn't find Steve Everett's *New Yorker* pieces... I had to write back straight away telling him not to address the ABA citing this case - I had this vision of people from the ABA ringing me up about this new precedent.

One wonders what Andrew did, as a child, that made him feel so guilty that he thought he deserved the death sentence?
I think it was simply my first image of death. I've got two kids and I've noticed that there's definitely a point when they discover death. For one of them, he was really angry when he heard about it but, a day later, he'd incorporated it into his knowledge of life. For the other one, the whole notion of it frightened her.

I say now that I understood Beachum's predicament when I turned 40 because now, I too, am on death row.
Only half way there.

I covered a lot of court cases in my limited experience as a reporter and what I found was that the police aren't Sherlock Holmes, they just know who the bad guys are because they know the neighbourhood and the circumstances. The guys who do the killing aren't master criminals, and the motive is usually drugs, money or passion. Once they know you've done it, they are more than willing to bend the rules to get you. So, because of that, there is every possibility that they could make a mistake.

America is obsessed with imagery, so it's not only important to be seen to be doing justice, but to be seen to be doing it in this very fair and proper way. That's when you get people being on death row for 20 years filing one appeal after another.

This, to me, is utterly ridiculous. If we're going to have a system with capital punishment, I would prefer one that worked quickly so that at least it fulfilled the one official purpose of the sentence, which is to work out the rage of the society.

If I attacked you, and you killed me, everyone would say that was self-defence. If I attacked you, and you knocked me out, tied me up and then killed me, that would be a very different thing. That's what's so disturbing about that long time between sentence and execution.

There is something quite chilling about a society which kills with exacting premeditation - like the fictional serial killers we adore. It is almost an egotistical display of power.

A woman prosecutor in Philadelphia, who is one of the biggest supporters of the death sentence, has said that one of the things it is about is giving people a sense of control. I think that is a pretty amazing statement for someone to make who is sending people to the death chamber.

With such a long space of time between sentence and execution, can Death Row be considered a kind of torture?

I don't feel any sympathy for murderers - they are not my favourite people - but I do feel that it must be torture for the families of the victims. If the judge says the murderer goes to prison for life with no parole, that's the end of the case and the family can get on with getting their life back together. If the murderer is on death row, appealing against the sentence again and again, 10, 15, 20 years on, that must be torture for the family of the victim.

The case is essentially unresolved. How can the family live for themselves when they have to continue living for a dead person?

This is, paradoxically, a problem with the parole system. I don't think that the families necessarily want to hear that eight years after the murder, the murderer is back on the streets. Over the past few years capital punishment has become very popular and has swept through the States. For example, when I started *True Crime*, I couldn't set it in New York state because they didn't have a death penalty but, by the time I finished it, it did.

All the people who got into office in our last election got in on the death penalty, even Bill Clinton. He let a guy, who was thought to be retarded, die in Arkansas because he was afraid he would be seen to be soft on crime. It was disgraceful.

One of the good things is that it has forced states to adopt sentences of life imprisonment without parole which I think, for certain people, is a very good idea.

So, right now, it is not such a good idea to commit a crime in America. The crime figures are dropping too.

It seems that you had a much better deal to commit crimes a couple of years ago.

Yeah. The market has dropped out of crime.

Each of us see ourselves in the fullness of our humanity, but we see only the shell of other people. Books allow you to take somebody, like Everett, and inhabit his mind whilst you're reading the book. I think that it's sometimes a good exercise to inhabit someone you might not immediately like. You can inhabit his mind in safety, and understand that he does see himself in his humanity, and that he abuses other people as well as himself.

In some ways, Everett is a better reporter because he wants the pure truth, what actually happened, without the veil of perception in his way. That's what makes him so obsessive, because it's impossible for him to find the truth without asking for other people's perceptions.

Everett is imprisoned and overwhelmed by other people's versions of the truth. One of the things that is both great and terrible about Everett is that the minute he hears a version of the truth, he doubts it. So even if the version is to 'do unto others... etc.', he rejects it, because he knows that beyond one kind of truth is another truth.

There's also a belief that, if he gets to the truth, everything will be all right with the world.

But even if he gets to the truth, all the problems he has will still be there.

And, of course, in his pursuit for truth, he causes problems along the way.

The impossibility of his quest is also attractive to him. He feels he can achieve it.

True Crime comes from a long line of race-against-time stories like D W Griffiths' film _Intolerance_, and Cornell Woolrich books like _Phantom Lady_ and _Black Angel_. So what is it about this book that makes it so different?

I've been trying to make books that _move_ like thrillers, but also have a lot of emotional resonance to them. It's very difficult because, to move like a thriller, you don't have much space to create your characters. I also try to plot so that the characters emerge naturally, without hampering the plot. It's like writing a sonnet - working in a very limited form. I find it great for discipline.

This is a new breed of thriller, where there is little or no physical action, where tension and excitement is created by the characters talking, yes talking, to each other. And by golly, it works.

Virtually all the characters in *True Crime* are amoral and they live in an amoral world. It's a world where things can just as easily go wrong as go right.

I can't see how, given the facts, you can write about the world in any other way. Some people say that after we die, everything is worked out for the best - I don't know, I haven't been there - but I know that it's not the case in the world we live in.

The thriller doesn't have to have a happy ending, but it does have to resolve itself - the knot has to snap and become untied. I try very hard not to impose unhappy endings when the story demands a happy one, and vice versa, but, at the same time, I try to make the story exist in the wider world where all the things that really happen, happen.

The plot has been resolved but the people haven't.

Exactly. There's no happy ending for Michele in *True Crime*, and her life is as important as anyone else's in the book.

Storytelling is the core of the novel. I think that the relationship between the storyteller and the listener is a really deep one. I get bored with people who write stories to elucidate stories instead of writing primary stories which are meant to elucidate life. For a while, modern fiction was in danger of going the way of modern painting, writers talking to themselves about themselves. One of the good things about the thriller form is that it is a place where writers still talk directly to readers, unobstructed by critics.

It all started around the campfire, people telling each other stories. We've developed all sorts of sophisticated devices to help tell stories, and our perceptions have altered as a result, but it would be a shame if everything came down to stories that only tell you about themselves.

There have been several terrific books recently which have taken techniques from all the experimentation of the sixties and used them to tell stories. However, the thriller requires more subtlety of experimentation than other story forms. You have to be more disciplined, experiment without people knowing it.

For example, you move from first to third person throughout *True Crime*. I read a review where someone said they couldn't handle it. Personally, I found it okay, although there were a couple of instances where it tripped up.

Presenting the novel as a *True Crime* book gave me the chance to use a narrative technique - it's written in the voice of one person, Everett, who writes the points of views of other people. This pushes the unreliable narrator one step further.

I was interested in the fact that Everett was willing to create other people's characters. There's one very telling line where his wife turns around and says *'you*

ANDREW KLAVAN

don't know anything. You just assume that people are like that.' When you hear her say that, you have to think about the whole book and wonder which characters he's done this to.

But also, why did he put that line in the book?

Exactly. That line makes you question the entire narrative.

To what extent has the narrator made things up in order to present a conclusion to the reader? Is Beachum innocent or guilty?

Read carefully - you don't know.

Journalism is always a form of storytelling but each media has different requirements. And these requirements frequently supersede an exact representation of the truth. I remember, for instance, cutting tape of Ronald Reagan. He would stutter and stumble for three minutes and, in the middle of that three minutes there would be a five second sound bite that made perfect sense. Now, you can't fill your report with three minutes of the President going 'duh...duh...duh...', you have to go with the coherent sound bite, so Reagan goes over the air sounding as if he said something very concise and intelligent and cogent. But I did that, with a razor. That's a requirement of storytelling in journalism.

You lean on certain rapid assumptions that people make. For example 'mothers love their children' is a good assumption to make. In a story where a mother watched her children trapped in a car sinking to the bottom of the lake, you make that assumption. If you find out two weeks later that she actually put them in the car, and put the car into the lake, it's shocking because of the assumptions you made.

That sort of sentimentality is assumed by and required of reporters today working in newspapers, radio and TV.

Another good example is that the media always assumes that if something happens, it's somebody's fault. If something goes wrong, who is to blame? How can it be corrected? There's a lot of good things that come out of that assumption - a lot of scandals that needed to be uncovered - but there is also a lack of a sense of tragedy that some things just happen and no-one is to blame.

That is about a sense of control, as though we can control the world we live in. Your books go against that.

Exactly. There is a surface sanity that we have some sort of control, but there is that underknowledge that we don't. That's another media assumption. It's not that the people in the media conspire to do that, it's just the natural way of the story.

At one time, Andrew worked for a small newspaper in Putnam County, New York State - a very small outpost of a very large newspaper empire. His novel Corruption *is based on that period.*

The book is the battle between a powerful sheriff and this little small town newspaper office. It examines the way that people are thrown into the position of judging each other, of passing judgements on each other whilst not dealing with the corruption within themselves.

Seeing the mote in other people's eyes, but not the plank in your own.

Exactly. The newspaper people and even the sheriff, start out being decent people. They are put into the position of having to judge people, having to take sides, and having to make the decision that something is newsworthy because it's corrupt. The people in the newspaper are trying to be objective when it's very clear from the story that they're anything but. They have every reason not to be truthful.

I suppose if you know people intimately, live with them all day and night, like they do in small communities, where everyone knows everyone else, it's a much more delicate situation. You don't want to offend people you know and have to live with all the time.

When you know so much about people, you prey off their insecurities and their weaknesses. These two people, Sally Dawes, the editor of the bureau, and the sheriff, are locked in this almost erotic hatred of each other, and they play off that eroticism throughout the book, and that preys on their lack of objectivity.

I know how it is working in an office, where you quickly learn what people are like, their foibles. To get your work done, you may have to use their personality to get things done. But, of course, they may be doing exactly the same thing to you.

After Watergate the American press took on this incredibly pompous, sanctimonious aura, acting as though they were the last spokesman or shield of the people against untruth and corruption, and I think that, in some ways, *Corruption* was a reaction against that.

I don't like this false concern in papers for the welfare of people they are using. It's tabloid journalism. It's insincere. Take the instance of that woman who was having the eight babies, the way the press hung around her, like ghouls, waiting for her babies to die. I found that disgusting.

It's depressing the way the papers play off people's worst emotions and desires. I think it's less true here than in America. In America, even when they do that stuff, there is an aspect of sanctimoniousness about it, a pseudo-serious attitude, almost as if the press were an arm of the government, that really makes it unpalatable sometimes.

They believe themselves to be the moral outlook of the world.

For a news junkie like me, you see how biased it all is. One thing I like about British newspapers is that they're openly biased. There's no attempt to disguise it. You know that if you buy *The Guardian* you're buying a left paper and the *Telegraph* is more to the right, whereas in America there is a pretence of objectivity which I find really distressing.

The press in America is not liberal, but kind of left of centre, and it's just amazing the assertions it will print wholesale if they come from the mouth of a feminist, for instance, that they would never accept if they came from the mouth of, say, the

National Rifle Association.

There is a political correctness to their reporting.

To be fair, the one thing I remember from being a reporter is how you were thrown into situations about which you know nothing and were expected to be an expert by that evening. There are many good journalists doing their best, but biased reporting is frequently presented as fact.

Reaction rather than reflection.

It's happening very fast. There are lots of flaws in the system but, if that is the case, there should be an attitude of humility. Every time I hear a journalist, like Jeremy Paxman, say *'oh, come on!'* to an interviewee I think *'what does that mean?'* Does the interviewer know better? If so, why don't they answer their own questions? That really bugs me. I think a certain amount of humility is needed in that job.

Does a reporter have to take responsibility concerning the consequences of their actions?

Of course. They have to. If they can take credit for the good things they do, then they should also take the blame for the bad. But the press are past masters at rationalisation. They will put a camera into your bedroom and when you say, *'you shouldn't really do that,'* they say *'well, it's a character issue.'* What does that mean? Just because they come up with a phrase, it doesn't mean anything. It's not relevant that a Senator or MP is sleeping with someone they shouldn't be. It's not our business. You wouldn't be allowed to ask that of a prospective employee going for a job, so why should you have to ask it of a politician?

The only thing you want to know is whether they can do the job or not. And talking of politicians, are you corrupt?

Well, in the sense of the novel, which takes in spiritual corruption, I would answer, *'who isn't?'* As a matter of fact, it matters to me not to be. I'm not somebody who cuts corners, sneaks off. Everybody cuts corners and commits sins but I'm not one of those people upon whom it sits lightly. I frequently wish I was.

Are you very conscientious?

Yes. I don't want to be guilty of the sin of pride, but I think I take care with this stuff and I try very hard to walk honestly - at least, if not with other people, then at least with myself.

Do these books represent your point of view?

My policy is that each character should reflect their own point of view. I think that's what you should try for - negative capability, an emptiness through which the story flows. You try to let the story tell itself as it's supposed to. You try to let the characters speak as they're supposed to. You let them see what they would see as whole people. But, it's my vision, it's me it's coming through, so there are things I'm not going to write about. I'm not going to write about a lonesome woman on the Kansas plains - it's not interesting to me.

So the subtext of the books comes from you.

I try to let the subtext grow out of the story and, as I come to understand it, I try to deepen it and put it in places where I feel it can appeal to the reader more strongly. What I try not to do is sit down and decide to write a story that says, for instance, 'war is bad.' I can't think of anything that would be a greater waste of time. If I sat down to write a war story, the theme would be 'war is...' and 'if war is..., what is it, what's it like?'

So, in a novel about corruption, I'm not sitting, thinking about what the moral of the story is. I'm just thinking about the ways in which each of these people are corrupt. Frequently, the title comes later when I begin to realise what the subtext and themes are.

The Animal Hour contains a lot of elements which have been used in other thrillers but they've been put together in, I think, a very original way. It's basically the story of a woman who goes into work one day and nobody recognises her. She says, 'I'm Nancy Kincaid,' and they look at her and say, 'No, you're not.' It goes on from there and works its way out.

When you say something is an experiment, it lets you off the hook in some ways because it allows you to pass the buck if it fails. I think *The Animal Hour* is kind of original for what it does and, since then, I've used some of the techniques more successfully in other books. There are a couple of moments of extreme violence that I wasn't comfortable about when I wrote them but I would do them the same way again if I had to.

The story reminds me of *The Last Of Philip Banter* by John Franklin Bardin, which is about a man who comes into work each day to find typewritten pages on his desk saying what is going to happen that day - and, no matter what he does, everything comes true. It's all about identity, what makes us us.

That is the theme of *The Animal Hour*. Who are you, and how do you know, and what does it mean to be somebody? What I was proud of was that it works out an extremely complex vision of identity - sexual, personal - and works it out without ever mentioning anything about it. The idea of that book, the experiment, was to try and work this out totally through action. I get very bored with characters thinking on the page so I wanted it to move like a bullet but still manage to work out these incredibly complex ideas. When the story comes to me, I let it tell itself in the most efficient, yet richest, way it can. *The Animal Hour* has so many ideas, seeds for future work, that it still excites me when I think about it.

Do you get excited when you're writing?

Sure. That's part of the thrill of writing. I get excited when I do a scene that's really warm and human and alive. Also, when I write a scene I've never seen written before, that works in a new way. I get excited when I read stuff like that as well. Patrick O'Brian, for instance, writes action like I've never seen before. It's fabulous, and he's incredibly innovative without you ever knowing. I think that only another novelist would realise just how innovative he is.

Are the themes you talk about in your books related to your personal life or are they abstract?

I don't sit, like a philosopher, picking abstract themes out of the air. I think all my themes come from my own life and thoughts. The way life tells itself to me is through stories. These stories come to me, I think about them, and that's how I work out my relationship to life. They're personal in that sense. In fact, when I was writing *The Animal Hour*, I was going through a period of loss of sense of identity and a sense of not knowing exactly who I was and, when that happens, the terrible thought occurs to you that you don't know what it is to be somebody. When you say 'who am I?' what the hell are you talking about? That is really where the force of the story came from. By the time I finished the book, I had come out of that period.

We often define and, ironically, lose ourselves in our routines: daily, weekly, monthly, yearly. It's a safe way of always knowing where you've got to be. When that's disturbed, interrupted, it's very frightening. I've been made redundant a couple of times and there is an absolute terror because you literally don't know what to do with yourself, your time. Your security is lost, you don't have to be up at a certain time, at a certain place, you lose contact with people you spend most of your life with. It's terrifying.

It's funny to me that you can walk down the street and a madman can just walk up to you and shout an insult at you, and you feel bad for the next hour and a half. It's an irrational connection between us.

I've been laid off too and know this terrible sense that you're not worth anything, you've been rejected, the ground has opened up underneath you, and how fragile your sense of well-being and identity is.

I just steal as much as I can from the company before I go and I feel much better for it.

The pencils, the paperclips, anything you can get your hands on.

Oh, I'm much more ambitious than that.

Don't Say A Word. **Please do.**

I like this book a lot. It's the first pure thriller I wrote after the books I wrote as Keith Peterson. I decided to teach myself to write a plot that just sings, y'know? It began when my daughter was quite small. I remember constantly going into her nursery to check that she was still breathing - this was for five years! There was a fairly large living room between my bedroom and her nursery and, halfway across, I would think 'what if I looked in, and she wasn't there?' That's where that one started, and I worked it out from there to the furthest degree I could.

I like that book a lot because it's very moving as it develops - the central character's relationship to himself, for instance. I'm particularly proud that some of my thrillers have a lot of emotional content, and you don't see that in most thrillers.

What makes it so difficult for a thriller to have emotional content, to make you really care for the people in it - as opposed to worrying whether or not they fall off a cliff - is how fast a thriller has to be to make it thrilling. That's why I compare it to a sonnet because you just don't have a lot of space for people to sit, rub their chin and reflect on life. They've got to be in the story, constantly, but you have to get their characters on the page through action as much as you possibly can.

People are defined by their actions. It's almost existentialist!

It is. You are also forced to do things at certain times within a thriller. You can't have page after page of conversation - there has to be action.

There's always a shock beginning, an introduction of characters, the peaks and troughs of action/emotion on a rollercoaster ride to the terrifying denouement.

The shock beginning of _Corruption_ is when the boy is in the river being dragged away by the current. I wasn't reading it, I was watching it in my head, remembering other scary river scenes - _Night Of The Hunter, Deliverance_.

For me, it's more about creating the scene in your mind than writing beautiful phrases. Writing beautiful phrases is the seductive thing about writing, the thing you have to cut out a lot of times because the last thing you want is somebody stumbling over your writing to get to the scene.

You know someone's a good actor when you forget they're acting. It's the same with writing.

Exactly.

I'm sorry to say this, Andrew, but when I forget you're a writer you're at your best.

(laughs) I get the point.

The Scarred Man is a story I've pillaged since because I've always wanted to tell it again but in another way. It's about a young man whose boss introduces him to the boss' daughter and falls for her at first sight. They're young and have this very passionate attraction for one another. They get together for Christmas and he tells her a ghost story around the fire, she starts to scream, runs out and won't talk to him again. It turns out that his ghost story has been her nightmare for years. The rest of the story is them trying to work out how this could possibly be. It's basically a love story on the run.

At one point they become convinced that they're brother and sister and, since they've been having an intense love affair, it becomes quite uncomfortable for them at that point. It became uncomfortable for a few movie studios as well.

The Scarred Man _was the first book Andrew sold to the movies._

That was a big moment, like winning the lottery, because the day it sold I was literally wondering how I was going to pay the rent. It's been written and rewritten, even I did a draft. It's a funny thing, and I probably shouldn't be saying this...

Don't worry. I won't tell a soul.

...but I use a lot of cinematic techniques, so my books have frequently been bought for film. But when screenwriters sit down, they find they cannot adapt it because it is all internal.

Klavan moves very quickly from one character to another, between different time zones, flashbacks within flashbacks. And all within a few paragraphs. Impossible to film as a linear storyline.

Although *The Scarred Man* reads like an action novel, everything that happens involves people reading something. It's a real problem portraying the act of reading as exciting on the big screen. When I sat down to write it, I knew about these problems, and I still couldn't produce a good script.

Another problem was that it had a thread of incest in it, which they wanted to cut. But that's the point of the story!

When he sold the film rights, Andrew wrote screenplays for Rough Justice, Don't Say A Word *and* The Scarred Man *but they didn't work because...*

a) I was bored telling the story again, and b) I was too attached to the story to see how to change it. I've also tried adapting other people's work, but I don't read too many books that I can see as a movie. What's I'd like to do is write a script from scratch. I've tried a couple of times and had them optioned, but I was never very happy with the scripts.

Scriptwriting is a completely different form. I don't care about it as much as I care about the novels. It's the difference between being an architect and a carpenter. As a novelist, you plan it, you build it, you put everything into it. As a screenwriter, you're just putting up the framework for somebody else.

Mrs White *was Andrew's first book, written with his younger brother Laurence, was published in 1981. Andrew wrote it because his wife was pregnant and they were broke.*

We needed a hundred pages and an outline to sell a book. Laurence and I wrote the first hundred pages in three days and, after we had sold it, we wrote the rest in another three days. It was a marathon, but absolutely hilarious because Laurence is a really funny man. On top of that, we were so exhausted at the end of the three days that anything would make us laugh. We spent a good deal of time on the floor, curled up, laughing hysterically. Also, we thought the book stank. We meant to sit down and write this terrible potboiler. After it had done very well for me (sold well, won an Edgar award) I went back and looked at it. I realised that it had a certain energy and the plot was pretty good. I did the plot, and it was that that made me think I could do this for a living.

On the first page, we told you who the serial killer was. The next hundred pages was just his wife and her everyday life, and about how very, very slowly the fact that he was what he was broke in on her consciousness. We made Mrs White relentlessly simple. We didn't make her a strong dynamic character - she was almost dowdy and simple and decent. The energy of the book, especially in those first hundred pages, comes from the fact that you know and she doesn't. After that, it becomes a fairly efficient chase.

Do you believe in evil?

Most days I believe in evil, sure. I think that it's entirely possible to say that there is evil in human life without necessarily implying that there is cosmic evil. Certainly, I believe that there are things that human beings do to each other, knowingly, which are wrong no matter what. I frequently find it frustrating when people find excuses for evil because it happens to be convenient. If a person does enough bad things then I think they should be classified as evil.

You don't think that the world is evil, or that there is a force of evil out there, but evil exists within ourselves?

I think that the world is, evil is and good is. These are things which are. I think that you have to choose sides in life. It's one of those things which is really complex, I think, for a novelist because he tries not to choose sides. He tries to let every character speak his mind. Then that 'discussion' comes back into the novelist's real life and helps him make moral choices.

Are your novels warnings?

I would not say so. I would simply say that I believe there is something very, very important about telling made-up stories in as honest a way as possible. I've never read a convincing description of what the importance of it is - I only know that there is a reason that people line up to see movies or devour books into the wee small hours of the morning. I think there is something really essential to our self-understanding and to our self-renewal in the relation of stories. This is why my allegiance is not to anything but to the story. It's not to giving moral messages, not to being politically correct, not to anything but to the inner integrity of the story. I believe in the story and that there is a purpose to it beyond what we really know. It just seems to me that you cannot regenerate yourself and keep yourself fresh without hearing stories.

When people talk about the collective consciousness, or a communal mind, I've often wondered whether stories are it. We tell stories to continue knowledge and understanding, otherwise it will be lost.

That's a lovely thought. I think that stories are certainly part of the process of connection, which is what we sense to be our central purpose. We sense it in love and kindness, and telling stories allows us to connect to all those emotions. I think the morality of storytelling is different to the morality of life and that's why, as John Keats said, an artist takes as much pleasure in creating an Imogen as an Iago. You owe as much to your evil characters as much as you do to your good characters for that very reason. The integrity of the story is another morality.

Isn't it easier to create evil characters, things which destroy, rather than those that create?

Y'know, I find it difficult to create evil characters that I believe in. Evil in real life is frequently quite dull. I mean, I love to read a creation like Hannibal Lecter but the truth is that guys like that are really pretty boring. So, it's interesting to find different ways of creating villainy. To be honest with you, I find it may be easier to create an evil character because his scope is limited.

They are easier to define.

Yeah. It's much more fascinating to create characters who are decent because decency is such a fluid thing. They don't know, in any given situation, what is the right thing to do and people who think about that tend to be more interesting to write.

Bibliography

NOVELS AS ANDREW KLAVAN
Face Of The Earth

"Face Of The Earth *has all the flaws of a first novel and more, I'm afraid, and belongs in what feels like a different lifetime. The one thing it has is an interesting plot which could easily have been written as a thriller."*

Darling Clementine

The erotic, philosophical story of a female poet , "Darling Clementine *is very dear to my heart. It's an obscene, philosophical, offbeat novel. It's a book I look back on, like* Animal Hour, *knowing it's for a small number of people, but the people who like it **really** like it."*

Son Of Man (1988)

"Son Of Man *is a collection of poems retelling the Gospel that I linked together with prose. The central poem, about the transfiguration, is the one I can still read without flinching."*

Don't Say A Word (1991)

A thriller bestseller, in excess of 100,000 copies sold.

The Animal Hour (1992)

"*I've been experimenting with different ways to make the thriller work in a richer way.* The Animal Hour *is the most experimental and is usually the one that thriller experts really like."*

Corruption (1993)

The story of an editor of a small town newspaper exposing a corrupt Sheriff who's put himself forward as a candidate for the local elections. "*This is more of a character study than an out-and-out thriller."*

True Crime (1995)
Agnes Mallory (1995)

The media likes to show one facet of people, one dimension, but Andrew has written other books which are more difficult to categorise - I suppose most people would call them 'literary'. "Agnes Mallory *was only published in the UK, partly because in America it's more important to be a brand name. Britain is much more accepting of eccentricity."*

Agnes Mallory, the celebrated sculptress, has been dead ten years and the only person who knew her well is Harry Bernard, a recluse impervious to biographers. When he meets a young girl very reminiscent of Agnes, the pain and pleasure of his memories throw him into turmoil.

NOVELS AS KEITH PETERSON
The Trapdoor
There Fell A Shadow
The Rain
Rough Justice

These all feature reporter John Wells. *"I'm pretty happy with the books as a series of straight-forward mystery stories. They were about the coming of info-tainment, which I lived through, and he's my stand against that. The Rain won an Edgar, and I like that too."*

The Scarred Man

"The book that really convinced me to take thriller writing seriously was Woman In White (1860) by Wilkie Collins. Dickens never wrote anything as dark, or as sexually charged. I wrote The Scarred Man after I read that. The Scarred Man is a transitional book for me and I had the credit as 'Andrew Klavan writing as Keith Peterson' because I wanted my name on that book. It's my first real thriller and I've written thrillers ever since.

"I also liked those old spy thrillers by Eric Ambler and Graham Greene. I love the moral ambiguity that runs through them, the sense of alienation, the sense that the world is coming apart at the seams. Then there's Dashiell Hammett - his books are hell on happy endings but they do have resolutions. The classic last line of The Thin Man was when Nora Charles says '...it's all pretty unsatisfactory.' That's what I'm looking for. I'm looking for endings that give the reader a sense of release but, after they start to think about it, they will feel that it is pretty unsatisfactory. That's life, I guess."

NOVEL AS MARGARET TRACY
Mrs White (1981)

A serial killer book written by Andrew and his younger brother Laurence in six days. At the time this kind of book was called a woman-in-peril mystery, so it had to be written by a woman. Andrew and Laurence took part of their wives' names to make up the pseudonym Margaret Tracy. It won an Edgar award and was filmed as *White Of The Eye* (1986) by Donald Cammell, co-director of *Performance*.

SCREENPLAY
Shock To The System, *based on the book by Simon Brett.*

"It annoys me when screenwriters say that they don't get taken seriously enough. They do, because they are just a small part of the whole film. When Michael Caine walked on in Shock To The System, I remember thinking that his face was more important than anything I had written in the script. He created the character on the screen."

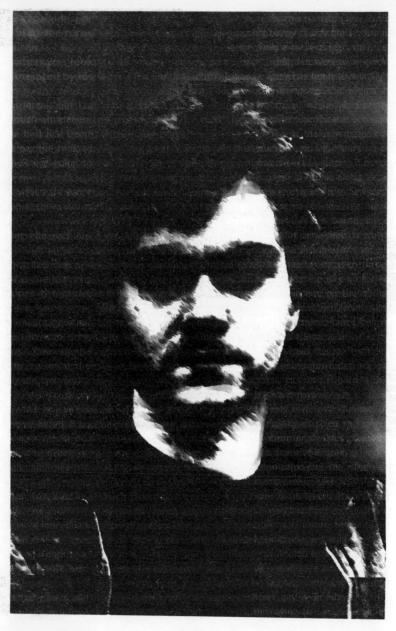

Jakob Arjouni

IT'S DIFFICULT, AS AN OUTSIDER, to get a contemporary picture of Germany. All our thoughts and knowledge are directed towards the past. The World Wars, the Holocaust, the Cold War, the terrorists of the seventies. We think of the German people in terms of media stereotypes. The upper crust general with a monocle epitomised by Erich von Stroheim. The stern, mechanical bourgeois boss who shows no compassion. The sluts and lowlifes in the paintings of Otto Dix and George Grosz, and the films of Rainer Werner Fassbinder. The political, religious, social and sexual guilt in the novels of Günter Grass and Heinrich Böll.

After the war, prevented from doing anything else, the industrial machine reassembled itself and gradually cranked up the gears until it had a stranglehold on the manufacturing world, much like Japan.

The postwar generation came of age in the seventies and found themselves trapped in a world their parents made. Their only release was anger and violence. Noise not quiet. Action not thought. Their disillusionment turned to apathy, which lead to an affluent stability throughout the eighties. Then, reunification came, like a bolt from the blue, and Germany was once again caught in a whirlpool of violence and uncertainty. What a great place for a crime novel!

Jakob Arjouni, writer of hard and fast crime novels featuring private eye Kemal Kayankaya, filled me in on what Germany is like today. He lives in Berlin, and has his finger on the pulse.

Outsider

One Man, One Murder

'Pitch-black noir' *La Depeche*

Jakob Arjouni

Before reunification, there were a few criminal bosses, but no trouble. Any trouble was between gangs. Ordinary people had nothing to fear. Since reunification, the Russian mafia have come in to make their money. They are more violent.

There are also a lot of grey areas, like currency exchange and buying and selling houses. Houses that were cheap, are now worth ten or twenty times more. A lot of people got rich very quickly - it was like winning the lottery.

And where there's money to be made, you'll find criminals. Jakob and a friend were going to write a piece about the house prices for a paper, but were warned by a friend that it would be too dangerous for them. I know real estate is supposed to be a cut-throat business, but...

Arjouni points out that Frankfurt is also full of criminals - it is full of banks.

With the Iron Curtain drawn, one would expect a lot of cross-cultural events, people mixing, a melange, but it seems not.

East German youths don't venture into the West because they feel vaguely afraid, out of place. At the same time, West German youths burn down houses for political refugees.

So, after years of oppression, fighting for equality, reunification, it seems as though Germany may still be divided, in spirit if not in name. Be careful what you wish for, because you might just get it. This is the theme of Arjouni's novel, Magic Hoffmann *(1996).*

The story is about a young guy and his two friends who want to go to Canada, so they rob a bank. He ends up in jail for four years. Reunification takes place in the mean time, so when he gets out, he goes after his money and his two friends. It's about how people lose their dreams, and also about the loss of Germany's dream - the bubble has burst after reunification.

The world changes, either remoulding or forgetting the past as it feels fit. Case in point, the four streets around Frankfurt rail station which are the setting for the Kayankaya novels. In his early teens, Arjouni spent his weekends playing cards among the seedy sex shops, hookers, drug dealers, Turks, old people, bars. It was a little town, market, circus, full of strangers, 'guest-workers' of all nationalities. Everyone got on. There was an equality. It wasn't judgmental, racist.

Now the money has moved in, taking over the houses and shops, forcing prices up, making it difficult for ordinary people to live in the area.

Arjouni captures the time he was there in the Kayankaya novels: Happy Birthday, Turk!, More Beer and One Man, One Murder. He wrote the first one when he was 19 (he's said 18 in other interviews because it sounds better).

Kemal Kayankaya is a private eye born in Turkey and raised in Germany. He's always drinking, always getting beaten up, always getting wet in the rain. He makes sure that the bad people are caught, even if he twists the law for his own ends. Sounds a lot like Dashiell Hammett to me.

When you're 18 or 19 you don't have your own style. You take from the people you know. In this case, the first pages of *Happy Birthday, Turk!* are me saying 'Dashiell Hammett is an influence.' (Not

More Beer

'Pitch-black noir' *La Depeche*

Jakob Arjouni

Raymond Chandler - he is too artificial, too arch.) It was something I had to learn from, to allow me to develop my own style.

Arjouni was born in Frankfurt, in 1964. He did a lot of travelling when he was young, ending up in a French boarding school, where he felt like a stranger, an outsider.

It wasn't anything dramatic, just a feeling of not belonging.

Not having many friends, he read Hammett, Chester Himes and all the other crime writers. He wanted to tell crime stories and paper is cheap enough to have a go and fail.

Looking back, I had a very professional attitude to writing, very organised. I'm also surprised by what I was thinking back then.

So, writing crime stories is great, but why a Turkish hero? In Germany, Turks are the street cleaners, the labourers, the people who get the shit jobs. They are perceived as the underclass of society, and are looked down upon. Germany invited the Turks over as 'guest workers' and, when they don't want them, ship them back to where they came from.

When I was 18, I read about a man named Kemal, in jail, about to be deported to Turkey. He didn't want to go, so he committed suicide, jumped out a window.

I was shocked. I had always been interested in politics, the way the world worked, and was fascinated by the stupidity of racists and nationalists. So I decided to use racism as a metaphor to show the troubles of Germany.

Germans are always angry at outsiders and a Turk is the most outside you can get. But, in Frankfurt, the Turks are second or third generation. They have never seen Turkey. They are German. So racism against them is illogical!

Racism has nothing to do with logic. It's about fear of losing power and money to others who presently have less power and money than you. The 'others' are grouped for easy identification by the colour of their skin, their accent, or dress. These groups then become the focus of the hate.

The only message in my books is that you should only judge on what you know. A person is an individual. When you see a person, they are new to you, you judge them on that. If you like, you like. Similarly, if you hate, you hate. I talk about this through Kayankaya.

Arjouni gets angry when he is judged by people because of his outward appearance, so he expects Kayankaya to get angry as well.

And, in modern Germany, Kayankaya has no choice but to be angry all the time. Kayankaya also has the ability to rub people up the wrong way in world record time.

If you're writing about a Turkish hero in Germany, he can't be too good.

The books are very sparsely written and take place over three days. There is very little time for thought or reflection. The characters speak through their actions or reactions, and these are often violent. In other words, you can only rely on what you see, your first impressions. Even for the central character. In the first two books, there is very little substance to Kayankaya's life. He eats fast food and has no personal relations.

Life is boring, routine. Only a half hour in a month is important. That's when decisions are made, when you find out something about yourself. These books contain that half hour.

Kayankaya is more complicated than can be shown in one book. As the books progress, you find out more about him. He becomes more real, more rounded. It's like getting to know someone over a period of time.

In *One Man, One Murder*, his professional and private life become more mixed. The fourth book, which I'm writing, will examine Kayankaya's private life even more.

The Kayankaya books have been very successful in Germany and around the world. They have been translated into eight languages, and Arjouni is very happy that they are in English.

All the best crime novels are in English. It is a fresh, direct language, like German. Other languages, like French, are not so vital because of the rephrasing and words that have to be used.

In 1992, Happy Birthday, a film of the first novel, was a big box office hit in Germany. The director, Doris Dorrie, is one of Germany's biggest directors. Jakob thought the film not very good.

It was a leftist liberal view of the world, concerned with the 'Turkish problem' and about Kemal 'getting in touch with his Turkish roots.' This is not what Kayankaya is all about. There are no problems with the Turks, or anyone else in Germany, that food and a roof over their heads wouldn't solve. Nobody seems to complain about having 'problems' with rich Turks!

Arjouni has now joined the ranks of modern German crime writers, so I wondered what he thought of them.

I don't like their work. They are trying to write crime stories that change the world and, at the same time, seem embarrassed to write in the genre. They are trying to write 'literature.' They are full of 'deep insights' which, upon reflection, turn out to be quite shallow.

What will become of Germany? Will the affluent West Germans allow the poorer East Germans a piece of the economic pie? Will the Iron Curtain continue to segregate Germany, this time acting as the division between rich and poor? Will the East Germans become 'guest workers' in their own country? And where will that leave the Turks?

Whatever the answer, Arjouni will be there to report his own findings. Still a bit of an outsider, an individualist, ploughing his own way through life, ruffling feathers, putting people's noses out of joint.

Yeah. Sounds good to me.

Bibliography

Happy Birthday, Turk! (1985)

A Turkish worker is stabbed to death in the red light district of Frankfurt and nobody cares. Except for his wife, who hires Kemal Kayankaya to find the killer. Kemal finds answers, but not the ones the family want to here. He finds the dead man's mistress, who's a whore. He finds a police cover-up. And he finds four knuckles on every fist beating him up along the way.

More Beer (1987)

Four members of a radical ecological group are accused of the murder of the director of a chemical plant near Frankfurt. While admitting to damaging the plant, they deny murder. According to witnesses, there were five of them, so where's the fifth man? The defendants' lawyer hires Kayankaya to find him.

One Man, One Murder

A distressed artist comes to PI Kemal Kayankaya for help. His girlfriend, a Thai girl, has been kidnapped. Kayankaya's raised eyebrows bring protestations of love. Kemal confronts obstructive racist officials and corrupt cops in his trawl through the immigration offices and brothels of Frankfurt. It seems that young women fugitives and asylum seekers are disappearing into the Frankfurt night.

JAKOB ARJOUNI

THE THIRD DEGREE

144

THERE IS A LAUDABLE TRADITION *of American socialist fiction. People like John Steinbeck writing about poor white folk during the Depression, eating dust, being thrown across America in search of work, of the promised land full of milk and honey. It's the American Dream, for God sakes!*

But the American Dream for whom? What happened to the poor black folk? Where were the black authors telling their story, their history?

Mention a black author and most people think of novels about racial tension in the deep South, tortured young men unable to make their way in the white world, interracial sex. It's always black in relation to white. It's rarely about black people living and mixing in black communities.

Walter Mosley is doing his bit to redress the balance. He has a private eye, Ezekial 'Easy' Rawlins, grow up in front of our eyes starting, aged 26, in 1948 Los Angeles. A war veteran, laid off from work at the aircraft factory, Easy must pay his mortgage, so is forced to find a man for money. His life as an investigator begins. In each of the books, which are set at different times in Easy's life, he is forced to make moral decisions. Easy's best friend is Mouse, a volatile man at the best of times, who is quite likely to kill at a glance. Mouse is chaos incarnate. Mouse makes it difficult for Easy to make moral decisions.

(Easy Rawlins is a pun, isn't it? He's not hard, he's easy. He's not boiled, he's raw. Okay, so it doesn't fit exactly, but I thought I'd give it a shot.)

They aren't many black crime writers: Chester Himes (Coffin Ed and Gravedigger Jones, two gun-happy cops in hysteria-fuelled black comedies), John Ball (Detective Virgil Tibbs) and more recently, Donald Goines, Gar Anthony Haywood and Mike Phillips. Walter Mosley is not like any of them. He is playing with the traditional themes of the private eye novel established by Dashiell Hammett, Raymond Chandler and Ross Macdonald. He's placing these themes into the life and times of a black man.

Starting with Devil In A Blue Dress, each of the Easy Rawlins books has a different colour in the title, and there are going to be about nine in the series. Walter Mosley has also completed RL's Dream, a novel about an old black man who's dying, and whose only claim to fame is that he once met legendary blues musician Robert Johnson. It is a novel about pain and about how people deal with it.

Paul Duncan talked to Walter Mosley.

Historyteller

You were born in Watts (that's south central Los Angeles) in 1952, and grew up in LA. Did living in LA at that time have any effect on you writing about LA in the Easy Rawlins' books?

That's a fun question to ask a writer because if a writer says yes, you shouldn't believe them, and if they say no, they probably don't know what they're talking about. It's hard to say.

Yeah, it probably had a big effect on me but I don't know what it is. It's like, I have a scar on my hand here, and I know what caused that scar but my upbringing...? I don't know. It's very hard to say.

I know LA very well. I was in Watts until I was 12, and then moved to west Los Angeles, to a mixed middle-class area and I know a lot about that area as well. I also know a lot about areas I've never been to at all. I wrote a lot about Riverside in *A Red Death*, but I've only been there about four times in my life. Yet, people from Riverside seem to think I know it.

Robert Campbell, who writes the LA-LA land novels, also writes a series set in Chicago about a detective who's part of the political machine. After about the third book, a guy said to him that he must really have been involved with the Chicago machine to have written about it so well. Robert said, and it's true, that he'd never been to Chicago in his life. But he understood the way political machines work.

So, it's a hard question to answer - I'm not trying to avoid it. I'm just trying to answer honestly.

Walter's parents had a mixed marriage. Both his black father, Louisiana-born LeRoy Mosley, and white Jewish mother, Ella Slatkin, worked for the local board of education. Walter schooled in Victory Baptist Day School, the only private black elementary school in LA, where he had a wonderful time. In 1964, before the riots in Watts, the family moved to a mixed middle-class area in west LA. His dad's Houston friends would visit and tell stories about the old days. LeRoy grew up in Houston's Fifth Ward in the forties and was forced into burglary, witnessed knife fights, crazy women and love gone wrong, before migrating to LA.

As a long-haired black youth during the sixties, it wasn't uncommon for Walter to be rousted by the cops - wryly, he comments that it's not surprising to him that you don't see many black writers writing police procedurals. When he was old enough, he moved east to Vermont to study at Goddard College, where he was asked to leave. Later, Walter studied political science at Johnson State College, then later went to political theory school at the University of Massachusetts at Amherst. There was a move to Boston before ending up at Greenwich Village, New York as a computer programmer.

I was a computer programmer from the early seventies, 1973, until 1989. I programmed in Assembler, RPG and Cobol for businesses. Nothing very interesting.

I wanted to do something other than programming. I didn't like going to work every day. I didn't feel in any way edified or satisfied, or that I was doing something in any way creative. I wanted to be creative. I would have been happy to be doing anything. I was a potter - I did that to make a bit of money. I was a painter - I painted a lot but didn't make any money doing that. I love music but I can't really play - I'm not tone deaf or anything but I don't have that facility. I like to cook. It turned out I was good at writing.

How did you find this out?

Just by writing. I had thought for a long time, even when I was a kid, that I was good at writing - not fiction, but papers for college and stuff like that. One day, I started writing, just for fun, like I did with potting, cooking and painting, and I liked the sentences. But, unlike the others, this worked and I could make money from them.

Walter wrote a series of letters to his wife and friends, who said he wrote wonderfully. This sparked him to go on a graduate writing program at the City College of the University of New York in 1985. It was a very artistic course, not commercial at all. He began by writing short stories. His first attempt at writing a novel was Gone Fishing *in 1988.*

It's about Easy and Mouse in their late teens, early twenties, in the American south of 1939. It's the first book in the series, telling you why they're friends, so *Devil In A Blue Dress* is really the second book in the series. I thought *Gone Fishing* was a successful attempt but people at that time didn't think so, but I'm still going to publish it, and soon.

There's a reference to Samuel L Clemens (who wrote as Mark Twain) in *Black Betty*, and Twain is one of your favourite writers. Are Easy and Mouse like Tom Sawyer and Huckleberry Finn only written by a black writer?

There's a lot of confusion about racism. There's a good reason for that - it's confusing, it's hard to see. I can see some people saying that Mark Twain is a racist because he said this and that, and people shouldn't read his books. Really, his books speak to the hearts of a lot of people who had that experience, Easy being one of them. Easy understood that experience.

When people think of literature, they think of literature that is important to them, that talks to them, is close to their heart. And very often, it's linked to their past experiences.

And reading is an experience that can affect you.

In *A Little Yellow Dog*, Easy goes to see a white gangster, who's reading a book - the Modern Library edition of *Meditations* by Marcus Aurelius, who was a very literate and intelligent emperor of Rome. The gangster expects Easy not to have read it, but Easy knows that Aurelius wrote it during his military campaign against the Germans. They have a conversation and, as Easy is leaving, the gangster asks Easy how he knows about the book. *'Well, Rome is a lot closer to Africa than it is to here,'* Easy says.

It's just a little statement. I'm not very didactic in the novels, I'm not trying to teach people lessons. Easy wants to reclaim what's his. Very often in Black America people say that all that stuff that happened was long ago and we should be back in Africa. Easy says, no, we've evolved everywhere so everything belongs to us as it belongs to everyone else. Easy is reclaiming those things in the novels, however mildly. Often I include that attitude in my novels and stories.

When I learned how to read, people taught me how to read, so that I knew everything I read was there for a reason. Part of the reason is to tell the story, part of the reason is to move the story along, and then there are trace elements like the writer's or characters' ideas and philosophy. Or they are making a statement about the time, politically, educationally or whatever. People don't read books like that any more but I still like writing like that. That's why I write novels.

I find it interesting that, very often, people who read for fun often see these things in my books but the reviewers don't, they don't look at the books they read very closely. They sit down to read a book with a mystery, or about black people, or about rape and they get confused when these are mixed into one book.

In my experience, I think that people who read for enjoyment are much more open to new ideas and concepts.

They take in more. Also, critics sit and read a book, and very rarely read that book again before writing about it. But I think 90% of reading a book is sitting down and talking to other people about it. You discuss scenes, characters, themes and go back and read the book again. That's when you really read the book and know you've read it.

You extended the relationship between Easy and Mouse from *Gone Fishing* and wrote a mystery story that turned into *Devil In A Blue Dress*, your first published book. Do you have a particular love of the mystery genre, or does it happen to fit into what you're trying to say?

I love writing and I think genre fiction can hold a lot. There is also the question of audience. You can get a larger audience if you write genre. You say the story's about a farmer in Iowa whose wife has died and the farm is going under and people turn off. You say it's about a detective and somebody's killed his daughter, then people's ears prick up - they're interested.

Devil In A Blue Dress is set in 1948. Since then the following books have gone through the fifties and sixties, reading like an alternative history of America through the eyes of a black man.

It is, but I didn't do that on purpose. It just turned out that way. Even now, it is not my main concern, although historical events are included or mentioned in the books. For me, it's the story of Easy Rawlins' strange relationships - it's not strange because he's a black man but because it's his life. I did that because very often events are coloured by other things. When you ask him what did he think of D-Day, his response is *'My mother died on D-Day'*, which means there's a whole other story going on. It's interesting because the whole world is affected on that day, as Easy is affected, and there can be a similarity or difference of emotions associated with it.

I do think it's also interesting that black people have an unrecorded history. Even where it is recorded, it's not taken very seriously. So, in *RL's Dream*, in which Robert Johnson is a character, as popular as he is nowadays it's very hard for people to take him seriously as a genius, whereas the guy telling the story in the novel obviously does consider him a genius.

It's interesting in the novel that meeting Robert Johnson seems to be one of the most important things in Soupspoon's life. It's his only legacy.

It's like one likes to touch the leg of the deity at one time in your life, and that affects the rest of his life. So the book becomes a personal document to Soupspoon and, also, through him a historical testament to a man who represented a whole group of people, the bluesmen. These men changed the world.

There is a discussion in the novel, saying that Europe never produced anything worthwhile. A very famous American writer - I won't tell you her name - was in England. She read that chapter and she said I was saying in the book that the only thing that European culture ever came up with was guns and stealing stuff. Then she said, *'But what about Michelangelo's painting on the Sistine Chapel?'* I could have talked about Catholicism and the rape of the rest of the world, but I didn't get into that with her. All I said to her was that I didn't say that, my character was saying that, and he was talking to another character. Yes, but you wrote it, she said. That was so interesting to me because a writer, a very good writer, was saying this to me.

This character I created doesn't know the truth, he's just telling what he believes. He's speaking from the heart, from whatever he knows, and we see another part, or another view, of history from his perspective. I'm not saying whether or not Europe has created anything that's culturally valid which, of course, it has, but this man hates the way his whole life has been blocked out. He tries to block out this writer's whole life, and she bites. So she now feels the way he does.

You're presenting different points of view through different characters. It's very interesting that Easy and Mouse are together, forced together, yet they have such widely different points of view. There doesn't seem to be a reason for them to be friends unless, of course, it's explained in *Gone Fishing*.

I'm having a discussion with all the characters in my books, and some of their points of view are ones which aren't often considered. For example, in *Black Betty*, Easy talks about his experiences in World War Two. He was surrounded by a mountain of dead people. He realised it wasn't the Germans who killed them - they were dying too - but it was the Generals who sent them out to be killed.

I try my best to be a good writer. I try. I want to be a good writer. I want to make good books. I want them to be novels - I don't call them crime or mystery stories. I write them as novels and that's how I expect them to be read.

On the other hand, I'm not like Ernest Hemingway, who came in and changed the way people look at fiction, the form. The way he wrote sentences, the way he structured things, was very unusual and influential, even though it had been used elsewhere previously. Very often, I'll write something which people say has never been written about before. If I decide to write about Watts or the Mississippi Delta, then no-one's written about it before - certainly not by somebody who's black.

When I think of black writers, I think of Chester Himes, Richard Wright, James Baldwin and people like that.

Richard Wright is a great writer, and he's written about the American south, but the emphasis of his work is a brooding, political psychology. It's a black man in relation to a white man and America. Very often, in the books written by these people in this period of time, the black man ends up going to France.

If you go back far enough, there're some incredibly wonderful writers like Langston Hughes and Zora Neale Hurston. These people wrote about the black experience in the Harlem Renaissance of the twenties and thirties. Zora was almost like an anthropologist. *Their Eyes Are Watching God* is one of her novels. Langston Hughes wrote lots and lots of short stories, novels and poetry. These people were actually celebrating black life, which is something that I do.

There is a guy, a friend of theirs, who wrote the first black mystery novel, *The Conjur Man Dies*. Even though he did that, and even though Chester Himes wrote crime, I'm entering the genre in a different way.

In your books you don't emphasise the confrontation between black and white, but often show confrontations between black and black.

There's a conflict in Easy about what racism is and isn't. In Easy's opinion, most white people in America are racist and accept racism as a natural thing, but not everyone is a racist. Along the way, he has to figure out who is and isn't racist. And there are also black people along the way who are warped spiritually and psychologically by racism and poverty. One of the things I want to say in the novels is that, in real life, black people are always unclear about where they stand. Who can I trust? Who can't I trust?

Easy can't seem to trust anyone.

It's very difficult for him, but he can trust Mouse. And that's a big reason for them being together. Mouse is violent, and unpredictable, and may kill a few people, but he'll never turn on Easy. Easy can always trust him, although Mouse can't always trust Easy.

Mouse is like moving nitroglycerine, he might just blow up. But Easy knows that. He can trust Mouse to be Mouse, but he doesn't know who other people are, what they are going to do. It's always hard for Easy to trust new people, and it's specifically hard for him to trust women but this is something I hope he works out over his life.

As Easy gets older through the books, his priorities are changing. For example, in *Black Betty*, he doesn't want to go out and hunt for some girl when he could be safe at home, playing with his children.

To a certain extent, he is becoming prosperous but, when you look below the surface, he is still trying to survive and he is motivated by his survival instincts.

Every once in a while Easy has these dreams of being prosperous but I'm never really sure how that's going to work out for him. He's such an idealist, basically. He so much wants to do the right thing by people. Like in *A Red Death* there's an old lady in the apartment building he owns who can't pay the rent, so he eases off and watches out for them. This isn't capitalism - he's not going to make money by doing that.

Money is a major concern for Easy, but there are other things which are more important even though he doesn't want them to be. I think he sometimes wants to be somebody else, but he's not.

He's almost acting the hero, going in to sort out bad situations, and gets into trouble because he's not a superhero.

Mouse is the superhero, but he has no sense of right and wrong like Easy.

Easy is idealistic, but he does do things which are outside the law. His truth is different to what the law may be. And at that time the racist laws were prevalent throughout America.

Nowadays, you can say that those racist laws shouldn't be, and if you are ignorant, you would say that there aren't any racist laws any more. All you have to do is look at the video tape of Rodney King being beaten up by the cops. Obviously, the law is not being applied to him the way most middle-class citizens are having the law applied to them. Then, people who are ignorant about the way the law works, say that Rodney King was a rare case. No, this happens at least once a day, every day in every big city, and more often in the prisons. Then they won't believe it's happening. At this point you have a basis of understanding the reason Easy has to make decisions differently from the way people who think the law works do. These people know how the law works for them and think it applies to everyone else - as if their children eating a full dinner every night means all children eat a full dinner every night.

The whites have one law for themselves and another for blacks, therefore the blacks have their own laws too.

But there is no one set of laws. Everyone has their own set of laws. Individuals have laws. Groups, whether religious or political, have laws. And then you have Mouse's law - do whatever you want, but don't fuck with me or else I'll shoot ya.

Is this why it's become so tribal in America with the Hispanic and black gangs?

America and everywhere else. This is why you have skinheads and ravers and whatever else you have in London. A lot of it is about being poor. Once you have a certain level of money things change. You might still be treated unreasonably but as soon as people know the colour of your money they change. 'Oh yes, Mister Jones, please come in, we want your money.' This is not just a black thing, it's also representative of a lot of poor whites in America.

I was talking to a woman the other day who said her Irish grandfather, who was a staunch Republican, said to her *'I like Clinton a little more.'* She was shocked. *'Why?'* she asked. *'Because President Clinton said Walter Mosley was his favourite author. He's my favourite writer too. When I came to America, my life was just like Easy Rawlins. If something went wrong, it was the Irish man did it. And the police - there were no Irish police then - they grabbed you and beat you up and threw you in the street and didn't think twice about killing you. It didn't matter.'* So I think a lot more people could identify with Easy and his situation because a lot of it is purely to do with poverty.

I like a few blues singers like Leadbelly and John Lee Hooker, but I've never really gotten into Robert Johnson.

I see Leadbelly as a storyteller, a balladeer, singing a lot of angry, powerful songs. Robert Johnson is much more like a poet. Johnson'd say something like: *'You better come in to my kitchen because it's bound to be cold outside,'* some music, *'I woke up this morning, went to the front door, I said Hello Satan, I guess it's time to go,'* some music, *'I'm going to beat my woman till I get satisfied,'* music, *'You can take my soul and bury it down by the highway and my evil soul will catch the Greyhound and ride.'* This means something, and it means something really deep. It's hard to figure out but, maybe, if you were living in the Delta at the time, it would be unbelievably more powerful. I think he was crystallising the sense of doom, which is why I wrote about him. I don't think Leadbelly does that. Robert Johnson was also a wonderful musician, a great guitar player.

Leadbelly is more of an entertainer.

Yeah. There's nothing wrong with him or Howling Wolf, Blind Lemon Jefferson, Muddy Waters and the rest, but Johnson was bigger.

The theme of *RL's Dream* seems to be physical and emotional pain.

Emotional pain for Soupspoon, physical pain for the people around him, especially Kiki.

It's a painful book to read. It is touching that these two people in pain get together and try to comfort each other.

I think that Kiki really got something out of the relationship with Soupspoon. He really helped her to stand up on her own. She robbed the place she worked, hurt the guy who hurt her, and got revenge.

A case of doing bad to do good.

The world doesn't really care about you. One day it can turn around and you lose your job. You're 52 years old and unemployed, and nobody'll hire you, you've got no retirement. Unless you've saved for 52 years of your life for this moment, you probably haven't got any money. That's all. There's nothing fair about that. So what happens to the guy? He might go off and rob a bank to survive. I might put him in jail but I'm not going to blame him.

If a guy, without any compunction, rapes a woman in an elevator, but he's the boss, nobody's going to listen to the woman. If the woman killed him, I might arrest her but, again, I wouldn't blame her.

Mouse commits a lot of bad acts but I can't really blame him for them because he's basically a good person. He's not evil.

Do you believe evil exists?

I think that some people can be evil. I haven't written about that. I haven't written about those kind of people.

Since the publication of his first novel in 1990, Walter has won awards, been publicly praised by the President of the United States, and had a fairly decent movie made from Devil In A Blue Dress. *It's a meteoric rise.*

I think about my career in a very pedestrian way. I don't know where I'll be next year or where I came from. It's impossible to assume that you're always going to be doing great. I have no control over that. But, I would like everything I do to be the best that I can do at that time. I have complete control over the books, so if they don't work it's my fault. The movie I couldn't control, but it looks and feels good, so I'm very happy about the way it's turned out. As long as I can continue to put out things that I can look back on and still be proud of.

A Name When I Lose

In *Deacon Blue* Steely Dan make vocal the basis of most noir fiction:
'They got a name for the winners in this world,
and I want a name when I lose...'
History is written by the winners, noir fiction is life from the point of view of the losers, the doomed and the disinherited.

The nature of noir fiction depends therefore on the nature of the society that author and protagonist inhabit. In most American noir the nature of loss is financial or class-based - the characters that populate many seminal noir works are economically disenfranchised or have lost their 'place' in society. American society being notionally a meritocracy, a 'classless' society, the theme of class is a particularly potent one, which recurs countless times. Elsewhere in this volume Elliott Leyton says 'in America, if you're less than middle class you're just a worthless failure...'

But the lure of the 'Great Society' is that people can transcend their status - that unlike the UK, where accent, schooling and the 'age' of the money you spend define you as much as the money you have - acquisition can lead to a better life.

Imagine your class is marked on your skin and however much money you have you can never aspire to the things the society you inhabit values.

Welcome to the world of Walter Mosley and Ezekiel 'Easy' Rawlins.

At the start of *Devil In A Blue Dress* (1990) Easy Rawlins is ensconced in Joppys bar, over a butcher's warehouse. A white man walks in and looks at Easy, and he feels a thrill of fear; then he explains;

'..but that went away quickly, because I was used to white people by 1948.'

Easy has been to war, fighting for freedom. The freedom to sit in a bar stinking of rotting meat, it seems. He has recently lost his job, and is about to lose his house, so when he is offered a job by the white man, to find a woman 'with a predilection for the company of Negroes' he accepts. He has little alternative.

This is the starting point of all the books. Easy's needs - financial, sexual - are manipulated by others so Easy does what they want. What they want varies, but Easy's part in getting it never does. It's bad luck for Easy all the way.

Devil In A Blue Dress also introduces us to Mouse, a kind of evil Huck Finn to Easy's resigned Tom Sawyer. Mouse is a killer, a sociopath, with little love for anyone except Easy, and later his son. Mouse has been accused of acting as a deus ex machina in the books, but in fact he is more like Easy's dark shadow. In a way Mouse *is* Easy - an Easy who faces the world with a grim realism and acts according. *Devil* is a slick performance for a first novel, conjuring up both our accepted vision of forties LA, as seen through the vision of Raymond Chandler and an infinitely harsher world of pain for Easy.

If *Devil* remakes the traditional forties PI novel from the point of view of a black underclass, *A Red Death* (1991) examines the 'communist menace' and questions of ownership. Since *Devil*, Rawlins has become a property owner and landlord, albeit a clandestine one. The motive power for the book is the arrival on his doorstep of the tax man, anxious to investigate his affairs, or more accurately to use their knowledge to force Rawlins to help them investigate a 'red', Chaim Wenzler. This sits hard with Easy, who likes Wenzler. At a pivotal point in the plot, Wenzler says:

"And that's why I'm here... because Negroes in America have the same life as the Jew in Poland. Ridiculed, segregated. We were hung and burned for just being alive"

Wenzler's words conjure up a memory of Rawlin's childhood in the south - of the death of a family friend's family by burning, a burning that we are not told was intentional, but have little doubt about. By the end of the book Easy's sense of betrayal will have lead him to his first steps towards a genuine responsibility to others, as he adopts his first child, Jesus.

In *White Butterfly* it's 1956 and someone is killing young black goodtime girls - no-one is interested until a white girl is killed. Then Easy is involved, once again against his own volition.

"I wanted to feel better but all I had was the certainty that the world had passed me by - leaving me and my kind dead or making death in dark causeways."

In *Black Betty* (1994) Easy is older, tired, broke and his wife has left him. It is 1961 and Kennedy is in the White House and Martin Luther King in the news. Mirroring the action of Devil, another white man, Saul Lynx, offers Easy some business. Lynx has been hired to find Elizabeth Eady, known as 'Black Betty.' Easy's reputation for 'finding people in the coloured part of town' has gone before him. Betty has left her job with a white family and disappeared, and they have hired Lynx to find her.

Easy has known Betty from childhood, and using an old black and white photo of Betty and his memories of her, he searches for her in the black community of LA, the desert, the jail, and the farm of the Cain family where Betty had worked.

Even after he is taken off the case by Saul Lynx, he continues the search. He tells his daughter, *"It's a secret and I'm trying to find it out."*

And, after a narrative that moves evenly between the search and the problems in his own life, Easy finds our what has happened to Betty.

In *A Little Yellow Dog* (1996) the year is 1963, JFK is President and Easy Rawlins is on the straight and narrow. Well for the first few pages of this book anyway. He's custodian of Sojourner Truth Junior High School in Watts. For the two years since the events of *Black Betty*, he's been getting up early and going to work. But that's about to change. Rawlins comes in one morning to find one of the teachers already in her classroom. She has a dog with her and tells him her husband's gone mad. Lust and indecision leave him holding Pharoah - the little yellow dog of the title. Before the end of the day the bodies have started piling up and the police coming round.

The police, in Mosley's fiction, are often the motive force for Rawlins' detective activities. If he doesn't *find* the culprit there's always a reasonable chance he'll end up *as* the culprit, courtesy the LAPD. This book is no exception, and Rawlins is on the trail, aided by Mouse.

Mosley now has an enviable control of a fully realised fictional world. Plot, dialogue, and the world view of his characters are welded together to create a view of American society from the bottom up that is as hard to accept as it is brutally compelling. Often in reading Mosley's work I have to step back and remind myself that this is not simply a novelist's stylisation, but a world that, to a lesser or greater degree, actually exists. A world of unrelieved harshness for black Americans, detailed with a clarity that is as enviable as it is uncomfortable. It is an ironic point that Bill Clinton, Mosley's most prominent fan, is currently helping recreate this world.

Rawlins escapes with his skin; others, JFK among them, are not so fortunate. The plot grips, the dialogue's tight, the mood is blue.

WALTER MOSLEY

JAMES SALLIS IS A LIAR. *And what's more, he gets paid for it.*

He writes novels featuring Lew Griffin who may, or may not, be writing the stories. But, of course, James Sallis is writing the stories, isn't he?

Lew Griffin is a black private eye, operating in New Orleans - well, the bars, really. Or rather, he's a debt collector who ends up, so the story goes, giving money to people to pay their debts. No, that's not quite true. Lew Griffin is a murderer, I'm sure. No, tell a lie. He's a lecturer on European literature. Nope. He's a novelist. Or he is all of them.

How can one man be so many things?

The same could be said of James Sallis. A trained musician, he plays French horn, violin, guitar, mandolin and Dobro. At one stage, to earn money, he was doing club gigs on weekends, music lessons in the week. There are a couple of failed marriages and alcoholism in his life. More recently, James has been working at the bedside of critically ill or dying adults and newborn children. On the literary front, he's an editor, reviewer, teacher, musicologist, essayist, translator, poet, novelist and short story writer.

In a world where we are pigeonholed by marketing statistics, stereotyped by our appearance, analysed by rote, it is satisfying to meet someone who defies categorisation. Someone who falls between the cracks.

Paul Duncan braved a tube strike, smog, sweltering heat, and a gaggle of Scandinavian air stewardesses to meet James Sallis. As they talked in a deserted hotel bar, Oasis were singing Don't Look Back In Anger. *No fear of that - James was constantly smiling and laughing, happy to be in London again.*

Professional Liar

An avid reader of SF since he was a child - his first book was The Puppet Masters *by Robert Heinlein - James began writing in the mid-Sixties.*

SF had always been a genre with a lot of potential, and I thought that, in the Sixties, science fiction was extremely important, largely because of *New Worlds* magazine, which was edited by Michael Moorcock, and all that was going on in London. For the first time, it seemed to me, someone had said that this stuff, SF, could be literature. Nobody had seriously thought about this before. Reading Jimmy Ballard was exciting. It fed my love of the surreal and edge literature.

I just recognised something in SF for which I hungered. Like pregnant women crave things, I craved this literature.

I'd been writing forever, but only then did I begin writing seriously, to finish stories, polish them. I ended up selling my first story to three people at once, which was rather embarrassing. I finally sold it to a guy in the States because he could pay me money, where Mike could only offer me hula hoops and any other door prizes he could scrape together. The story sold for $300, an awesome amount of money at that time. I can't sell a short story for that amount of money NOW, which is why I'm writing novels.

I was in college and, after selling some short stories, decided to drop out to write full time. Mike had already published a couple of my stories in *New Worlds* when he came over to the States to attend a writer's workshop organised by Damon Knight. We met, spent a lot of nights talking till dawn. At the end of that Mike, who wanted to back away from editing and just remain publisher, invited me to become the editor of *New Worlds*. I knew nothing about editing and had no money, so I said sure.

James' first visit to London was in the late Sixties, where he became fiction editor, then editor of New Worlds. *He solicited and edited Harlan Ellison's famous short story* A Boy And His Dog. *Other writers whose early work was published include J G Ballard (*Crash, Empire Of The Sun*) and D M Thomas (*The White Hotel*). When the magazine ran extracts from* Bug Jack Barron *by Norman Spinrad, questions were raised in Parliament, and* New Worlds *was banned for obscenity.*

You know how these things are - you're never really told. There was a lot of criticism, and one of the large bookstore chains refused to carry the magazine, which completely wiped out what financial base we had. The magazine sputtered on for a little time. Meanwhile, I went back to the States to try and save a marriage - which I didn't save - and was just too poor to come back to London, which I've regretted ever since.

James went on to edit two SF anthologies, The War Book *(1969) and* The Shores Beneath *(1970), a recent issue of* The Review Of Contemporary Fiction *about Samuel R Delany, and* Ash Of Stars *(1996), a critical anthology of Delany's work. There is a collection of SF short stories,* A Few Last Words *(1969), and James continued to write SF short stories throughout the Seventies.*

I don't read too much SF nowadays. I did a SF column for the *LA Times* up until recently, which kept me up-to-date. I haven't stopped writing SF, it's just that I don't write it that often, probably 5 stories in the same number of years. I don't write many short stories anyway, since the market isn't there. I sold consistently to *Amazing Stories*, now they've gone under. Economically, I can't afford to spend a week writing a short story which probably won't sell or, if it does sell, will 'sell' to a literary magazine for a free copy.

To me, the literature of the Sixties was when everyone swore and wrote about sex (Henry Miller, William S Burroughs, etc.), and when everyone played with the form of storytelling. Of the two, the later seems to be the one that has come through into the mainstream. Like fashion, where the outrageous is seen on the catwalk followed by the toned down version in the chainstores, the experimentation of form done in the Sixties is often seen in mainstream books today.

I agree with you completely. It's been my contention for years - Norman Spinrad contests this, but Mike and I agree. Years ago a friend of mine was saying that we thought we were doing important things in *New Worlds*, but since then, SF had become unreadable - although it's gotten better since. He told me: 'Jim, what you don't realise is that you didn't change science fiction, you changed literature.' And I think that's what happened. Certainly, we raised the standard of literacy in SF, and expanded the ways you can tell stories, but I think the most important aspect is that our influence spilled over into the most important body of literature and really changed it. I don't think you would see books like *The White Hotel* by D M Thomas if it hadn't been for *New Worlds*. There again, this is my opinion, and perhaps I think we're more important than we really are. 'Things in the mirror appear closer than they are.'

It was whilst editing New Worlds *in London that James became a fan of crime literature.*

I had not read much of it. Mike gave me his copies of Raymond Chandler's books and I read the complete works in three days and nights. I've never been the same since. I've tried very hard to keep up with crime fiction since then and fill in the gaps in my knowledge. There are many American writers who are out of print and virtually unknown in their own country. Chester Himes is one, Horace McCoy is another. I'm writing about McCoy now.

I've read the three Lew Griffin books and I can't remember the plots.
That's because there aren't any!

The subtext of the novels serve as the plot. Griffin never solves any cases. Griffin always loses. It's all very strange. Why?
When I first tried to describe the first book to people, I said - Well, he's a detective that keeps going on missing persons cases, and he never finds anyone.

I find plot very uninteresting. When I read crime and detective stories, I read for the atmosphere and the voice. I could care less for plot. When I put down a

Larry Block book, I couldn't begin to tell you how Matt Scudder found who did it. I don't care. When I read James Lee Burke, it's not for the occasional idiocies of the plot which he eventually works out, but for that wonderful atmosphere, the characters and the voice. The voice more than anything.

One thing I try to do in my books is to create the book I always wanted to read, but never could find. I love both 'literature' - for lack of a better word - and detective fiction, so why not have an amalgam which combines the best elements of the two? The edgy atmosphere and crisp dialogue of detective fiction. The pursuits and content of 'literature,' which is a study of character and milieu and how the two interact. That's what I'm trying to do. Write books I'd love to read, but can't find anywhere else.

Also, I get very bored with plots - as reader *and* as writer. I can't force myself to sit down and write them. I try to make it as obvious as possible that there are no plots. Lew is often saying that he just sat down and drank until someone tripped over his feet. This is a big criticism of my publisher, of course - he wants pumped-up plots so that he can sell 50,000 copies.

I can't see it happening.

Neither can I.

It's obvious that you're enjoying yourself. You can always tell when an author enjoys writing.

I like playing with the reader. If you're not aware that you're being told a story, that it's artifice, then where have you been for the past forty years? That's what 'serious' fiction - again, for want of a better word - has been doing. I want to keep it in the reader's mind that this is a game we're playing, that it's artifice, that Lew's stories and the reversals that occur in the books are just fun. I hope people enjoy that aspect, also that those readers who aren't aware of that aspect won't be bothered by it.

I try very hard to submerge the artifice so that people can easily read from beginning to end without stumbling over it. You'd be shocked to find out how many people read *The Long-Legged Fly* as just a straight detective story. They have no idea what the ending is all about. It amazed me when I got my first fan letters, from people who read nothing but crime fiction. What book had they read?

You can never tell how people are going to perceive the books.

Never.

You have presented a literary puzzle. Readers have solved, or ignored, it. But their solution may be completely different to yours.

Once I write the books, they belong to the readers, they can read whatever they want into them. The reader participates in any novel as much as the writer does. The book is whatever they make of it. Obviously readers *are* finding a plot, a story to follow. They're filling in all the bits I left out. I have my vision of the book and do all of the structural and symbolic things I can to try to enhance and realise as fully as possible my vision of the book. And while my vision of the book is not necessarily theirs, I hope I've written well enough and given them enough of the undertones and submerged rivers that, whatever they make of it will be similarly strong and structurally beautiful. Naturally, it's going to be a different book. You're British, Paul. You're a different age, have different experiences.

We've read different books.

Yes. And the books we read define us. Lew doesn't read in an organised way. He knows a lot about many strange things and almost nothing about most normal things.

He reads a lot of books, and a wide variety of them - all your characters seem bookish. The central character of _Death Will Have Your Eyes_ carries a book bag with him, even when he's on the run.

Wouldn't you? This is part of the playful nature of my books, telling you that this is a book, that it is of other books.

Your books could not exist without all these other books existing.

None of ours could.

The novels are literary criticism and teaching at the same time. One explains the plot of another, that each of them is based on literary works. For example, Lew seems to be equally damned for what he didn't do as for what he's done, which is your interpretation of Camus' _The Outsider_.

In _Black Hornet_ everyone believes Lew killed a man, yet he actually tried to save the man. All these stories are told about him. He's completely passive, doing nothing, and everyone is coming to visit him.

People like Lew, who are opaque, on their own, whom no-one understands, often get stories told about them - sometimes they encourage the stories. Because they're not understandable, people try to come up with a reason why they are like they are.

Especially with someone who has Lew's contradictions of character. Why can he open someone's belly with a leather-worker's knife and then, pages later, take a foundling under his wing and let her live in his home?

It's circumstances. People act and react under different circumstances. People go to war, kill, then come back and raise a family.

Maybe. Lew's a fascinating character. I'm always finding out new things about him.

Is he James Sallis?

No. There are lots of things about him that come directly from me. I kind of play with the details of my life in the same way that he plays with the details of his. That's part of the mirror, the game playing, but no, Lew's not me.

Certainly, I share a lot of his self-destructive instincts - that's what I tap into when I'm writing. Like Lew, I do wrong things, even when I know I'm doing the wrong things. I drank extremely heavily for many years, probably for much the same reason as Lew. I've made bad choices that, looking back, I'm appalled by.

I'm not violent - I think I've gotten into two fights in my life. Still, Lew reads the books I read, lives where I live, eats the same food. I appropriate a lot of the details of my life, but the things damning and confounding Lew's life don't damn and confound mine.

The Long-Legged Fly developed from a long short story. I just had that first scene in my head, the oil derricks heaving. I wrote it in an hour or so. At first, I wanted to just create a character who did something unforgivable and then make you love him. Afterwards, I wondered where all his rage came from. Twenty pages in, I realised this man was black. That was the only thing that could explain all this rage and anger boiling out of him, usually at inappropriate times. So I went back and started writing it again, and found out more about who Lew Griffin was. I discovered these things about the character as I wrote the text. I didn't decide on format or character before I started - and I'm still eliciting from the character as the stories are being written.

They're all improvised, I hasten to add. I never know where I'm going when I start the book, even where I'm going from one page to the next. I gave up writing well-made stories many years ago. For it to engage me, I have to improvise, have to wing it.

But you are a controlling force on the book. You have to know whether what you've written is good or not. Do you rewrite?

Endlessly.

You have to know when to stop writing, to know when you've made your point.

Yes, but it's wholly instinctive, Paul. I'll write a scene or chapter, read, and wonder whether it did what it was supposed to do. It's all about feeling. A lot of times I don't consciously know why I reject a scene or a chapter. There's a controlling influence, sure. But that's a complicated thing that occurs while I'm writing. I'm making lots of choices as I'm writing. Endless choices. And I revise a lot.

When I was writing *The Long-Legged Fly*, I wanted a small book, everything boiled down. I'd write scenes, dialogue, then cut it all by half.

Because the books are cut so fine, the reader devours them quicker. Things are missed, so the reader has to go back and re-read the book. I don't think that's a bad thing. They're so short, it's quite easy to go back and read them.

I worry about that sometimes. Perhaps I should put up the equivalent of road signs like those we have in Arizona reading Slow, Watch Out For Rocks or Animals Next Ten Miles. Lots of readers tell me that they go back and read the books two or three times.

I think of my writing in these novels as a kind of poetry. Everything's just so condensed. And so quick that people miss things. My agent does. She'll ask me a question, and I'll explain the answer is obvious, it's on page so and so.

When I think of your writing, I think of it in terms of jazz rather than blues, even though the blues features strongly in the novels.

It's always specious to make comparisons between different arts, but... I would say blues has become a symbol for me because it's trimmed-down, no fat, stark, telling-it-as-it-is storytelling. My writing's also similar to jazz insomuch as I'm improvising, playing off major key forms, figures, looping back and doing variations. Any writing has that analogy with jazz, but I may be more aware of the improvisational element.

As I'm writing, I listen to music all the time. There's a scene in *The Long-Legged Fly* where Lew is writing about his Cajun detective and listening to Cajun music. I do the same sort of thing, playing different kinds of music depending on the scene. I'm sure it affects me. When I was doing the Raymond Queneau translation I played a lot of old Forties French accordion torch songs, which was highly appropriate.

Lew Griffin is a black character. Have you researched the black experience in New Orleans?

Yes. Quite a lot. In New Orleans and outside it. The earliest influence was Chester Himes. A lot of Lew's character traits come, not so much from Chester's characters, as from Chester's life. Lew's passivity, for instance, the way he lets himself be moved from crisis to crisis. His almost exclusive love of white women. His inchoate rage, which Chester had. Acting out inappropriately at the worst possible times. Alcoholism. Some of the sections when Lew's out of control I intentionally tried to pattern on Chester Himes' *The Primitive* (1955). It's the book I most admire. I buy copies at second hand stores and give them to people.

As I got into this, and was doing the research, I read a lot of black literature. I already had an interest in black music - jazz and blues - and was fairly knowledgeable about that. I grew up in the South and played exclusively with blacks up until the age of ten, when I was told I couldn't do that any more. I didn't understand why. A lot of this dovetailed into the books. Some of the things in Lew's early life are transformations of things which happened to me.

As for New Orleans specifically, I've spent a lot of time in cheap bars and cheap restaurants talking to people of every sort, and I tend to steal what I can.

Have you run into any trouble with people saying you're a white writer writing about blacks?

I keep expecting it to happen, but so far it hasn't. Every time I'm at a signing or reading, I truly expect anger to be projected towards me, but everyone's been gracious. Not to say that there haven't been some very surprised faces at signings, when they realise I'm not black.

There have been other white writers, like Ed Lacy (in *Black And

Whitey) and Shane Stevens (*Go Down Dead*), who have successfully written black characters. The whole argument is slightly ridiculous because it's like saying that Walter Mosley can't write white characters. Or that Charles Dickens couldn't write women and Jane Austen couldn't write men.

You're playing with time and form in the books, making a lot of literary references.

Far too many, according to my publishers. And a lot of my readers.

You're expecting a lot from them.

Not really. I don't expect them to pick up on all the allusions. They don't need to know all this stuff. They can read on past the literary stuff, concentrate on the characters and the adventure. However, if they want to take note of and track down the literary allusions, then they're free to do so - there're plenty of them. My French translator amazes me because she'll pick up on these tiny, little phrases - her ear is so good that she can tell it's an allusion, but she won't know to what.

Albert Camus, Raymond Queneau and W B Yeats are mentioned by you within the text. You're obviously widely-read, write essays, poetry, short stories. But why is this all in a crime novel?

Why shouldn't it be? A lot of the literary stuff underpins the artifice. You have to remember Lew, or whoever, starts off writing a very conventional detective story. As the book progresses it becomes more and more literary, more and more autobiographical, so that you think, in the third section, when Lew says that he's writing so close to his life, pretty soon he's going to have to start writing what he says next. Then, at the very end of the book, the narrator says that he's been lying to you all along. He just made up this character called Lew Griffin, you don't know who's really writing this.

The stories are written so that you don't actually know what Lew is thinking, even though they are supposed to be written from his point of view. He tells you he's walking down the street. Then he tells you he hits someone. There's no guarantee of an explanation.

There are two levels to the books that seem contradictory. On one level there is Lew Griffin as a made up character, which is written as a story. On the other level, there is Lew Griffin as a real character, which is written as an autobiography. Those are both goals, and I don't think they are contradictory. I think the stories most important to us are the stories we tell ourselves about ourselves. They are fictive. They allow ourselves to get through and over bad things in life.

It's like the stories your parents or grandparents tell, and tell over and over again with different details. They are exaggerated, to make them entertaining, palatable. Sometimes they are full of outright lies, but they hold grains of truth, which is their point.

That's why I repeat so many things. Some reviewers find it annoying that I repeat little bits of narrative within the books. What they fail to say is that the story's told differently each time.

Lying is important.

Lew talks a lot about dissembling. That's what the black experience has been all about - saying one thing but thinking another - having to lie and not say what you feel. Lew talks about things in the books, but he really means something else - much of the point is what's not said.

Lew seems very intelligent in the books, but it is his emotions which lead him astray.

Painfully so. It's the whole dichotomy between the head and the heart. For me, that darkness and light is what is so compelling about Lew. He is such a smart person. He understands so much about other people's feelings and about what they need - again and again you see this - yet he can't understand himself. He can't figure himself out at all - he's a complete mystery. And he never gets control of whatever it is inside himself which is tearing him up. He goes through periods when he's able to function and has a safe existence, but life always turns dark again.

In Dashiell Hammett's Continental Op stories, the detective is invisible. You don't know what he's really feeling. You know his intellectual approach and his moral outlook, but essentially he's a commentator on the world around him. Very much like reviewers and essayists, and I think Lew Griffin fits perfectly into that role.

I agree. I certainly tried to keep that in mind. There are all sorts of little homages to Hammett, Chandler and other crime books.

You haven't had a happy ending yet, have you?

Could Lew ever have a happy ending?

The happy ending depends upon where you end the story. Lew's life story is told over a long period of time and you chop and change and spindle parts of his life into a solid form. Surely there is something he did which ended happily?

I suppose I could always do a David Goodis and tack on a happy ending that makes no sense to the rest of the story.

You make it seem that Lew lives such a terrible life.

But it's not so terrible. I mean, for all the crap that goes on, how many of us have friends like Don Walsh and LaVerne and all the wonderful women Lew meets. He has success as a writer and as a teacher. He loves fine food. He doesn't really have a terrible life - it's just he has a lot of things going on inside him. What the hell's a happy ending? In the end, we all get thrown into the dirt. You have moments, islands, when things are okay, then something bad happens.

Obviously, because this is edge literature, I'm not focusing on these islands of happiness, but they're there. I think the final scene of *Black Hornet* is a beautiful romantic scene, where LaVerne comes up the steps and Lew reads her a passage from a book he doesn't really understand. They hug. It's a tender, hopeful moment - and at a time when he's young and really just getting fucked up for the first time.

A nice ending, but not for long.

They never are.

If I read your non-crime writing like _Renderings_ (1995), _Limits Of The Sensible World_ (1994), and the upcoming _Gently Into The Land Of The Meateaters_, would I find the same concerns?

Yes. I don't see that much distinction between my writings. _Renderings_, for instance, is science fiction, although you could just as easily read it as a surreal fantasy. It started as a long novel, but I super-condensed it down to 100 pages. Most of the editors who read it said it was too bookish. It does have a plot, but you pick it up as you go along. As in the Lew Griffin novels, there's a lot of talking about books, thinking about the fictions we tell ourselves.

Limits Of The Sensible World is a collection of what I consider to be my very best short stories. They are very intense and have the same feel and penetration as the Lew Griffin novels.

There's little distinction between them all. It's just me explaining, in words, the way I see the world, and they all have the same preoccupations.

I don't like the way publishers pigeonhole writers, categorise them into marketing genres and sub-genres. Was HG Wells just a science fiction writer? Was Rudyard Kipling just a children's author?

I do have this problem with publishers in the States. I write a lot of different things and so have multiple publishers.

James listed his literary influences as Julio Cortazar, Tom Disch, Boris Vian, Theodore Sturgeon, Chester Himes and Raymond Queneau. James translated Saint Glinglin _by Raymond Queneau in 1993, and Queneau is mentioned in_ Moth.

Queneau was a French writer who came in at the end of the surrealist period, became involved with them, overlapped into the existentialists and the Pataphysicians.

What were they? It sounds medical.

They were a group who loosely patterned themselves on Alfred Jarry (author of the play _Ubu Roi_) and didn't take anything seriously. It was said that if you gave a Pataphysician a form that had three duplicates, he'd fill out each one with different information.

When I was editing _New Worlds_ in London, I got a lot of continental books to review and discovered Queneau, the first French writer I fell in love with. For me Queneau is the ultimate artist as artificer. His books are very strange and unworldly, very obviously books. He plays a lot of jokes on the reader, on himself, on expectations. There's nobody like him in English. In fact, there's nobody like him in French.

He was a complete man of letters. He was an excellent poet. He wrote popular songs. He translated. He was a great editor. He oversaw a huge encyclopaedia project that is supposed to cover the entire knowledge of mankind. He even wrote an autobiographical novel in verse, *Chêne Et Chien*. He wrote a play where a character just decides to leave and walk around real life for a while.

Why did I include him in the Lew Griffin books? Probably because I was reading him, or thinking about him, at the time. There are two set pieces in *Moth*, one of which is a lecture Lew delivers about Queneau. All the information is wrong, everything is mixed up.

You're telling lies.

Yes. I think Queneau would have heartily approved.

I'm a binge worker, so I tend to work on one book at a time, and work on it intensely. Now that the short story market is dead, I'm essentially just writing novels, and doing occasional book reviews.

Some work sits around for a year or two before I finish it. *Renderings* was in manuscript for years before I finally found time to work through it.

I try to write full time, and can usually manage this for two to four years at a stretch, then something happens and I have to let go and earn some money. The last time was when I wrote *Death Will Have Your Eyes*. It didn't sell at first, so I had no money for six months and went back to work.

I'm a respiratory therapist. I work with people on ventilators, especially and by preference with newborns. I do that when I can't make a living writing. When we first moved to Arizona, things were really bad; I worked full time as a respiratory therapist for about four or five months until we could get our savings back up.

All that stuff about being at the bedside in *Moth*, that everyone thought I'd researched so carefully, was all off the top of my head. I've done this for almost twenty years off and on. I'm licensed, can pretty much get a job anywhere and at any time I want.

I think it's important work for me. One, because it's so different from writing and everything else I do, and two, because I'm dealing with extreme situations - these kids are gravely ill, crack babies, chronics, and many of them die. Makes me think about things a lot.

I could never do it. It's too much like facing reality.

Exactly why it's important to me. Most of us, in our lives, are not up against death all the time. When I'm doing this, I look it in the face twelve hours a day. If I do something wrong, even if nobody does anything wrong, this baby will die. I work in one of the major centres for my part of the country, so there are many extreme cases, emergencies flying in all the time.

It must be very distressing.

It can be. And it's both physically and emotionally exhausting, which is why I don't do that and write at the same time.

Your work is subversive. I wondered whether there was an element of sticking two fingers up at society. You're playful, but there is a serious message in your work. It's about people who are not happy about the world they are living in.

I don't think people are happy - how can they be for more than a moment at a time? We have to try to laugh at our lot in life. Laughter through tears as Chekhov says again and again. Nobody seems to mention this, but Lew's a funny guy.

It's a dry sense of humour. Very dry. Very English.

Yes it is. Quite English. We laugh, we form connections with people that endure. We tell stories to ourselves and to each other that help us forget the real world we live in, how miserable everything is.

Stories are the fictions we tell ourselves to go on. It's a very Wallace Stevens existentialist kind of thing. We know they're fictions, but we go ahead and tell them, and we choose to believe.

How important are they?

Vital. It's the only way we ever come close to understanding ourselves and others. That sounds dreadfully...but I think art is urgent.

You are trying to understand people, to find out why they are the way they are.

Absolutely. What else is fiction about? We try to see the world through different eyes, get into others' heads.

But, once we see the world, understand it a little more, can we then change it?

Ultimately, no, we can't.

We're supposed to be human. We're supposed to be able to change things.

You can cultivate your garden. You can strive to make, keep, strengthen the friendships and connections you have in your life. You can strive to maintain a sense of humour about all this. You can strive to be the best man you can. To understand as much as possible about other people and their needs. You can try to find stories that make sense to you and make you more viable. You do have a choice: stories that paralyse you, or stories that liberate you.

Would you say you are subversive?

All art is subversive.

To what end?

There's a poem by Lawrence Durrell I love called *Style*. Durrell talks about finding a metaphor for the way he wants to write and goes through all these rather grand concepts like, *"Ovations of leafy hands accepting"* wind. Eventually he comes down to *"Grass - an assassin of polish."* And he describes the way you see grass, touch it because it's pretty and green, pick it up, and how only after you've thrown it away do you realise it's cut you: *"the thread of blood from the unfelt stroke."* Art has to be subversive. It has to hurt a bit, has to be not quite what you want it to be. You have to feel that thread of blood from the unfelt stroke.

Popular literature assures you that everything you believe is correct - and that you're a good boy for believing it. Real art conveys Rimbaud's message: Everything we are taught is false. Nothing you believe is correct, or even close. Let's think about this for a while.

Popular literature is comfortable, makes you feel good. In fact, popular literature often affects your body, makes you sweat, your heart pound, arouse you. The thing it doesn't do is affect your emotions, or make you think.

I like the Lew Griffin novels because I can go back and read them again and again, and they will make me think. They also affect my emotions, but I don't really know why.

I don't really intend people to put down the novel and start thinking about the purpose of life. As with the grass, I want it to be getting to you without your realising it is. I'm very pleased when people write or tell me that my work has moved them, made some deeper connection.

Old Words

The Long-Legged Fly (1992)

The first Lew Griffin. The title comes from a W B Yeats poem, which describes the long-legged fly as sitting above the stream of time. Yeats goes on to describe Julius Caesar, Helen of Troy and Michelangelo during moments of silence and reflection. Sallis' novel takes place in 1964, 1970, 1984 and 1990. During this saga, Lew kills a man, and a series of women disappear. We meet lots and lots of people, Don Walsh, LaVerne etc., in bars, offices, rooms, cemeteries and police stations. The act of doing good does evil, and evil does good: this is a theme running through all of Sallis' books. Nothing I say will describe it accurately. This is brilliant. One of the best books of the decade. Available as a No Exit paperback.

Difficult Lives (1993)

This is a collection of three long essays about Fifties pulp/noir writers Jim Thompson, David Goodis and Chester Himes. Published at $12.00 by Gryphon Publications, PO Box 209, Brooklyn, NY 11228-0209, USA.

Moth (1993)

The second Lew Griffin. LaVerne is dead. Lew, now a novelist and lecturer, searches for her daughter. Lew is drawn into a series of searches for missing people. Like a moth to the flame, he cannot refuse, resist, retreat, no matter how much it hurts him to find them. Lew's interest is in the search, that's the attraction. Once they are found, he is lost. Available as a No Exit paperback.

Saint Glinglin by Raymond Queneau (translator, 1993)

Published at $19.95 by Dalkey Archive Press, Fairchild Hall/ISU, Normal, IL 612761, USA.

Black Hornet (1994)

The third Lew Griffin. Lew is a debt collector. A sniper has killed five people at random. He moves around the city. Lew was standing beside the sixth victim, a white woman he just met. He is accused of the murder. To investigate, Lew does not move. He stays in his room and people turn up at his doorstep, wanting something, but giving Lew clues/information. The comparison is to Albert Camus' *The Outsider* - you are damned for what you don't do, as well as for what you do. Available as a No Exit paperback.

Limits Of The Sensible World (1994)
Collection of short stories. Published at $7.50 by Host Publications, Inc., 2510 Harris Blvd., Austin, TX 78703, USA.

Renderings (1995)
Novel. Published at $10.95 by Black Heron Press, PO Box 95676, Seattle, WA 98145, USA.

New Words

Death Will Have Your Eyes (1997)
This is James' new spy novel. A network of now-unemployed spies are being killed, and one man is called in to sort it. He runs away to catch the killer and, on his journey, everyone he meets is part of the conspiracy. The book's bizarre, ironic, witty and great fun. It's one of a kind.

Eye Of The Cricket (1997)
The fourth Lew Griffin. James is presently working on this and hopes to complete it in time for Fall publication.

Big Green
Screenplay. A thriller based on a treatment (in French) by Simon Reggiani, to be directed by Patricia Mazuy.

"There are several novels I want to write. One is half done, called Bottomfeeders, *which is about a bunch of street people who gang together to find a cop killer. It's a gentle take-off of* The Seven Samurai. *I've another in mind, in which a man condemned to death for murder and another, rising from a nine-year coma, come together. And I want to write a novel from the point of view of Gilles de Rais, who was Joan of Arc's captain and a child killer."*

"Most British murders are practically accidents..."

Elliot Leyton

CONCEIVED DURING AN EARTHQUAKE *and born during a deluge in Hollywood, California - Edward Bunker knows how to make an impression, and to overturn your pre-conceptions. From the age of ten he was in and out of reform schools. Ended up dope dealing at sixteen. Yet, he saw William Randolph Hearst on the day he died and enjoyed a sunset swim at San Simeon. Aged nineteen, he was the youngest con in San Quentin. Listening to Caryl Chessman's typewriter clacking on Death Row, Edward Bunker was inspired to start writing.*

Twenty years later, after master minding robberies, extorting protection from pimps and madams, forging cheques, running a drugs empire and getting on the FBI's Ten Most Wanted list, his first book was published - No Beast So Fierce (1972). Filmed in 1978 as Straight Time, *starring Dustin Hoffman, it provided opportunities which put Bunker onto the straight and narrow.*

*Besides his hard-hitting crime novels (*The Animal Factory *(1977),* Little Boy Blue *(1981)), Edward Bunker has also established a career as a respected screenwriter (Oscar-nominated film* Runaway Train *(1985)) and occasional bit-part actor (the most famous being Mr Blue in* Reservoir Dogs *(1992)). He recently completed a screenplay of James Ellroy's* Suicide Hill, *and published his newest novel* Dog Eat Dog *after a fourteen year gap.*

Paul Duncan talked to Edward Bunker.

Top Dog

Edward Bunker was born December 31 1933 in Hollywood, California. At the time, palm trees were floating down the canyons due to torrential rain. His parents were Edward N Bunker, a stage-hand/grip/set designer, and Sarah (née Schwartz), a chorus girl in stage shows and Busby Berkeley musicals. His first clear memory was, aged four, seeing them fight and the police having to be called out.

When his parents divorced, Sarah couldn't take care of him, and his father had to work to support him, so Bunker was ferried from foster homes, to boarding homes, to military schools for years. He used to run away, jump on trains, always in trouble. Eventually, aged eleven, the police picked him up and put him into juvenile hall.

You grew up in juvenile institutions. Do you ever think what your life would have been like if you'd lived in a normal home?

I may have been more. I may have been less. You can't speculate about these things. My family had no money, so I wasn't destined for Stanford University, y'know?

You tested very high in IQ tests, but you never had the education to back it up.

I had an education up until I was ten years old, then I started going to juvenile hall, so I'd only go to school for one or two days a week. When I was ten, I was two full years ahead of school because when I was in homes there were no summer vacations, and there'd be a teacher for teenagers. It was intensive. I started reading when I was six, and really started when I was seven. I was a voracious reader.

One of the things I thought was interesting about *Little Boy Blue*, which I think is the best of your four books,...

My wife does as well.

...is that a lot of it takes place during the second world war, but the war's hardly mentioned. I wondered how you judged the passage of time? Did you take any notice or interest in the outside world while you were in prison?

From around 1942/1943, when I was in the boarding and foster homes, yeah, I followed the war. I was conscious of the big murder cases, like the Black Dahlia case in 1947. When I started to go to juvenile hall and being locked up in institutions, no, the world outside was totally erased, you only exist in the environment you're in. I was aware of when the war was over and the bomb.

I remembered when President Roosevelt died, in 1945, because I was an escapee from juvenile hall, living in a giant abandoned industrial washing machine about fifteen feet from the railroad tracks. I'd wrap up in burlap and sleep there at night and the train'd rush by so close I'd vibrate. I remember walking down the street and seeing the headlines that Roosevelt had died - he'd been in since 1932 so I'd never known another President.

It was in juvenile hall where Bunker first became acquainted with the whores, pimps, queens and dealers of society, and also with the incredibly harsh rules of survival. If you don't want to become a punk, you have to fight and win. If you want people to leave you alone you, you have to be crazier than anyone else, willing to go further. Bunker had to slice a seven-time killer, Billy Cook, (used a razor blade in a melted toothbrush handle) because Cook wanted to meet in the showers. He was bounced around the system, always in trouble with nowhere to go. He was beaten by guards. He started a riot. He would retreat from the horror of life by reading books. Knock On Any Door by Willard Motley. The Fountainhead by Ayn Rand.

I was at a nuthouse for psychiatric observation when I was a kid, when I fucked up on a juvenile ward, tore it up, they couldn't handle me. They put me over in a regular, adult ward and most of them were junkies and alcoholics - I wrote about that in Little Boy Blue - and there was an old man there who was a boozer. He was there for alcoholic commitment. I guess he had been a newspaper journalist. He was working in the linen room, writing a book on a typewriter. I thought that was a way-out thing, and I put him on a pedestal because of that.

Bunker eventually stabbed a guard, but the judge couldn't bring himself to put someone of Bunker's age away, so he was put on probation. Bunker's lawyer, Al Matthews, was friends with Louise Wallis, wife of legendary Hollywood producer Hal B Wallis - when Hal went to collect the Oscar for best picture as producer of Casablanca, the Warner Brothers arranged for their cronies to instantly fill the aisles so that Hal couldn't get to the stage. Louise got Bunker to drive her around. Bunker thought she wanted a gigolo or something but she showed him what life could be like, what he could achieve if he worked at it. He drove her to Marion Davies' house, where he saw old, frail William Randolph Hearst in a wheelchair. From there Louise and Bunker drove up to San·Simeon, Hearst's extravagant estate, where Bunker enjoyed swimming in the twilight. Hearst died that day.

But Bunker still had friends in the life, the only friends he knew, and the inevitable happened. He was carrying weed and the police wanted a chat. He drove off. A car chase ended with him crashing into three cars and a mail truck. He wasn't charged for selling weed, which was a serious offence back then, but for a probation violation. He was sent to San Quentin. At nineteen, Bunker was the youngest guy in San Quentin, where he served almost five brutal years.

In a way, prison was a new adventure every morning. A crazy Mexican told me - he was a maniac - he was weird - he got out and never came back - he escaped, got deep into Mexico and married some broad and owns a shoe shop in Guadalajara - he said that every day, every morning, he got up, went to the yard and it was a new adventure.

For example, one morning, first thing, you come out for breakfast, some people go to work, some people go back to their cells. I went back to my cell. I came out on eleven o'clock unlock. San Quentin, if you can visualise it, has two or three thousand convicts. A guy comes over and tells me "Dickie Bird's gonna stab Fat Albert." Dickie Bird is a maniac from back East, not a California boy. Fat Albert was a compulsive gambler and he had stolen cigarettes from his cell partner to pay his debts.

On the yard it's cold and the lighting, let me tell you, is weird because the walls to the cellhouse are a putrid green. On a rainy day it's kinda grim. You wear these blue clothes. And the guys at work, which is about half of them, have these bright yellow raincoats. So, it looks like some kind of Impressionist painting but, because of the light, it's hard to see anybody or focus or identify anybody until they're very close to you, right on you.

One of the guys in a raincoat tells me to come over and watch. So all these guys in the Aryan Brotherhood are standing up on a bench along the wall, next to the prison block, so I get up in the line. We're all standing in a line watching the yard. So here comes Fat Albert winding his way through the crowd asking people *"Have you seen Dickie? Have you seen Dickie?"* Someone says, *"You'll see him in a minute."* And here he comes through the crowd holding a fourteen inch kitchen blade. He comes behind Fat Albert and two-hands this blade straight through the neck, down the back, to the hilt.

And this is one of those weird things - the guy don't go down. He tries to reach behind him, to get the blade out, but he can't. He wanders off into the crowd. About twenty feet away two bulls - two cops - are standing around, hands in their pockets bullshitting. And Fat Albert goes over to them and points to the handle of the knife in the middle of his fucking back. I've never seen anything like this in my fucking life.

He had to turn around and show them. Man, they about fainted. He just turned around and walked across the yard to the hospital. It wasn't no little knife either. Fourteen inches is a lot of fucking knife.

Later on, they called me on the speaker. I had to report, and the guards had to report what they saw. I saw the x-ray photographs and the knife went all the way in and missed everything. It didn't hit anything vital, just pushed things aside. They put him in the hole for a couple of months and transferred him for his own protection. That's the sort of shit you saw on the yard.

Was this violence a daily occurrence?

I wouldn't say daily, but they'd have fifty murders a year among a population of three or four thousand.

That's a lot.

Yes, it is. But, when the race wars got started in the late sixties and early seventies, it got worse.

After watching crime, gangster and prison films starring James Cagney, Edward G Robinson and Humphrey Bogart, most people think that they know what criminals are like, what they say. Whilst in San Quentin, Bunker found out that, unlike the movies, no-one protests their innocence. Conversely, no-one admits their guilt, but say what someone else said they did. It's always 'The prosecutor said that I...' or 'They say that I...'

Bunker was at San Quentin when Barbara Graham was executed - she was the subject of I Want To Live, *the film starring Susan Hayward. For a time Bunker was in* the hole, just behind Death Row where Caryl Chessman would be typing away day and night. Chessman was sentenced to die for a series of robberies and sex crimes on Mulholland Drive (which he probably didn't do). Chessman sent over a copy of Argosy, which had a short story, soon to become the first chapter of Chessman's book Cell 2455 Death Row.

I talked to him, but not very much because he was on Death Row, but I saw him once in the bullpen at the LA County Jail when he was down there for a hearing, for about an hour and a half, waiting for the other cases to be heard, the bullpen thinning out. We talked about a lawyer, about his case, my case. When I stabbed a guard, I'd had a lawyer who'd helped me out, who was Chess' advisor - Chess was defending the case himself. This lawyer, Al Matthews, had been a public defender, and the best one they ever had, but he went into private practice. He rarely won a case, all his cases were no-hopers before he started. He was a legend because he took on all the tough cases.

After that, I'd see Chessman walking across the yard from Death Row - two bulls accompanying him, they'd clear the way for him - that's where the expression 'Dead Man Walking' came from. I knew him well enough to call 'Chess' - he had status so it gave me status to know him.

What are your views on the death sentence?

No doubt some deserve to die - but the devil is in the details. How do we decide? I refer you to Camus' monumental essay: *Reflections On The Guillotine.*

Do you believe that there are purely evil men?

I've known killers and murderers, the former being like predatory leopards, the latter more reptilian. I've known mass killers (Stephen Nash, who killed thirteen) and young boys who killed their fathers, not to mention 'hit' men and tough guys. Nobody I've ever known would I consider 'evil' in the demon-possessed sense. If I knew them enough, I could always see the why of what they were, how they had come to be.

*Chessman wrote three non-fiction books (*Cell 2455 Death Row, Trial By Ordeal *and* The Face Of Justice*) and a novel about a violent prize fighter,* The Kid Was A Killer. *His writings were often seized to prevent publication, but he made secret copies and smuggled them out. The money from his writing helped finance his defence. Chessman spent twelve years on Death Row, during which time he had eight stays of execution and became a celebrity, even appearing on the cover of* Time *magazine. He ran out of his nine lives on May 2 1960. Two films,* Cell 2455, Death Row *(1955) and* Kill Me If You Can *(1977), have been made about Chessman.*

Encouraged by the fact that a convict could get published, Bunker, already an avid reader, learnt how to spell and punctuate, then started writing. Louise Wallis sent a typewriter and a subscription to the New York Times Book Review *to help him out.*

I really began to read. At first, I would go through the bookshelf, read every book, and once in a while I'd get a book and it'd be different. I didn't know why, just that it was different, like when I read Sinclair Lewis. But I didn't care whether

I was reading that or *Bomba, Jungle Boy* or *Thuvia Maid Of Mars* or whatever. Then I would read the *New York Times Book Review*, see who the different writers were, and went through them. I was more focused. I used to read five books a week from the library. If I got a big, fat Dreiser, I'd get a little, small James M Cain to even it out a bit.

I didn't read too much about politics outside. The Rosenbergs I knew a little bit. I read Theodore Dreiser and Thomas Wolfe and read all that shit. Truth to tell, when I read something that was hard to read I would discard it because there was always something good that was accessible and I didn't have to struggle with. Later on, I went through the French existential writers, Camus and Sartre, and I think they were really influential on my first book *No Beast So Fierce*.

It has often been said that criminals transgress against society with deeds, whereas artists are transgress with thoughts. Do you agree?

There are criminals of all kinds. The rapist is as different from the thief as he is from the postman. Thieves are the extrapolation of laissez-faire capitalism. The similarity between the artist and the criminal is that they are both iconoclasts - and both tend to have high sociopathic traits on the tests.

When I read your work, it reads like an old book, pre-Dashiell Hammett. It's not a clipped, hardboiled style. It's longer sentences, closer to Jane Austen.

That's great, man. W Somerset Maugham is who it is. He once wrote an essay on style, about clarity, simplicity etc. After a million words, you know how to write, he said. I know sometimes my sentences are a bit long...

I'm not complaining! I like it.

Thank you. I'm complimented by that. I think they were better writers. I don't like all this post-modern stuff.

When you were writing for years, writing novels and short stories in prison, did you talk to anyone about writing?

In most prisons, there was always a large group, who were readers, who passed around books. There was a group of us who wanted to write, including Paul Allen, he died last year, and Jimmy Postman.

I thought Jimmy had the most talent. He was very facile, a master thief, a small, skinny guy, pretty-looking. He was a couple of years older than me. He had heart, but he was very smart. When I went into San Quentin, I wondered why people respected him. He was the assistant dentist, the clerk to the dentist, he would get people's teeth fixed. He was the richest guy in the pen, you know what I mean? You couldn't get to the dentist unless you paid him off. Man, what a thing to control!

Everyone likes to have good teeth.

Or some teeth!

When the dentist dropped the extractions in the pan, Jimmy'd have the gold, man. And during the dentist's lunch hour, he'd do his own gum work, which he wasn't supposed to do, bridges and crowns. I thought he was the most talented of us.

Paul had a great facile mind, he was the best editor I ever had, but he couldn't physically write - he couldn't spell or punctuate at all. Right from the beginning, I told him to take a course in this and that, but he wanted to jump right to the chase.

Jimmy was so talented he went on to do a whole lot of others things - he wasn't solely committed to writing. But I was. I kept at it and persevered.

At age twenty-three, with the help of Louise Wallis, Bunker got out on parole and was good for a year but found that society had locked him out. There was no skill he could use that would let him join society, so he resorted to master-minding robberies, forging cheques, and extorting protection from pimps and madams.

I always made money. My reputation was of never being broke, of always being moderately on top. I was never a big kingpin, but I was always driving a nice car, wearing nice clothes, living well. Guys would listen to me because I had the front of doing good.

You are the exception. Most criminals are poor, living in awful conditions, living badly. Why do they become criminals if they're not making money out of it?

Because they don't know how to do anything else. They're not emotionally or psychologically equipped to work. In fact, they can't stand authority. It isn't their choice. They get that way by default because of the other things they can't do.

Why were you successful?

Because I was smarter and, like anything else, I studied my craft when I was young. I was an insatiable learner. The older guys in jail would tell me things. One time an old card mechanic came in for sixty days for being an addict. He was a card mechanic - that's how he hustles, man - and he was showing me how to make a slick sleeve, how to work it, how to hand off and break off, and deal from the bottom of the deck and shit. I was in jail for hours with nothing better to do than to practice dealing from the bottom of the deck, and the seconds, and hold the card out. I was like that. Another guy was telling me about being a great safe cracker. He showed me by drawing a diagram. Other people wouldn't do it. I would hear stories about people playing sucker games, about the psychology, and give little bits of advice. When I got out, some of these same guys would be emotionally driven by being hooked on drugs, or some broad, or they needed the money quick, so much so that they would not follow the advice, the methods and techniques, that they had given me.

Another reason why I was successful was because most people commit crimes on very momentary impulses or needs, so they drive around until they find something to get. No. No. No. I would do the preparatory work of going out and looking, finding the place, sitting on it, checking it out, scheduling it. For a while this was my hustle. When a guy'd come out of the joint, he'd be a wild man. I'd tell him to take it easy, put him in a room, tell him about my plan, what to do and he'd go out and do it. He wouldn't get a million out of it but he'd get $15,000 or $20,000 and I'd take 25% of it.

It takes a certain degree of intelligence and nerve to plan crimes. Do criminals have to be more intelligent than non-criminals?

Criminals have the same intelligence range as the general public, but they tend to have less education. Only a tiny fraction of crimes have any thought or planning whatsoever. Nearly all are impulsive, a predator prowls the jungle and strikes on opportunity.

Women do not, generally, seem to have a central role in the lives of criminals. Why is this?

That's true, women are usually peripheral to a life of crime, but there are, occasionally, powerful women drug dealers, and now and then some woman controls her man, who has power. In the world of crime, the toughest reign. Women seldom fight as well as men.

Bunker's freedom lasted for a couple of years before he was put away again, this time for seven. He realised that the only skill he had that would get him accepted into society was his writing. Being locked up for eighteen or more hours a day gave Bunker an opportunity to read the great literature of the world, and write as much as he wanted. He edited a prison newspaper in Vacaville and wrote legal briefs, as well as articles, short stories and novels. Bunker used to sell his blood to get the postage, $16 a throw, every three or four months. Writing was the only thing he could do inside, to keep his mind occupied. There were laws about what he could and couldn't write about, so he concentrated on trying to smuggle some of the things out. Eventually he sent novels to a New York literacy agency, but they said they couldn't sell them.

Outside the cell, on the Big Yard, it was a different place.

There were gangs. One white, two Mexican, and one black, and the Muslims. When these gangs started, they were loose. Then they began to have the structure of organisations, so that if somebody goes the gang continues.

The two Mexican gangs are at war with each other - like the Mafia families are at war - it goes back to some prison shit in San Quentin. In California, you talk about the Mafia and the people aren't scared. You talk about the Mexican Mafia, they're legendary, and people are scared. You heard of the drive-by shootings in east LA? The Mexican Mafia stopped it in the Mexican neighbourhoods. They told the kids that if they went to the joint for that they were going to fuck them when they got there. That's the Mexican Mafia and they're at war with the 'Familia.' It started a long time ago when the Mexican Mafia were at low numbers in San Quentin. All the other Mexicans, they were country boys, from small towns, they did a vigilante act and attacked and killed a couple of the Mexican Mafia. They attacked on the lockup bell, caught them at their weakest point, and got away with it. Then they became pariah in all the other prisons, and had to form a gang, get members and shit. It's gone on since then. There are murders on the streets, they break into each other's houses and tie each other up and shit.

So these gangs, these wars, continue outside prison?

Sure. The Mexican Mafia control the drugs in east Los Angeles. It's a huge market, like controlling drugs in half of London, but with three or four times the volume.

Is it just drugs, or are there other sources of income?

Just drugs because the money's the greatest in drugs. Most of them are Catholics so prostitution is not gone into that much.

Then there are the black gangs. The Crips and the Bloods have gangs all across America, in all the small towns. They have outposts in Indianapolis, Chicago...

Were the race riots in the prisons an extension of the civil rights riots in the outside world?

Yeah, it overlapped, but it was more extreme inside. The Panthers had this ten-to-one policy - they took ten lives for every one lost. In prison they substituted political rhetoric for literal truth.

Why do people join the gangs?

It's often not a question of choice. As in the outside world, in prison, people have a desire for status and power. Sometimes it's a matter of protection, to belong makes them stronger. Some people don't join and they're okay.

I never joined. What happened was that I was from another era. When the gangs started, as a point of fact, I was a legend, highly respected. I was able to get down in any way they wanted to get down, you know what I mean? I was as crazy as anyone else, but I didn't fuck with anyone. I respected people, but don't fuck with me. On the other hand, I was very smart. I was a jailhouse lawyer and I kept political jobs in prison.

For my first nine years, I was wild, but after that I had what they called politician's jobs. At that time, convicts ran the prison. In essence they were the clerk for the cell move lieutenant, but they'd make the cell moves and the lieutenant would just sign it. They were the clerk for the job lieutenant, y'know what I mean? There were several of these jobs in the prison. I never had the very highest job which was the associate warden's clerk but I had very powerful jobs. I was the cell house clerk for 2000 cells. I could do anything. I could hire the convicts and assign them for the work crews. I could do whatever I wanted in that cell house. The bulls on the Big Yard would chase me, close in on me for drugs on the yard and I'd sidle into my cell house and I was safe - the sergeants would tell the bulls not to fuck with me, to leave me alone, because I did their work.

By the same token, the guys who did these jobs were not trusted by convicts. They're suspect. And I wasn't suspect because I'd proved myself, and continued to prove myself even then. As I described in *Animal Factory*, I smuggled drugs, ran books and shit. I ran a scheme where I put a ticket out, say on American football, you pick four winners and could get 10-1. I called it Bunko - my brand name.

I'm not a violent person. You have been. In your books, you seem to be saying that the social conditions you were brought up in forced you

to do the things you did.

Not forced. No. It contributed to it. You always have a choice within the parameters. I believe that there's a fatal circle, a big circle outside which we can't go as an individual, where we have no choice. I mean, you can't be a Tibetan monk. There are things you can't do. But within that frame you have a choice. I'm not totally a determinist, but I believe that you are what you're taught to be depending upon your individual character. Two people can be taught the same thing and react differently but can also play different games and come up with the same result. Still, I believe we are what we're taught to be. Every one of us is what we're taught to be.

I don't really like violence either, but I came to understand quite young that if I didn't want violence but I wanted my rights and status - I wasn't as husky as I am now and I was younger - if I was crazier than everyone else they wouldn't fuck with me, I wouldn't have trouble.

I had a reputation for being a crazy motherfucker and no-one came near me. I wasn't actually insane, but if I was going to do a thing I would carry it through. I was hot-tempered but I wasn't psychotic.

But when you talk about not being violent, what sort of situation do you mean? When it comes to a certain situation, when you're sufficiently afraid...

Or during war.

Right. Or at what point when someone's fucking with you? When do you become violent?

There's another thing that happens in the joint. You always have the image that one guy owes another guy, the guy doesn't pay, so the guy owed kills the guy that owes him. No. No. No. It's the guy that owes the debt that kills the guy he owes. The guy that ain't gonna get no money is going to huff and puff, but the guy owing the debt is scared, y'know what I mean? It's more times, ten-to-one I'd say, it's that way. It's almost always the guy who owes who kills and the bully who gets it.

In fact, in Folsom, two guys owed this guy, Chuck - he was a bad motherfucker, looked like he could have been a longshoreman on a dock, an organiser. He was kinda stocky but he was terrible, big thighs, muscular. He was like a fucking tank. These guys owed him, but the debt wasn't due for two weeks. They knew they couldn't pay him when the time got there, so they killed him today. Down the line, he would have been dangerous, he would have been on his guard, so they busted him on the head with something and threw a piece of wire around his neck and hung, one on each side, and garrotted him, and he dragged them fifty feet down the tier before he went down. He was out.

So is there honour amongst thieves?

Yes and no. Wealth in drugs and money often changes hands on one's word, sans contracts or suits at law. In prison it is often said, *"I don't have anything left but my word..."* The test of honour comes in the police precinct... Are you willing to go to prison to maintain your honour as a thief? On the other hand, I have had criminal friends whom I trust without reservation.

If a man's word was his bond, that that's what he was worth, then if a guy owes money, doesn't pay it, and then kills the guy he owes the debt to, what do the other convicts think of him?

The guys with sufficient status on the yard would pass judgement. It depended on their response, and everyone followed. In the case of Chuck, they found it very funny, they found the humour in two guys trying to kill a man and him dragging them all over. Besides, he was an evil sucker.

In Folsom there're these old guys who have an absurdist humour in the evil, sick twists of the fucking thing. They laughed when that guy Juan Perona killed those workers and buried them in an apple orchard in Orange, California. They find humour in those things.

In earlier years, it was accepted that people were in prison because there was something mentally wrong with them, but as Bunker experienced it, crime was mostly caused by social conditions. This was the key to his novel No Beast So Fierce, *which was written in San Quentin and Folsom (and yes, he saw Johnny Cash sing in both prisons). Bunker's agent said he could probably sell* Beast.

Meanwhile, Bunker was out again.

I was kinda wild. I was mad when I got out the second time. I just wanted a gun. I just wanted to rip, y'know? Before that I would never think about pulling a robbery myself, y'know?

He went up to San Francisco, set up a little drug empire.

What I brought to it was the connection - I had the connection in Mexico, to get whatever I wanted delivered to me in Los Angeles. I had a partner, a guy I'd known since childhood, who'd been on the streets in San Francisco. I told him, *"well, we're partners, I give the stuff to you and you make the arrangements."* So we found some dealers. It took us two or three weeks. A couple of them burned us right from the start but you weed them out - you take that as a loss - they're short of money, or blah, blah, blah. But after a couple or more weeks you're left with four dealers, and each one of them is bringing us $2,000 or $2,500 every day, every fucking day, seven days a week, y'know what I mean? There was between eight, ten, twelve thousand dollars coming in a fucking day. That's in 1972.

I go to LA and pick up a load of shit and I come back and leave it in some third rate bust-out hotel, not my apartment, then tell the dealers where it was at. Later, I'd go back to the room with my partner and we'd open the bottom drawer and it'd be full of fucking money. I thought I was so cool because I didn't deal with anybody.

This operation got him on the FBI's Ten Most Wanted list.

They knocked me out using Squeaky Fromme - she was the Manson girl who tried to kill President Ford. She was one of the girls outside the courthouse when Manson was being tried. She'd written a letter to *Prison Life* saying she'd written a manuscript about being with Manson and I wanted to see it. So I was in LA - this was before Beast sold - and I was going to this hotel room, to read the manuscript. When I got to the eleventh floor, the door opened and all these fucking FBI agents came out with all their guns and shit. They found the dope and let her go. Then they made a deal with me to get the connection, for me to get him across the border to the US, so I said *"yeah, just let me out."* So I immediately got out, called him and told him *"hey, man, blah, blah, blah,"* and told him I'm going over the border to Mexico to see him.

So, I went to San Francisco to pack all my shit, 'cos my car was in San Francisco. I drove to LA, didn't get in touch with anybody. I knew about this bank in Beverley Hills, known about it for about ten years - I might as well just get a little finance, get it easy along the way. It's just a one-teller bank, one of those ritzy, exclusive banks which deals with heirs and trustees, so it's got a lot of change and it's real soft. Well, I said, I'll take it on the way.

So I robbed the fucking bank and, as I'm robbing it, I looked up and somebody's at the window, looking in with their hand shading their eyes, and I recognise the face - I didn't know the name, but I knew if I recognised the face it was one of the cops who just caught me - so I ran out the other door and the chase was on, a helicopter and five carloads of narcs following me. I kept losing them. They kept finding me. I didn't know, but I had a beeper on my car, a homing device. They ran me into a building and I threw my gun down - all my friends got down on me 'Punk! You threw your gun down.' I didn't want to die right then, you know what I mean?

It was 1972. Five publishers rejected Beast, but one said they'd take it if he cut it by a third and polished it. Sure, why not? Whilst waiting for sentence, the book was accepted. From 1953 to 1972, Bunker had written five 100,000 word novels and over fifty short stories and never sold a thing. On the day he sold Beast, he also sold his first essay, War Behind Walls, *which was about the prison race wars in San Quentin. He was a three time loser, going down for a bank job, expecting twenty years minimum, yet, due to letters from famous authors, he got the lightest sentence of his life - a nickel, five years.*

Bunker maintains that this wouldn't happen now because of Jack Henry Abbott and Edgar Smith. Norman Mailer championed Abbott, who wrote In The Belly Of The Beast, *and got him released. Abbott later killed a guy in a restaurant. William F Buckley championed Smith, convicted for killing a fifteen year old cheerleader, who wrote* Beyond A Reasonable Doubt *and* Brief Against Death. *When released, Smith killed a clothing factory worker and then admitted he really had killed the cheerleader.*

Firing on all cylinders, whilst at Terminal Island, Bunker wrote the novel Animal Factory *and had articles accepted in* Harper's, The New Yorker, *the* New York Times *and the* Los Angeles Times.

When I think of prison cells, the image I always get is of a small, completely black room that's damp and cold, with rats.

Yeah, it was like that in San Quentin. Prisons have gotten worse over time. In a way, they've gotten more diabolical than they've ever been, in an Orwellian sense.

What I mean by that is that now you're untouched by human hands. They've got individual lockups that have cameras on you and shit. They don't come in and beat you up, they stand outside the door and shoot you with a taser, or they jolt you with 600 milligrams of thorazine and turn you into a vegetable. They lock you in a cell and you can't talk to anybody. There're little games going on. They come up to the door and be silent. The glass is frosted so you can't see the light. The bulls bring food and slide in the paper-wrapped sandwiches on paper plates, the bones taken out of the meat. To me that's Kafkaesque - it's worse than the kick-your-ass stuff. And they can get brutal too, they'll get physical.

If a guard beats up on a prisoner, I see that as being criminal. Do prisoners see it that way?

They see it as the way it was. Did they put any moral value on being beaten? No. It just confirmed their attitude that everyone was a dirty son of a bitch - they ain't no better than us really. They have the power. They don't have any moral supremacy.

Very few bulls commit crimes, but invariably a prison has one or two who have been co-opted to smuggle, and there are always some who take pleasure in being brutal.

The film rights to No Beast So Fierce *were sold in 1975. The star, Dustin Hoffman, came down a couple of times. The screenwriter, Alvin Sargent, came visiting every day as the pair of them wrote and re-wrote the script. In 1975, Bunker got out and has never been in trouble again. He puts this down to circumstances, not personality - he was hired as technical advisor on the film for six or eight months, which meant he had money in his pocket and food in his mouth. Circumstances.*

But what happens to the people who can't write? Who don't have favourable circumstances?

In all truth, I think very few people plan to commit crimes when they get out of jail. Very few are pumped up with that attitude. I think seventy, eighty, ninety per cent want to make it, go out and go straight, get a job, and they fail. Why do they fail? There are many instances where it depends upon whether they find a niche, a spot, where they can fit, which demands things of them but provides for them as well.

But, of course, they gravitate back to the people they know, who face the same situations they've always faced, with the same equipment they've always had - I'm not the same person because my circumstances changed and I changed with them. Originally, my circumstances didn't change, it was just that I wasn't going to go out and do something stupid, you know what I mean? I had a book published which was a success, I was off to make a movie with Dustin Hoffman, and they were giving me a job on the movie that lasted for seven months - I wasn't going to go out and do something stupid. I didn't want to go out on the yard and those convicts tell me 'you fool,' laughing at me and ribbing me 'man, you had everything.' Man, they'd get on you about that, man. I'd feel so bad...

In many senses I've gone far beyond I ever imagined I would go. The people I

EDWARD BUNKER

know. The people I associate with. The places I go for dinner. No convict has ever gone that far or done that.

As well as the co-scripting on Straight Time (1978), as the film version of Beast was called, Bunker had his first acting job. This is something he's continued from The Long Riders (1980) to Runaway Train (1985) to Reservoir Dogs (1992). He's been in about thirty movies, and will be getting a pension from the Screen Actors' Guild. Bunker knows how to play the game, use friends and influence to keep in work, get his health insurance sussed. Who can blame him? He's got a wife (married in 1979) and child (born 1994) to support.

Bunker has been polishing scripts for a while. He wrote the first half hour, all the prison dialogue, for Runaway Train (1985), which was directed by Andrei Konchalovsky, based on story by Akira Kurosawa, and starred Jon Voight and Eric Roberts (who both got Oscar nominations). It's an existentialist prisoners-on-the-run movie which turns into a trapped-on-runaway-train movie. There's a scene in the middle of it I like:

Buck: That's what I've been dreaming about, a really big score, y'know what I mean? Then I'm gonna par-tee. I'm gonna go to Mardi Gras, to Vegas, and I'm gonna go with enough money in my hip pocket to catch them fine bitches, y'know what I mean?

Y'know, I spend almost every night of my life dreamin' about this kinda shit.

Manny: Dreaming? That's bullshit.

You're not gonna do nuthin like that.

I'll tell you what you're gonna do, you're gonna get a job. That's what you're gonna do, get a job, some job a convict can get, like scrapping off trays in a cafeteria or cleaning out toilets, and you're gonna hold onto that job like gold, because it is gold. And let me tell you, Jack, that is gold.

Are you listening to me?!

And when the man walks in at the end of the day, and he comes to see how you done, you ain't gonna look in his eyes. You're gonna look at the floor, because you don't wanna see that fear in his eyes when you jump up and grab his face and slam him to the floor and make him scream and cry for his life. So you look right at the floor, Jack.

Pay attention to what I'm saying, motherfucker!

An' then he's gonna look around the room to see how you done. And he'll say, 'oh, you missed a little spot over there,' 'jeez, you didn't get this one here,' 'what about this little bitty spot?' And you're gonna suck all that pain inside you, and you're gonna clean that spot, and you're gonna clean that spot, until you get that shining clean.

And, on Friday, you're gonna pick up your pay cheque.

And if you can do that. And if you can do that, you can be president of Chase Manhattan, corporations, if you can do that.

Buck: Not for me, Manny. I wouldn't do that shit. I'd rather be in fucking jail.

Manny: More's the pity, youngster. More's the pity.

Buck: Could you do that kinda shit?

Manny: I wish I could.

Bunker thought they ruined the end of it, that it wasn't realistic, consistent. At the end, Voight stays on the train to die with his enemy. Bunker thought Voight's character, the ultimate hard man, would never give up, that he'd jump off the train, try to survive, no matter what.

When you write screenplays, you're collaborating with other people and what you write doesn't necessarily make it into the movie.

They make up for that by paying you lots of money. It's really a drag to do it when they don't get it, get the point of the script.

I learned a lot from Alvin Sargent and from doing scripts. I didn't know I could do it and I wrote a script, *Slick Willy*. I sent it in to a fellowship award in New York with about 600 others. The judges read them blind and mine was judged to be the best. So then I knew I could write scripts, although I've never been able to get it made. I've almost had it made several times.

Slick Willy is about an old thief who breaks out of the LA County Jail on a firehose. He's in his fifties and he thinks he's dying of cancer. He's been a booster and a shoplifter but now, he thinks, *"Fuck it, if I go down again, I'm going down for life,"* so he starts robbing banks with a toy gun. It's a comedy. Every time he goes in, something happens. One time he makes a loan application instead. Eventually, he steals a bank but the money's got dye all over it so, as he hands it over to people, the people keep getting accused of being the bank robber.

Writing something and getting it made are two different things altogether.

Right. If you can write something on spec and sell it, you can make beaucoup money. Otherwise they hire you for much less to write their ideas, rewrite other people's scripts etcetera. They bring me in to write scenes set in prison, so that the dialogue is right.

Quentin Tarantino was at Robert Redford's Sundance Institute, which helps film people develop ideas, scripts, skills by having established movie makers divulge their opinions and experiences. Tarantino studied Straight Time there and, when he cast Reservoir Dogs (1992), Chris Penn (a friend of Bunker's) suggested Bunker. Bunker played Mr Blue in a couple of scenes. He didn't give any technical advice. For starters, if a team of thieves are going to do a job together, they must know and trust each other - they can't be complete strangers à la Dogs. Also, dressing identically? There'd be no chance that the waitress at the beginning of the movie would fail to remember them. Bunker could go on about it but, ultimately, he realises that the film's about other films, not about real criminals.

Bunker was a consultant on American Heart (1994). This film is about Jack Kelson (played by Jeff Bridges), just out of the slammer and trying to go straight, picking up a job cleaning windows. Nick, his son, joins him, trying to form some sort of family environment. But, the low-life environment gets to Nick, who embarks on a life of crime. Jeff had Bunker sit by a monitor for every shot and tell him what he thought.

He was a technical advisor on Heat (1995). Coached Robert di Niro some, went out for a long talk. The actors were escorted to Bunker to meet him, to find out what criminals are all about, what makes them tick. The film sure feels right. And Jon Voight, still friends since Runaway Train, is made up to look like Bunker.

Dog Eat Dog (1996) is a novel based on stories Bunker had heard in prison, rather than purely extensions of his own experiences.

There were fourteen years between Little Boy Blue and Dog Eat Dog. Why so long between books?

Although Little Boy Blue got great reviews, the publisher did not market it at all. It sold under 4000 copies in the United States. I'd worked a couple of years on it - I'm pretty steady and it takes me a year and a half to two years to write a book I guess. It did nothing. It just fell on its face. Then I got movie work, which paid better money. The book so depressed me, they so bum-kicked me, then I started to get published in France around 1990, and they loved me. I had a market and they published all my books. Then England came in, and No Exit have been doing a great job. Then James Ellroy got me a different agent, and he talked me into writing a couple of chapters on spec. I can't sell them, but I'm so far in I have to write the fucking book. That took me a couple of years and meanwhile I wrote a volume of memoirs (unpublished) and had other jobs writing screenplays. The reason it took me that length of time is money. I would like enough money on each book to finance my life for the next book. No Beast So Fierce did that, it was a pretty successful first novel. The others haven't been as successful.

There's a big difference between reading books and writing them. Why are you a writer?

I started because I loved reading. Later on I found out that historically, there had been many great writers who wrote in and about prison. I like good writing. I'm very interested in the truth. I like to tell the truth. I'd like to accomplish something. A lotus grows in the mud. Maybe I can say something that'll mean something, that entertains people. The job of a writer is to communicate to people. And make a living. I'm not adverse to selling myself to be famous, y'know, to have my books last. It's great that twenty years after the fact, my books are being reprinted. There are not too many writers who can say that.

What truth are you trying to communicate?

Really, just an overall truth that we should be rational, look at things rationally.

This applies to everything but I focus on crime and criminals. I treat criminals like human beings. In America, they are so afraid of crime and criminals - they're locked out not locked up. They treat them like 'the other.' In point of fact, they are not 'the other.' Society has a right to protect itself, first and foremost, but there must be some rationality to it. It's like this fucking three strikes law that they say will knock the crime rate right down - you're automatically in for life on your third offence. I don't agree with that. If you dropped the hydrogen bomb in east LA you'd knock the crime rate down too! That's not as wild as you might think - it all depends upon what you're willing to do and the antecedent realities of your actions. You can stop crime by repression but then you'll have a police state. In California, which is 30 million people, they have 130,000 people in jail. That's a lot, man.

Most of them get out once or twice, but none of them are getting out a third time now. I don't know who's going to pay for it.

In the early part of this century there were lots of movements to rehabilitate criminals, to make them fully functioning parts of society.

That's all gone. There's none of that. There's only punishment. This is because there's more violence, now, and it's more racial. 15% of the American prison population used to be black. Now it's an average of 50%. Some cities are as high as 70% black. So you can imagine the reaction of the monied public to helping violent niggers. America used to have a love affair with outlaw criminals, back to Jesse James. Even in the thirties you'd have guys like Pretty Boy Floyd, and people'd really like them. Now, people have been affected, somebody in their family has been hurt physically.

During prohibition people were often on the wrong side of the law having a tipple. Also, during the Depression, when a lot of people lost their houses and livelihoods to banks, they liked it when gangsters robbed the banks. Being working class, they saw the criminals as being like themselves, as human beings. Now, the rich white middle-class see the crimes being committed by the poor black unemployed-class and don't see them as human beings.

Yeah. They see them as 'the other.'

It also coincides with the fall of the professional criminal and the rise...

...of the wild man who just wants to get high and shoot people. They got no respect for people.

People listen to you. They have respect for you. Do you use that position?

I try to impart some wisdom. I'm not very good at argument. Most people don't want the truth, they just want arguments to support their position. They find the argument to suit themselves. In a way, I'm sometimes the same, but I'm more open to facts. Nothing can be true if it's refuted by a fact. All this other bullshit about what we believe is just a distillation of the facts and what the facts mean. Unless you can qualify, or find a reason for them being wrong, facts are supreme. You can't have anything which is violated by facts. A conclusion is supported by facts.

Your books are based on your own life, or on the stories you heard in prison. Do you see yourself writing stories which are not about criminals?

I try to write about the whole society, but I use crime as the lens through which I refract it. I think I'll only write using crime - I have so much material, I've hardly started to dig into it.

Do you regret your past acts against others?

I have regrets, but little guilt. If God weighed what was done to me to what I did, I'm not sure how the scales would tip.

Bibliography

No Beast So Fierce (1972)

Max Dembo is released on parole, intending to go straight. It's straight in his mind, he's all set. But, the only people who'll accept him are ex-cons, boosters, coke-heads. They come to give him money, or touch him for some. He doesn't know any other way to live. He tries to find a job, but he has no skills to offer, he has no work experience. On top of that, his parole officer is a hardass, won't bend, can't see that Dembo is trying to reform. The only way out is to stay in the life, and that's when everything starts to go wrong. This is a criminal's view of society. Step by agonising step, we see the tumblers click into place, locking Dembo into a destiny he cannot avoid.

The Animal Factory (1977)

Ronald Decker, middle class capitalist, goes down for a minor drug dealing charge and is incarcerated in San Quentin. Having never lived, breathed, conversed with real criminals before, it's a bit of a shock. Claustrophobic, brutalised, alone, Decker is in constant danger. Luckily, he hooks up with old-timer Earl Copen, who teaches him, protects him. It could be love, it could be a fatherly feeling, it could just be disgust at seeing someone else being dragged into the life. Decker is transformed - he realises that, to survive, he has to become a mad motherfucker, to stick the knife in first, to kill instead of being killed. It escalates out of all proportion, Decker can stand it no longer, so the pair of them plan their escape.

Little Boy Blue (1981)

This novel is an elegiac tale about a troubled eleven-year-old boy, Alex Hammond, who spends his life rebelling against the system. Beating a path through various foster homes and care institutions, he takes on the code and mores of his peers to survive. To prevent himself from becoming a 'punk' (i.e. being sodomised) he is forced to use violence. Alex is beaten and attacked by inmates and guards alike, so he retaliates with vicious fearlessness. The violence escalates and Alex is put in more rigid and oppressive prisons. Eventually he explodes and escapes.

With no parents, no guidance other than from his older peers, Alex swings between a yearning for knowledge and an anger at a society that won't let him live. As the book progresses, and his finer thoughts and feelings are submerged by an obligation to his corrupt friends, you realise that there is no hope for Alex. He knows no other life. Even the war - this is set, interestingly, during World War Two - comes and goes without comment because it has no bearing on life inside.

In the end, the best place for Alex is in isolation, reading books, because it is the only way he can escape from his life, and from himself.

This is a stunning wrongs of passage novel of boy's inhumanity to boy. Too painful to be anything but thinly veiled autobiography.

Dog Eat Dog (1996)

Troy, Mad Dog McCain, Diesel. Three friends. Two convictions. One last score. No more chances. That's the hard cell. This is probably Bunker's most action-packed book, the closest to a crime novel. It continues some of his earlier themes, in particular, the tension between going straight and loyalty to your friends, and the changing face of society and its values. The most important aspect is the relationship of the friends. Troy is indebted to Mad Dog for an incident in their childhood, but Mad Dog is actually mad, high on heroin most of the time. This, then, is a struggle between the old-style professional career criminal and the new breed of coke-heads who place no value whatsoever on human life. The tension is terrific, and the outcome... well, I'm not going to tell you.

EDWARD BUNKER

YOU CANNOT PIN PAUL BUCK down to any one medium of expression. For the past twenty-odd years, Paul has been reading, translating, editing, performing, directing and mostly writing about the darker side of passion, lust, desire. In a word...sex. But not any old sex. Not your sanitised, moralistic sex. We're talking sex crime here. The dirty, uncomfortable, dangerous sort of sex. The sort we flirt with occasionally in our daydreams, before they become nightmares.

Paul likes his research. He ferrets through the nooks and crannies of our sub-cultures, which gives him a unique view of the world. Ask him his thoughts about crime fiction, for instance, and he'll gladly talk about Jimi Hendrix, David Cronenberg, the anarchic stage drama of Artaud, and the latest on the S & M scene. Believe me, in the mind of Paul Buck they are all connected. What's worse, he makes you believe it.

To date, Paul's best known work has been The Honeymoon Killers, a superior novelisation of the film of the same name. It features a fat woman, Martha Beck, and a thin man, Raymond Fernandez, who are trapped in an obsessive relationship as they travel America killing lonely widows. Based on a true story, Paul's additional research brought to light new facts when the novel was published in 1970. François Truffaut, Michelangelo Antonioni and Jean-Luc Godard cite the film as one of the best ever made, and the book was translated into French to appear in the prestigious Serie Noir imprint.

Since then, Paul has written several unpublished crime novels: Bottle, Red Ascends, Fallen Corners and Tainted Love. The last two haven't been offered to publishers yet. We live in a world where the only books you can read are those that an editor/publisher feels they can market to a mass audience, sell TV, film and video game rights for, and franchise the brand name to fast-food chains. There are other books - books written for reasons other than for money. Paul Duncan talked to Paul Buck in Sidcup to find out what these reasons were.

Passion Victim

One of the reasons for not doing interviews, for not explaining your work, which I have a tendency not to do, is because you don't understand your own work. When you write something, you have certain preoccupations in your mind. When someone speaks to you some time later about it, you can't necessarily remember the reasons and preoccupations that were in your mind. So you start interpreting your work in terms of what your preoccupations are now. The answer I give is the answer for this particular moment, which is also not necessarily the answer I would give if I thought about it a long time, or even tomorrow morning after a night of torrid sex, or devastating nightmares... the razor woman coming to torment me again, for example. So I have a tendency to talk around my work, about the painters and writers I like, about the different media I'm involved with. People can get an idea of the locale, the area I'm working in, so they have a certain understanding when they actually read my work.

But people love to be told what something means. Unfortunately, once they have been told it means something, they don't think about it any more.

When I was young, I didn't read as many books as I should have - I listened to jazz instead. Being brought up a Catholic, and being rebellious, I was fascinated with Soho. I saw a book called *Adrift In Soho* by Colin Wilson, so I picked it up. I went through it, it turned me on, and I went out and bought *The Outsider*. I read about Barbusse, Camus, Sartre and thought 'Phew, this is what I should be reading. This is me.' I read them all, all the other Colin Wilson books: *Ritual In The Dark, Necessary Doubt...* I respect a lot of what Colin Wilson is about, but I don't like his style of writing - it's a bit clumsy. That's not his fault, he's a self-educated person, and the people he admires a lot aren't necessarily brilliant writers either. But, don't get me wrong, he's a great person for turning people onto the subject and onto writers they wouldn't have heard about elsewhere. He's important in that way. I don't think you have to be a great writer and win prizes. If you advance society, or encourage other people who become great writers, then you have served a purpose.

When I decided I wanted to write, I walked out of my science degree in college, got a day job in a bank, wrote at night. Six months and that was enough of that approach. I used what I'd saved from the bank to write, and when it was time to work again I thought working in a top bookshop was a better way, and set out to do just that.

I lived in the same house as Norman Snyder, a novelist who wrote the film script for *Dead Ringers*. I remember Norman saying that his friend David Cronenberg, a young filmmaker from Canada, was coming over bringing his 16mm films, *Crimes Of The Future* and so on. I took David down the BFI so that we could project his films there. We had loads of hassles trying to set that up.

In the sixties, in Notting Hill Gate, everyone lived just down the road, or round the corner, so everyone knew everyone else. I worked for Better Books where everyone bought their books. You'd see William S Burroughs, Francis Bacon, underground filmmaker Steve Dwoskin. These people are now famous, although they weren't at the time. I wrote for *International Times*, the first underground newspaper, and worked at UFO. UFO was the centre of the universe, really, where Pink Floyd and Soft Machine played, and Jimi Hendrix came down to jam, Procul Harlem, Arthur Brown, Tomorrow. The people who visited included Mick Jagger and Marianne Faithful, Paul McCartney, Pete Townsend...

It wasn't necessarily a glorious past. Everyone met everyone in these places, but I wouldn't want the past again. If you're involved in the arts scene from day-to-day, then you don't see it as something that's glorious, because you're just working. I'm always bumping into people in London - I met someone last week who I hadn't seen for ten years, but has since been to the top of the music charts, and now has a house in Kent and a new album coming out. But I'm always meeting new people. In the last year or two I've become friends with some well-known people, but I've met a lot of new, young writers and painters as well who I think are interesting. I do think there are less and less younger artists about. I see a lot trying to be artists without doing any work for it - they just do the writing or music or whatever without doing all the background study that goes with it. It's all instant. It's sad because it means that certain aspects of the culture are dying off.

Eventually, I wrote to publishers asking to become a reader. The most positive reply was from Anthony Cheetham at Sphere. I got a pile of books from him, mostly of a sexual nature, to read and comment on. After a while, he asked me if I wanted to write a novelisation of a film. Up until then, I had written poetry, a play, and some television plays which hadn't been produced but had attracted interest. Anthony suggested *Performance*, which had already been shot and was being edited at the time. I talked to co-director Donald Cammell (Nic Roeg was the other director), saw this absolutely brilliant film at a viewing theatre in St Anne's Court, got a copy of the script, and started writing straight away. I was stopped a week later because the movie company had already agreed that another writer would write the novel - a writer who never saw the film and thus wrote a pile of shit, because the book was only a dialogue transcript, nothing more - you had to see the film to see the context.

Anthony told me there was another film, *The Honeymoon Killers*, which was based on a true story, and asked me if I was interested. I went away, did some research into the murders, and agreed to do it. With the film script and my research notes in front of me, I wrote the book in a week.

I did not plan to write about murders and murderers, but I was already interested in them. Before *The Honeymoon Killers*, I read Colin Wilson's books:

PAUL BUCK

The Outsider, his novels, the first part of his encyclopaedia of crime history. I had also read a lot of European literature and thought (Camus, Sartre, Barbusse...), and it seemed to me that, in France, Ray and Martha might have gotten away with it as a crime of passion, compared with the way the Americans treated them.

Also, there is a very strong sexual theme to it, which is true of all my work. When I saw sexuality overlap with criminality in *The Honeymoon Killers*, the idea of psychopaths as sexual killers - lust killers, if you want - I became very interested in that. Of course, everyone is into serial killers now, but at the time no one was really interested in them.

The Honeymoon Killers was published in the Serie Noir in France, and a completely new translation later in Rivages Noir. So, I suppose because my work contains sex and violence, and my philosophy has to do with existential ideas, it tends to get classified into the Noir area.

Everything I do is subversive. I don't always intend that to be the result, but ultimately that's what happens. For example, one of my unpublished crimes novels, *Bottle*, revolves around South London gangsters. There are three distinct types of gangster and I have written them with their own dialects - not Cockney, but South and West London. I gave the book to various publishers and they said they couldn't sell the book in Australia, South Africa or America because of the dialect. I thought that was extremely patronising. When I watch a film, or listen to records, I'm expected to understand the sound and slang of people from all over the world. Just because I come from London, I'm expected to write in Oxford English or 'sumfing'. Okay, so I could easily take out the South London dialect, but that would destroy the construction of the book, because of the three language regimes of gangster in the book. The first is the contemporary of the Great Train Robbers, who has been in prison, read a lot, restructured his sentences, and so doesn't have such a pronounced clipping of his speech. The second level are the gangsters you would have seen in the film *Performance*, for example. Then there's the very young gangsters who don't have a sense of discipline, both in the way they behave, and their language - they swear more, they don't have a large vocabulary, and their syntax is different. Intertwined between these men are the women, whose language reacts as they move between these groups of men. So, because the language is so important to me, I decided to stick to my guns and wait until such a time as someone came along and wanted to print it.

In *Bottle*, the police are dumb and corrupt - just the way I like them. I'm not interested in the police, and there's a reason for that. Fifty yards from where I'm sitting now, lived a policeman called Commander Drury, who was the commander of the flying squad at Scotland Yard, and the first high ranking policeman to be jailed for corruption. That was the late sixties. I knew he was corrupt when I was growing up, I could see it for myself. He had a big flash Jag. There was an extension to his house, the first in the area, and there were various unsavoury visitors to his house. Police were discreet in those days.

This area where I live is really good because a lot of the police from Scotland Yard live round here. Also, the gangsters who make money have houses here as well. They don't live here at the moment because they're on an extended 'holiday' in Spain, or wherever. You can tell which houses are theirs because they have iron gates and fountains. We don't have any break-ins in this area - if you accidentally knock off a gangster's place you've had it, mate. And if you break into a policeman's place, it's just as bad...or worse.

I nearly ran over a policeman once. When I was eighteen, I was driving down a country lane at a phenomenal speed, crashed the car and just missed a small police station. If I'd been a better driver, I would have gone straight through the front bloody door. I'd come from a fancy dress party, and I staggered out of the car, into the police station. I was wearing a pair of pyjamas and a fez hat. 'Evening all.' They had the nerve to take me to court.

I've never been really interested in the police, in crime procedure, because they are about law and order. I write about transgressions. Of course, as a human being living in society, I don't want people breaking into my house or anything like that, but that doesn't mean I'm going to arm myself and shoot anyone who comes through the door. Ignore the machine gun on the mantlepiece, it's not loaded. I only put the bullets in before I go to bed. And the grenades are planted discretely around the house. The one-armed kid next door thought they were pineapples.

In *Bottle*, the women appear as though they are the standard women that appear in gangster books - being abused and trapped in bad situations. You think that this book is the same, but as the book progresses they fight their way back and they become the interesting characters by the end. If you want to jump the gun, and think the beginning is how it ends, that's your bloody problem - you shouldn't judge a book by its cover. But we do do that. We live in a world where everyone tries to make quick decisions, instant judgements. I'm just being perverse. I'm saying that you have to read on further than the first few pages to find out what the book is about. On the other hand, people who like the idea that women should be beaten, will suddenly find characters with depth to them and realise that it's not what they thought. I like my women - as characters, and in real life.

There is very little sex in *Bottle* - I cut it out on purpose - there is only gruesome violence, particularly in the use of language. However, I don't pour over the detail of violence like I did in *The Honeymoon Killers*. The scene where Ray and Martha hit the woman with the hammer was written with great detail because you weren't allowed to do that at the time. Then I followed the killing with a Henry Miller-type sex scene - another thing you weren't supposed to do. Even now, graphic sex scenes are not really allowed in crime books. I put the sex scene in not to shock, but to jar against the reader's expectations, to help them understand what was happening to the characters.

I think other people shock more than I do. A lot of people may say that the films I make are shocking, or the performance work is shocking, or whatever. My work has violence in it, and sexuality, but, in reality it isn't that shocking. For example, in the sixties, I made a 16mm film called *Thighs*. When I was filming, there was a naked woman in front of me, the camera was going all over the place and you could see everything. But in the editing, I cut everything out so that you couldn't see her pubic hair or anything. You saw her thighs, and her fingernails running up and down them, marks, scratches. When I showed the rough cut to the grant body a woman came up to me and said it was one of the most erotic films she'd ever seen. I thanked her. She said, no, it's terrible, she couldn't possibly show it to the panel to get more money to finish it and get a print. She knew she couldn't see anything, but it was the way I edited it. That is an example of how I do all my work. My work doesn't have much sexual or violent content, but the fabric of the work, the style and language I use, highlights that sex and violence.

This interest in sex comes from being a Catholic. My mother was Italian, so she made sure I was brought up as a Catholic. I think what happens is that most Catholics make the decision in their teens to either continue to be devote, with all their repressions, or they rebel totally. I rebelled, and it gave me a freedom to express my sexuality. Although many of my friends remained Catholics, I have found that many artists I've met over the years are lapsed Catholics. They recognise and use their repression in order to perform their art. If they went to a psychiatrist to clean it up for them they'd lose the thing which was driving their art, so they don't want it cleaned up.

An artist is unclean. Being an artist is a criminal act. That's the other aspect that interests me. Art activity is a transgressive activity, like crime. Art, crime, and sex all involve taboos, which is why I think they tie together so easily. A lot of people see art as therapy, a cathartic experience. I'm not into that, though I can see how it can be used as therapy.

I wrote *Red Ascends* six years ago. It's about the painting and gangster worlds, no police involved. (Oh sorry, two policemen show their ugly heads and get them blown clean off.) It's basically about a painter going back to his roots, to a funeral, having to take over the management of the life of an orphaned child, looking at what he has achieved...it's about his relationships with women - his ex-girlfriend, his agent's wife, his sister's orphaned child, his sister's sister who moves from a dancer to stripper to gangster's moll. Women always play a major role in my work, even in *The Honeymoon Killers*. Men don't develop very much in my books. They have a character that they pretty much stay solid on. The women are the main protagonists, and they evolve in the course of the books. It's not that I'm trying to be politically correct or anything, I just generally find women more interesting to write about, and I like women's writing, which has influenced me a lot.

In the Seventies, after *The Honeymoon Killers*, I wrote about a million words of true crime articles for a crime encyclopaedia, published in French by a Swiss-based publisher. I wrote many essays about psychopaths. Each essay would be about 20,000 words long, in English, and written very quickly. It was an interesting project because a lot of French literary figures wrote for the encyclopaedia, and I encouraged people in this country to contribute. It has been published in six different languages around the world, but not in English, the language it was originally written in. It was a good income for about three years.

At this time, I began researching a true crime book which I still haven't finished. I don't want to talk about the subject of the book because a book hasn't been done on it. It's to do with murders which have never been categorised. I've been researching it for 16/17 years, collecting bits of information in files, which I've now transferred onto the word processor.

I then edited *Curtains*, a literary magazine which had a lot of French translation in it, juxtaposed against British writers and artists who have since gone on to bigger things. I published work by Iain Sinclair and Paul Auster amongst others. The best way to understand a writer is to translate him, because you have to read intensely. I translated contemporary French writers, got very involved with the scene and went to Paris a lot. I recently translated Bernard Noël's French literary erotic novel *The Castle Of Communion* - I published some of his work in *Curtains*. It was at this time that I became very involved with Bataille.

Georges Bataille was a surrealist author who wrote intense erotic books like *The Story Of The Eye* (1928), and *Blue Of Noon* (1957). He wrote about the dark side of sexuality, connecting sex and death. My translations of Bataille's work in *Curtains* helped introduce the author to Britain. Ironically, since then, I have been accused of copying Bataille.

A gallery recently exhibited some art accompanied by my poetry from *Violations*, a collection of my poems, and my translations of Bataille. The art was based on Jack The Ripper and Dennis Nilsen. I didn't mind them quoting my work, as long as they dated it, to show I'd been writing this sort of stuff for a long time.

I ran a week-long Georges Bataille festival in 1984 called *Violent Silence* -

there were contributions from Bernard Noel, Derek Jarman, Steve Dwoskin among many others. I had heard that Marc Almond liked Bataille's work, so I went down to his office and asked if he wanted to take part. He said yes, we became friends, and we said we'd work together again once the festival was over. Three weeks later Marc rang me and asked if I'd translate a Jacques Brel song. I did, he liked what I did, and the result, and it just went on from there. We did two albums together. One was all Brel songs, and the second was French songs by Juliette Grèco, Barbara and others, plus some Baudelaire and Rimbaud set to music. They all have a sexual content. Marc is known for working in that kind of decadent area, so he attracts a certain kind of audience.

Marc wrote a song for Melinda Miel, a torch singer I worked with as manager and lyricist. The songs were about love and hate, sex and death. The music was mostly written, played and arranged by Steve Rowlands. The two albums were *The Law Of The Dream* and *A Kiss On A Tear*. She was particularly liked by the S & M scene and also had quite a gay following, because her songs appeared more open to interpretation for them, and because she took on the diva role for her public face. In the lyrics I played with the extremes of passions, enhancing her chosen image. And Steve's music only heightened it further. It was so intense that it was bound to collapse, but I bet you'll not see anyone else make such an extreme statement in that area again. We were way over the top. (I have written for and gigged with 48 Cameras, a Belgian art-music group, and have also written two libretti for operas by Stanislaw Hansel. I'm currently working with David Coulter (ex-Pogues) and other musicians, like guitarist Marc Ribot, with a view to recording and performing.)

At university I studied geology and, although I quit the course, some of the ideas in the subject apply to my work. For example, there are strata of meaning in the way I construct my work. There are fault lines, where everything slides against each other. There are precipices. In fact, I use words like 'precipice' a lot, but they are given further meanings, usually sexual. I think that 'crack' speaks for itself, as does 'fissure.' I use my own perverse vocabulary and, over the years, I've shifted the meanings of these words in my work. They are buried within me now.

My writing is layered. That happens without me trying because I'm thinking all the time, writing all the time. That's reflected in all the things I like. For instance, the films I like include Bertolucci's *The Conformist*, Welles' *Citizen Kane* and *The Lady From Shanghai*, Cammell/Roeg's *Performance*, and other Nic Roeg films like *Eureka*, written by Paul Mayersberg. I like layers of meaning and rich textures, like Dundee cake. I came out of the sixties and a strong European tradition of Antonioni, Godard, Rivette, Fassbinder. Underground psycho-drama movies by Maya Deren, Kenneth Anger. Italian art-gore, like Dario Argento. Painting: abstract-expressionism, Pollock, De Kooning. Hans Bellmer, who has a strong sexual content, Andre Masson, Giacometti, Tapies. Photography: Jan Saunek. Literature: French literature, especially Bataille, Artaud, Duras. William S Burroughs. Philosophy: Cioran, Wittgenstein. Periphery women writers: Jane Bowles, Anna Kavan. Theatre: I've got left behind on. Pinter because of the use of language. Music: I played jazz many years ago on the saxophone, and that evolved into the sixties with Hendrix, and now I'm into all forms of new music.

Every day I assimilate information, media, thoughts, ideas. I write in the morning when my mind is clear, before it gets cluttered up with the day. I get up at 6.30 am, am at the table by 7.00 am, and spend most of my day there. I leave it at about 2.00 am the next morning. I don't sleep much. That's seven days a week. Okay, so you have to go out shopping, watch telly, do the gardening, listen to music, but those are the exception. The rule is the table.

Before Melinda sang my words, I often performed my poetry, but I wanted to do more than just read from the page. I wanted to vocalise what was on the page in such a way that another layer of emotional meaning would be added. Eventually, I wrote pieces to be vocalised. They were quite extreme in an Artaudian sense. (Artaud created the theatre of cruelty, where he explored the inner emotions of people. He found ways of showing people's emotions on stage. This has assimilated itself into so many theatrical experiences that we just take it for granted now. It is generally thought that he only had people screaming, ranting and raving, but he had tapped into different cultures from around the world. I recently performed vocalisations of Artaud's texts at The Institution Of Rot and at the ICA as part of the Artaud/Genet weekend along with other artists like Peter Sellars, Jodorowski, Patti Smith and Pierre Guyotat.)

I investigated the writing structures of different music cultures from around the world. Then I wanted to improvise, like musicians often do. To do that, you have to practice your scales every day, and I did the same with language. I thought it was a bit pointless to practice all the time for two readings a year, so it transformed into performance. I became friends with various performance artists who used their body to express pain. People like Stuart Brisley, who's still around today, and Genesis P.Orridge, who's now famous for other things. They did performances which were very much to do with body art ideas.

I moved on from there. Not wanting to pursue it further myself, I wrote plays for other people to perform. I began to write songs for other people. I didn't want to perform myself. Eventually, to earn my living, I started teaching two days a week in art school. That's basically a three hour talk, which I now improvise. Back to performance again. The teaching drains that aspect of myself out in a creative way, because the lessons always include the work I'm researching at the time.

Another novel I'm presently writing, *Rear Entry*, has a different dialect, middle-class, set in London's art scene. This one is loaded with sex, not explicit sex, because Paul Mayersberg (writer of *Homme Fatale* and *Violent Silence*) is doing that sort of thing very well, and I don't want to get into that area. It's a heavy book, about incest, but not in the way that people normally approach the subject. It's very politically incorrect. It's very nauseating, intentionally so. I start off exploring one area and it leads me onto something else.

I talk about politics, religion, and the way society works all the time. It's in my work, but in a different way. In general, I see my work as extremely political because of it's subversive technique. Everything is based on language: laws, government, society. It's based on the fact that you keep certain rules to your language. If you start disrupting the language by changing the order of the sentence, the syntax, the meaning of the word, it is a subversive act. For example, no one can define obscenity, so a lot of people cannot be prosecuted for some of the things they do, because the goalposts of obscenity keep shifting all the time. If you have money, you can find the loopholes in laws. It's very funny, and also disgraceful in another sense, that because the education system is sagging so badly, people can't write any more, they can't structure their sentences properly, their punctuation is atrocious. Take that last point - I got an official document from the Enterprise Allowance scheme and a comma was in the wrong place, which totally changed the meaning of a very crucial condition of the scheme. So everyone who read that form would have to get that point clarified because of a comma. It's disgraceful. So, in a sense, society is doing it to itself. In the novels, and all the other things I do, it's not so obvious that I'm trying to subvert the meanings of words. I think that's a political action in itself. As a person to meet I'm probably very pleasant, but intense. It's the writing where I'm doing the damage.

I have channelled my life into the research of sexuality, criminality, and art, the philosophy behind these. In doing so, my research has manifested itself as poetry, music, crime writing, radio scripts and so on. I don't dictate how it appears, it just comes out naturally.

I have many diverse influences, so my work can be kinda strange, intense. If I really wanted to sell my books I'd have to water it all down to give the public what they want. The problem is that no-one knows what the public wants, otherwise people would have bestsellers all the time. If a major publisher in this country pays a good advance, they want the book to become more commercial in order to get their money back. That's not for me.

The way it works is that you do something that you sincerely believe in, and you present it in a professional manner, somewhere down the line you'll interest someone. I've tried to find a publisher in this country for a long while. They all realised I had something, but they couldn't categorise me. That's the big problem in this country, in other areas of the arts as well. In Europe, publishers are much more interested. Look at Derek Raymond's books, which were published in Europe before being published in the UK.

I think I have to do what I have to do, and that's it. A lot of people write novels because they want to write, not to pay the bills. If they just wanted money, they'd go rob a bank.

I don't write about a large number of people. I make it very personal. Although I know a hell of a lot of people, I work better when I'm talking to just one or two people. I don't go to pubs, or big gatherings. I'm interested in people, not the superficial side of it. I'll talk about someone, and Catherine will ask me to describe what they look like. I can't, because I didn't actually see them. I can describe their personality and what I thought about them straight away, but not what they looked like and what they were wearing. So in my books, I am more interested in setting up people's characters than the way they look. I'll find some way of describing them, somewhere, but it's not important to me. For example, in *Bottle*, the people are defined by the dialogue, the way they speak, because I've pruned away much of the narrational detail.

My favourite crime writers are not current writers, but those from the past, like Horace McCoy, Norbert Davis, Fred Nebel and Carroll John Daly. These were the Black Mask writers who were blue-pencilled all the time - every word that didn't contribute to the plot was ruthlessly rubbed out in blue pencil by editor Joseph T Shaw. I don't necessarily like them because of the content, but because of the way they wrote. I just can't stand stuff that is padded out, which is how publishers work today. The publishers want you to add another 100 pages so that they can add a pound to the price.

Harry Whittington is an example of someone who had a great use of dialogue. I remember in one book he had pages and pages of it without even the 'He said, she said', and you knew who was speaking all the way through. And this is a so-called pulp writer - far more relevant and invigorating than many 'literary' writers.

On my wall of crime books behind us, there are the Black Mask people from the Thirties, the Fifties originals like Day Keene, Charles Williams, Harry Whittington, David Goodis, and Jim Thompson. That includes Vin Packer, a woman writer, whom a lot of contemporary woman writers are totally unaware of. They all think she's a man, but she's also written under the name Ann Aldrich, and her real name, Marijane Meaker. There are hardly any contemporary crime writers on my shelves because you either have the journalistic type of crime writing, or the police/PI series characters. I always think these people are writing crime for money, not because they want to write. They could have chosen to be bank managers and done their job just as well...or badly.

As we're talking, we have the telly on in the background, and we're watching a film with a rollercoaster. At the end of the night, I'll turn off the telly and forget about it. In the same way, I'll read contemporary crime, and forget about it when I'm finished. I don't feel that way when I finish a book by Thompson or Whittington. I can read and reread their books. I don't care if it only took them days to write, and it took the newer guys a year.

The only comparable author is Derek Raymond, whose books are uneven - and he would have admitted that himself - but there's a passion there: 'a fucking passion' he would've said. Derek was great. *I Was Dora Suarez* is not an even book, but it's very deeply upsetting. I didn't enjoy reading it, but I'll read it again. I don't read a book purely to be entertained, which is the difference. I'll read anything which will challenge me, make me think, stir up my emotions.

I could easily do the necessary and join all the other crime writers who do it for money. But, if I did that, I'd be deeply unhappy, in the same way that I'd be unhappy to compromise whatever else I was doing. At the moment, I think there are a few, new young writers who are uneven in their writing, not really concerned about getting everything politically correct, or writing what the so-called public want them to write. There are also a couple of new publishers getting started who are more open to publishing in this new area.

The new writers are influenced by the previous generations who have been reprinted and rediscovered - Thompson, Woolrich, Goodis - as well as serial killers, and horror/gore films. All this is coming together and being presented as crime novels. But these novels probably won't be structured as crime novels, with nicely solved murders at the end. They'll blast their way through, making up the rules as they go along. There'll be some disasters in this process, but I much prefer to read that than a book divided into good and evil, knowing that good will win.

I'm also interested in the screwball crime comedies of Jonathan Latimer. His books are about a private detective who's always drunk, who's effectively taking the piss out of crime writing. He solves things by not solving them. He does fuck all, but somehow it all works out. Latimer didn't write a series either, because he tried to make each book different, to have it evolve, which is why he wrote so few. The interviews I'd read with him showed that he simply got bored if he repeated himself. That interests me as well, the fact that he didn't just churn them out. It's subversive. There's some very clever writing in there. Latimer was brilliant really, as was Horace McCoy. Horace McCoy's books are about failures, and it wasn't until I did the research for an introduction to a collection of his work, that I found out how much of a failure McCoy was himself. It was Horace McCoy with *They Shoot Horses, Don't They?* who inspired Camus, Sartre and the whole Existential movement, not

James M Cain as is generally quoted. Another author I like is P J Wolfson, who's a big crime writer in France, yet no-one knows him in Britain or America. His books are about total despair, which is what I like to read about.

You have to decide what you want to do with your life. You can be a vegetable working in an office, being part of the machinery of life, living in the suburbs with a house and car. Or you can do something with your life. You might decide to become famous, or make a lot of money, or become an artist, or explore your interests. My interests, I've discovered, have been in all arts: music, literature, theatre, films. I'd be quite happy looking at films all day, listening to music, reading books. I don't think I have to necessarily create, but I do enjoy it, and I find I can drain off my energies through creating. I'm not a very violent person, but my work is violent. I often wonder that if I didn't drain it off through my work, whether I'd be a violent person or not.

You have to have a sense of humour about life, otherwise you're going to be completely depressed all day. We're watching the Yugoslav civil war on telly now, and the people dying in Somalia. I'm sure there are people who take what's happening around the world very seriously, because the telly tells you about it all the time. Years ago, you knew things were happening, but it wasn't rammed down your throat by the telly. Also, you sit there and you can't do anything about it, and your country doesn't do anything about it either. People talk about the ozone layer, the way we're destroying our environment.

People feel impotent. Then they become apathetic because they don't think they can do anything about the problems they're faced with. This is a very apathetic, docile country in many ways. Even the rebellious things that the young do, like joyriding and raves, are impotent acts. They don't lead anywhere. They're not done with any form of conviction, any long-term plan. They are little acts of spite before they settle down and become part of the apathetic mass. They don't see it like that themselves, but that's what they're doing.

In the sixties, we joked that the capitalist system in Britain, and possibly the world, would fall apart by the end of the century. And that's exactly what is happening. We said that the only way the county was going to survive was if everyone worked a 3 day week and shared jobs. Otherwise, we said, a few people would work and have lots of money, and the rest signed on the dole and had little money. And that's exactly what has happened. The problem is that the people in jobs do not want to give up their little power, their seat, their desk, to someone else for 3 days a week. People are still selfish, greedy. It was like that in the sixties, and it's still like that now. How can we change our society when that's people's attitude?

I think I'm a very moral person, and the people I associate with are moral people too. I look at today's newspapers and I think that the behaviour of the

PAUL BUCK

Duchess Of York and others seems to be very immoral. Whereas I know people who go to S & M clubs, and I think that they are moral.

I believe in honesty. An artist or writer can try to be honest, to get through to the truth, yet deal with a subject matter which seems to be completely immoral. My mother, and other people, said that my work is totally immoral, but I think it is actually quite moral. It's an exploration of morality. I am trying to find a sense about what life is about. I could easily take another approach and write a book about Somalia, how it got to be like it is, all the rights and wrongs. Or write a book about how all Governments, all political systems in fact, are immoral. The structure of society is rotten, and immoral. It probably always has been. That's why I concentrate so much on personal politics - because it's probably the only way we have a chance of working things out.

Since this interview, Paul has written two novels that concern themselves with crime and sex, thus making life difficult for himself in the commercial market, as they don't fit neatly into the crime or erotica genres. Fallen Corners is set in London, with a dubious Irish background that is always present, though the foreground of the book is about a relationship between a boy and a girl, with a heavy and very explicit and humorous account of their love life.

The other novel, Tainted Love, which plays with the title of Soft Cell's hit song, is about the sex life of a French psychiatrist, a woman, as she goes about her daily life in Paris and another unnamed city. Whilst being an equally serious novel with ideas and comment on contemporary society, this book reads as almost uproarious farce, with no concessions given to the reader as far as its sexual nature is concerned, nor in its violence and complete disregard for acceptable practices of social behaviour. Both these novels seem to be aside from the current climate in what is regarded as marketable books, so neither have been offered to publishers at this time.

Paul is currently writing a book about the underbelly of Belgian life, as seen through the city of Liège, a book that he started long before the current interest in the local paedophilia and political corruptions, subjects which he was already focusing upon as being at the core of what interested him about the Belgian unease. The book is called The Three Faces Of Liège.

At the same time, he is moving towards a completion of a long-term project around the film Performance, a book that intends to display a richness of interpretation of the film both in its analysis and presentation. As always, neither book is commissioned and tied to a publisher, though both have interested people awaiting the results.

PAUL BUCK

Martina Cole

I **T IS DIFFICULT TO ACCURATELY DESCRIBE** the novels of Martina Cole. They are full of extremes. Extreme violence. Extreme sex. They are about London families, about women holding these families together, about women protecting their own. I think of them as romantic crime sagas. Her first, Dangerous Lady, was a runaway bestseller and the subject of a TV drama.

So I turns up to meet Martina in a London hotel, not knowing what to expect. Her press photo shows her as a Joan Collins type, all shoulder-pads and fluffy hair-do. In the flesh, she's petite, blonde hair tied back, light blue suit, softly spoken but a surprisingly deep voice.

On the trip to the hotel, Martina's cabby told her about a fare he'd just dropped off. An Arab and two of his veiled women got in back. There was a disagreement for some reason, and the Arab started punching these women. The women were bloodied and defenceless. The cabby couldn't believe it, the violence, so he stopped the cab. The Arab calmed down and paid the cabby off with a large tip.

We sit and gossip for a while, Martina playing mother when the tea arrives.

A Dangerous Lady

My first boyfriend was an armed robber. I didn't know until he didn't turn up one day and I found out he was on remand for armed robbery. He got twelve years.

When women are married to villains - some know before they're married, some find out after - the husbands go out, do their job, come home and nothing is said. What she doesn't know won't hurt her.

The central character of Martina's fourth novel, The Jump, *hasn't got a clue that her husband's a villain.*

The Jump is about Donna Brunos, who lives in a stylish house, married to a very handsome Essex man. His father's Greek, his mother's Irish, and he's got the worst of both nationalities. She's given her life to him, been with him since she was seventeen.

As a used car dealer, and being involved with a construction site, she knows he ducks and dives a bit. Then someone grasses him up for armed robbery and he gets an eighteen year sentence. Donna is dragged through the underworld of Glasgow, Liverpool and Soho setting up The Jump - his escape from prison. As she does so, she finds out more than she bargained for about her husband's activities. But it's too late. The Jump is set up, and Donna can do nothing to stop it.

Why do women put up with that sort of life?

Perhaps they do it because the bloke's really exciting. Perhaps they love him, have his children, and accept him, whatever he is. The men look after their wives, have beautiful homes, beautiful clothes, and when he gets banged up for twelve years his biggest fear is that she'll find someone else.

A lot of The Jump is set in the prison. I talked to people in prisons, and found people who'd been inside. (I had a lady tell me one time that her son was doing twenty years for armed robbery, but that he was a nice boy.) You start talking to these people and they love telling you all about their lives and the people they met. One old guy said, 'You're a lovely girl, dear, and I love chatting to you but I feel like a grass.'

There is a kind of code among criminals, and they have rules about what is, and what isn't, acceptable.

If you talk to hard men about murder, they think that if a guy kills someone when he had too much drink on him, then that's par for the course. But if a guy batters his wife to death, then they are always put on Rule 43 because they're not welcome with the other prisoners, like rapists and child molesters.

Someone told me a story about when they were in a top security prison. A Rule 43 prisoner came in, waiting to go to Broadmoor or somewhere, and the screw settled him in a cell and went straight down to the Prison Officer and told him that the prisoner was there. They left him for half an hour whilst the PO and friends battered the hell out of the guy. Someone said that the same thing happened in another prison, but in this case the PO threw two pounds of salt over the guy at the end.

Regardless of the rules the prisoners make for themselves, the prisoner is there because he broke society's rules.

Prison is there to take the prisoner out of society. That is their sentence. There are people within the service and outside, who believe that whilst they are there they should serve another sentence. One guy was telling me about a prisoner who was on the block for eight weeks. The screws hammered the fuck out of him. They didn't allow him toilet paper, toothpaste or a bath. I don't hear him being on the news, or see Amnesty knocking down the door.

These prisoners suffer enough without these extra sentences. Their families are broken up, their wives remarry, their children grow up without them. If they're A grade, they're not even allowed out when their mum dies.

If, instead, they'd raped and murdered a woman on the street, they'd go to a special prison for a couple of years, then into a dispersal system that would let them out eventually. In England, the courts give bigger sentences to crimes involving property and money, than to crimes involving rape and murder.

It seems to me that something, somewhere, has gone wrong.

It's always amazed me that if I worked in Barclay's Bank, or wherever, and committed a £50 million fraud, then I'd get Ford Open Prison and have a lovely time. But, if I got £4,000 out of a Post Office with a sawn-off shotgun and no violence I'm looking at eighteen to twenty years. To me there's no difference between the two, but in the courts there's still a class distinction between white and blue collar crime. What's the difference? They're still robbers and thieves.

In the past, Britain has not had too bad a gun problem, but that could all be changing.

Drugs bring guns. You can buy a handgun in Brixton for up to £50 now. The drug problem in this country is far bigger than has been made out. There's E and crack cocaine all over the place. As the mother of a young son, you have to be so aware, look for all the signs.

Before writing her books, Martina does plenty of research, trying to get authentic stories and characters.

It's sometimes the best part, better than writing the book, because you're finding out about other people.

Her screenplay for The Begging Boys *is about boys living on the street.*

I talked to a rent boy - he was only thirteen. He came from up north, probably around Bradford judging from the accent. I asked whether he was frightened. 'Only when I was a spring chicken,' he explained, which is when they're virgin. As far as he was concerned, he was having a really good time in this house, watching videos and with money to spend. I realised that he had made the 'job' secondary in his life. Children can do that. They can justify anything.

I thought that if he survives, if he doesn't catch AIDs or get murdered, and becomes a grown man, he doesn't realise that all this will haunt him for the rest of his life.

The saddest thing, it seemed to me, was that everyone he'd dealt with didn't really seem to care about him. He said he'd rung his mam and she'd told him to eff off. He said he didn't care, but you could tell he would of loved his mum to come and collect him and take him home.

In all her books, Martina writes about a predominantly male world where the women are as violent as the men.

Or more so. I think women are more ruthless than men. Men get mad. Women get even.

My heroines are very, very strong. In *Dangerous Lady*, Maura Ryan kneecaps a yardie in London, then she orders her brother's death, yet people still sympathise with her and love her.

I came from an area where you needed to be tough, especially when you were tiny - and I've always been very tiny. My brothers and sisters are really huge, taking after my dad's side of the family.

Me and my older brother hated one another and always fought. I think it stood me in good stead later on because I learnt that you had to fight dirty to win. I remember once he was lying on the settee, I came running in, hit him with one of my mum's stiletto's, then ran out, slamming the door behind me.

Another time we were at the dinner table. I'm very fastidious about eating and he was loud and horrible so I stabbed him in the forehead with my fork. To this day, when he combs back his hair you can see the four holes.

It was at this stage that Martina asked if I wanted sandwiches, or something to eat. I declined.

Martina comes from an Irish Catholic family. Her mother was a psychiatric nurse who worked nights, and her father was a 6'4", 18 stone, red-headed Irishman who was always away at sea.

He was a complete and utter lunatic, but great, great fun. He'd come back from sea, get us out of bed at five in the morning, and we'd go out to the West End for the day. We'd go from pubs, to the films, and have a steak dinner at night. Me mum used to say we lived like the Bible: seven lean years followed by seven fat ones.

Martina could read before she went to school.

I read everything. My father wasn't really a reader, but he'd buy the bestsellers in America and bring them back for me, not realising what was in them. By the time I was ten, I'd read Harold Robbins' *The Betsy* and *Carpetbaggers*. I read *The Godfather* when I was eleven. *Luciano's Luck* when I was fourteen. I lived in a bit of a dream world, losing myself in Ernest Hemingway and John Steinbeck. I was only ten when I read *The Grapes Of Wrath* - the scene where they're in the car and talking about elephants stuck in my mind for years. The same with the scene in *To Kill A Mockingbird* where the son is ashamed of his father because he wanted his father to conform. Lots of scenes stayed in my mind, because they struck a chord with me and my life at the time.

Her interest in reading translated into writing, and her stories were put up on the wall at Holy Cross convent school.

I had no time for the regime there, but the funny thing is I'm now a practising Catholic.

A lot of women have been brought up to need men, to be supported by them. This is why many women find it difficult to survive on their own. As a result, they are used by men. In the case of prostitutes, there were some, like Mynah Bird, who made it their career to sleep around, and there's a sort of acceptability to it because they slept with barristers and aristocrats. Whereas some poor cow who's on an awayday in King's Cross to keep five kids on social security because her husband's pissed off, is looked on as the lowest of the low. I'm a great believer in circumstances. It could be anybody. You don't know what life has in store for you - nobody does.

I had my son when I was just nineteen. My mom delivered him. As an unmarried mother, I lived in a hostel for ages and it was horrible. It was bad then and it's bad now. I don't think not having a father affected my son's development into manhood. He's turned out to be a really nice boy, despite having a raving lunatic as a mother. When I was pregnant, I remember the social worker saying to me, 'Martina. How do you expect to look after the child when you can't even look after yourself?' There was a big stigma attached to unmarried mothers at the time. I hardened myself up because of that, but I think having my baby was that best thing that ever happened to me, because it gave me a goal in life.

We lived in some pretty rough areas and I worked, worked, worked. I ran an off-licence, was in a supermarket, nursing, a secretary. I used to work in Coral's betting shops as a relief, driving all over east London and Essex, filling in for people off sick.

My son was my career. He came first and work came second. I got a nice home together and eventually bought a house. (I live in a nice respectable neighbourhood. I know it's respectable because you can be dead three months before the neighbours notice.) Even though my son is a big, strapping lad, if someone tried to hurt him or upset him in any way I feel I'd want to kill them. It doesn't matter what age he is, I'll always want to protect him.

Coming from the area she did, Martina heard stories and knew of people involved in the underworld.

When you found out so-and-so's husband or boyfriend was 'away,' it was accepted because it was part and parcel of the life.

I've always been fascinated by true crime - I buy and read all the books. In fact, when I was doing *The Ladykiller*, which was about a serial killer, I went to the local paper and got everything they had on Peter Sutcliffe. I enlarged all the pictures

MARTINA COLE

and articles and put them on the walls. This man came to put in the fax and he came into the room and just stood there looking at these photos of bodies and things. I offered him a cup of tea. 'No!' he said. Anyway, I had to go out and this bloke asked my husband what was up with me with all these photos. My husband explained I was a writer. 'Ooohh!' the man said, 'I thought it was a bit of a weird hobby.'

What's really sad about it, of course, is that everyone knows Peter Sutcliffe's name, but if you asked anyone to name one of his victims they wouldn't be able to do it. The killers are turned into celebrities. I mean, women write to Peter Sutcliffe offering marriage - that's really sick. I can understand someone writing to a bank robber doing twenty years who's a handsome demon - for instance, Ronnie Knight, in his day, was a seriously good-looking bloke - but how anyone would want to write to an ugly bastard like Peter Sutcliffe, I just don't know.

To Martina there is a difference between the career criminal and the sex killer, and she thinks they should be treated differently.

Reggie Kray should be let out. I think he's done quite enough time for the murder of Jack The Hat. He's in his sixties and paid his price to society. It's all politics now - no-one wants to be the person to let him out. It worries me that if a Labour government got in, they'd probably let Myra Hindley out because it's seen to be more politically correct.

People ask me all the time if I know the Krays. I once read that I grew up with them! People love the glamour associated with crime, of being part of something. If I gathered all the people I've met in my life who said they used to drive for the Krays, I'd fill a multi-story car park.

Over the years, Martina has met a lot of people involved with The Krays.

There's a lot of rubbish written about the whole thing. What it basically comes down to is that whatever they did was done a long, long time ago. Hating them now is like hating the Germans for what they did during the war.

If the government had released the Krays seventeen years ago, it would have created a fuss and that would have been the end of it. As it is, they continue to be in the public eye and a mystique has grown up around them. Everyone else, like Chris Lambrianou, Tony Lambrianou and Albert Donaghue, is out and writing their books, making money. They would never have sold those books without a picture of the Krays on the cover.

I write about old-style villains. My villains all have hearts of gold. Basically they're nice people who do bad things, but always for the right reasons. It's a twisted morality, I know, but if you saw all the letters I get from women asking where they could get a Michael Ryan, a Patrick Kelly... They love them. I know I don't write literature, but I don't want to. I look on my job as entertaining people.

Bibliography

Dangerous Lady (1992)

No-one thinks a seventeen-year-old girl can take on the hard men of London's gangland, but it's a mistake to underestimate Maura Ryan: she's tough, clever and beautiful - and she's determined not to be hurt again. Which makes her one very *Dangerous Lady*.

The Ladykiller (1993)

George Markham has a nasty little hobby. He pursues it in secret, behind closed doors. But now George's little hobby is becoming an obsession, one that erupts into an orgy of vicious sexual depravity.

Patrick Kelly is a hard man - the most feared in London. His daughter falls prey to the Grantley Ripper, and Pat wants revenge. Kate Burrows is the DI in charge of the case, and her growing involvement with Kelly, a known villain, puts her career at risk.

Goodnight Lady (1994)

The infamous Briony Cavanagh: quite a beauty in her day, and powerful, too. In the sixties she ran a string of the most notorious brothels in the East End. Patronised by peers and politicians - even royalty, some said. Only Briony knew what went on behind those thick velvet curtains, those discreet closed doors, and Briony never opened her mouth - unless she stood to benefit.

The Jump (1995)

Donna Brunos worships her husband and is devastated when he is jailed for eighteen years for armed robbery. Georgio swears he's been set up and - terrified he won't survive Parkhurst - persuades Donna to help him escape.

Planning *The Jump* takes Donna into a twilight world she didn't know existed - a world of brutal sex and casual violence. And the more she sees, the more she's convinced her husband isn't as innocent as he makes out...

DR ELLIOTT LEYTON *lives on the edge of the known world, in an isolated cottage in Newfoundland, Canada. He didn't want to be just another dull professor in a sleepy provincial university, so he became an internationally renowned author of best-selling books about violence and crime, like* Hunting Humans, *the first book about serial killers. A social anthropologist by trade, he teaches one day a week at the Memorial University of Newfoundland, and has long-standing ties with police forces around the world.*

*   Men Of Blood: Murder In Modern England *is Dr Leyton's latest book. Using statistics and police interrogations as examples,* Men Of Blood *reaches the surprising conclusion that England & Wales have one of the lowest murder rates in the world (along with Japan and Ireland). Each year, an average of 500 people from a population of 50 million are murdered in England - a malfunction rate that would be the envy of mechanical system designers the world over. More people die due to road accidents, smoking, suicide or industrial disease. Of course, Paul Duncan didn't believe it, so he decided to interrogate Dr Leyton himself. They met at the Grosvenor Hotel in London.*

*   When we met, Dr Leyton was really pissed off at me for being late. He'd been waiting twenty minutes in the hotel lobby cursing my name. I pointed out that his watch was wrong, and I'd arrived on the dot. Elliott, as I now call him, was all apologies for the rest of the evening.*

Bloody Murder

Any book I've ever written is an attempt to explain to myself, and then to others, a phenomenon I can't understand. I came from a disordered, dysfunctional family, so my early books were about that, to understand my family.

Elliott was born August 21 1939 to Harry (a physician) and Lilyan Levson in Saskatchewan, Canada. After a stint as a junior reporter for the Vancouver Sun, *Elliott got his Masters degree and became assistant lecturer in anthropology at Queen's College, Belfast, where he legally changed his surname to Leyton in 1965.*

The early books, *Dying Hard* (which charted the effects of an industrial disease on a small mining town) and *The Myth Of Delinquency* (about young offenders), were only published in Canada.

For *The Myth Of Delinquency*, I studied kids in reform schools on the Eastern seaboard. I read all the literature, visited all the places. I found that experience so devastating, both personally and emotionally that, for then on, I wanted to be at least one step removed from actual live thugs.

Bearing this in mind, for several years Elliott looked for a new subject.

My wife was bringing home journalistic accounts of various serial killers, and I picked one up - *The Stranger Beside Me*, Ann Rule's account of her friendship with serial killer Ted Bundy. I found this man to be so utterly mystifying - the idea that a man would kill the woman he just made love to - that I had to find out more. I went to the library to check out the medical and psychiatric explanations for this condition, only to find that there was no literature, no explanations. That's when bells started going off in my head. I knew I'd found my life's work.

I began by reading everything written in English about real-life cases. Then I began creating a network of friends in police forces worldwide which, over the past twenty years, has given me access to people, case files and information.

At the end of 1984, I finished writing *Hunting Humans*, and nobody wanted to publish it. Nobody even recognised serial killers as a phenomenon at the time. Eventually, a couple of presses in the US and Canada very reluctantly, and only because they'd published my earlier books, agreed to publish it. The book sold like crazy around the world and, to this day, continues to sell.

Elliott does not talk to any of the killers he writes about.

I have read more interview-based books than most people and I have formed the opinion that the interview, as a data source, is a profoundly flawed instrument. When you interview a killer a long time after the event, he's got his whole act prepared and he'll tell you exactly what he wants you to understand. Whereas, I have found that police interrogations immediately after the event (where there is more chance they are telling the truth) and psychiatric evaluations are infinitely better material to work from than the interview books.

You have to be very careful, because this information could obviously contain the concerns and points of view of the police and social workers who write them. I try to be as judicial as I can. In fact, the interviews are quite good because the police are naturally very cynical people, they don't believe people tell the truth and assume that they are lying all the time. On the whole, I was impressed by the quality of the interviewing. It was pretty subtle.

At one time, Elliott was happy to help the police with their investigations, to build up a profile by analysing the information available. He also enjoyed reading crime fiction. He remembered one horrible day when he began reporting on a case and realised he was confusing crime fiction with crime reality. At this point, Elliott stopped reading crime fiction altogether. He also stopped helping the police with their investigations, but that was because he didn't want to confront real killers. Who does?

In the UK, crime is presented differently in the media than, say, in America. Although there is always going to be the sleazier end of the true crime market, in general, I would say, people react with horror and disdain to violent crimes and murder. Whereas, in America, violence and murder seems to be embraced, glorified and admired. For example, in the UK, violence is usually presented as having an immediate detrimental effect whereas, in the USA, violence is seen as a positive way of solving problems.

I agree with you absolutely, with one exception, and that is that the British media give the impression that Britain is more violent than it actually is. People believe this, and it's not true.

So who actually kills people?

There are different kinds of killers. Serial killers are basically recreational killers - they do it for fun. Mass killers are revenge killers, making their one big statement to society.

The commonest murders in the UK, as well as in other countries around the world, are pretty mundane and unsensational, committed by pathetic, limited men who probably have little education and come from a dysfunctional family, have no professional qualifications, probably have drinking/alcohol problems, chronic long term unemployment, brushes with the law throughout their life, no control over their emotions. Those are the people that do it, under enormous stress and tension, on the spur of the moment. Most British murders are practically accidents - very few are actually planned.

I read about these pathetic, limited, defective people over and over and over again in the police case files. I was surprised that they are often consumed with remorse and shame. In some cases, so much so that they commit suicide.

If most crimes occur as a result of losing control for a split second, in the heat of the moment, you have to examine the cause of them acting as they did in that split second.

Exactly.

When people are drunk, and they get in a fight, they're not thinking about prison or the punishment for their actions. They're just drunk. To reduce the homicide rate, the violence rate, you have to look at what there is in their life that allows them to lose control.

Britain has serial killers, but are they the same as, say, American serial killers?

You produce your share of serial killers despite the extremely low homicide rate. There is a distinctively English quality to your serial killers: the puritanical, avenging Peter Sutcliffe; the pathetic killing for company of Dennis Nilsen. Those are different to the so-called joykillers found in America and Germany, the recreational killers, as criminologists sometimes call them.

We don't like having fun in this country.

You don't like admitting you're having fun.

A recent TV programme said that criminals may be identified by their DNA. That there is something in their genes which make them killers.

That's a hoary old chestnut which gets trotted out every year, ever since Cesare Lombroso started analysing facial types or the Glucks started measuring the dick lengths of adolescent boys. Some people like the idea of criminality being biological because it would make 'them' different to 'us.' I'm sure there probably is some biological reason, but they sure haven't demonstrated a bloody thing yet.

The thrust of the programme was that the people under discussion were under stimulated due to a chemical imbalance, which made them restless and dissatisfied with their surroundings, and this led them to conduct acts which spiralled into criminal activity. Ironically, this seemed to lump both criminals and artists into the same category.

I know what these people are trying to say, and there is certainly an escalation in the levels of gratification that these guys need when they are on a killing spree. However, I don't know how this differs from anybody. An adolescent starts necking, then petting, then gets laid. This is a socially acceptable progression of behaviour, whereas other forms of behaviour are not socially acceptable. Putting criminal behaviour down to a chemical imbalance is just scientific hocus pocus. It could mean anything. I'm not dismissing or rejecting the theory, just saying that it hasn't been developed.

In the past, a lot of British convicts were sent abroad, to Australia, New Zealand, America. The idea of a gene pool, if there is such a thing, being sent, en masse, to another place, is intriguing.

Robert Hughes mentions this idea in his book *The Far Shore*. You would expect there to be an enormous murder rate in Australia, but there isn't - it's in the middle of the league - which leads you to think that perhaps murder/crime has nothing to do with genes.

What about learned behaviour being the reason for criminal activity?

I think learning from parents, from society, about what is appropriate, what is acceptable, what you can get away with, definitely has a large effect on people's development. I think that, perhaps, the importance of parents is emphasised too much and that society plays a much greater role in the learning process than is sometimes appreciated. If society did not have an effect, then there would be no difference between the crime rates of different society nations but, as you know, there are profound differences between nations. And the most reliable social index which varies the most between countries is the homicide rate. I think it tells you a lot about the nature of the society, whether it is the educational system, the family, or the mass culture. All of these factors have to be considered - I don't think it's just the one thing. The investigations into this area have not been done. Everybody makes plausible assumptions, but nobody knows for sure what the figures are.

Writing about serial killers may be a mass industry, but the books all seem to be the same. No-one is doing the background research, asking the sort of questions you're asking me now. I'm mystified. I don't understand why so many people in academia completely ignore this aspect of our society when it is so bloody interesting.

Elliott pointed out that the former white dominions (New Zealand, Australia, Canada) benefitted from the law and order systems put in place by the British Empire. America was the exception. The British Empire never had the chance to enforce law and order there. Would that lack of law and order in America's past have resulted in today's high murder rates?

It would certainly have contributed to it. In America, the state presently does not have the right to exact revenge. In many jurisdictions, if anything happens to your house or person and you call the police, they'll tell you to get a gun and take care of it yourself. This is terrible. American jurisdictions do not accept responsibility to protect you as a citizen. It's your own responsibility.

Most of the Americans I meet have extreme views on the punishment of criminals. They tend to approve of the death sentence and life imprisonment meaning life. In the UK, most people believe that life imprisonment should mean that and not being released after 20 years or so.

There is a very different system here, although it looks the same. In the UK, when you're released, you're still on licence for life, whereas in America, when you're released that's the end of it.

I'm not surprised that Americans are that way. They come from a society which is much more aggressive, there's a lot of tension, and their judicial system is one of the most punitive on the planet. They exact the most horrendous punishment for all crimes, including violent crime. How many nations still have the death penalty, for God's sake? Yet, it has had no effect whatsoever on their extraordinary level of violence. So they just pump up the punishment even more...

In the UK, we are less likely to kill because we can use the law, whereas in America people are more likely to kill because they cannot rely on the law. But how did this all come about? Elliott has gathered the work of many eminent Medieval scholars in one coherent chapter of Men Of Blood *to explain how the origins of the legal system in the UK allowed everyone equal access to the law.*

Laws everywhere are designed for the people who design it, and they are usually the ruling elite, the rich.

In the UK, it began in the 15th Century when the monarch seized control of the state and, to consolidate his power, declared homicide an offence against the Crown. The original motivation was to protect the estates and the persons of the ruling elites, but it was soon extended to everyone. By the early 18th Century, if I was your serf and you were a great lord of the estate, then if I was in trouble for any reason you would pay my legal fees. So, by default, the law became universal.

It wasn't just a legal thing, it also set in motion a set of ideals, propagated by the ruling elite, about aggression being inappropriate to settle disputes. It conditioned and taught people that civility, politeness, courtesy and respectability were qualities to be admired.

I find it interesting walking around London, today, looking at how people interact on the street. This is one of the largest cities in the world so it should be a lawless, scary place, but it's not. People act with such civility here. In London, public discourse is very courteous. People are always saying 'please' and 'thank you.'

Elliott told me about the time he was in Belfast, trying to catch a train to Dublin, to meet his wife, but was late. He was clueless. He didn't know how to use the phone. A passerby told him how to use it, dialled the code for him. Elliott didn't have the right money, so someone else gave it to him. He was amazed by the way people just stopped to help a total stranger, a foreigner even.

There is a sense of responsibility to each other, and to the community. I have more faith in British justice than in any other.

This faith in Britain extends to the police force.

I'm relieved to see such a profound difference in the actual style of policing in Britain. The confrontational/adversarial relationship between police and civilians in the US is horrifying. I remember, a couple of years ago, I was going down to the FBI Academy to visit some friends. I wasn't accustomed to the freeways and got very confused about where I was. I saw a police car parked on the freeway, so I pulled over to ask directions. I thought, as well, that it'd be interesting to see how the police handle civilians. Anyway, immediately, the policeman's hand was on his gun, he was shouting at me to get back in the car and I ended up with a ticket for stopping to ask him directions. It was horrifying. And I'm white! Imagine what it'd be like to be black living in a slum area...

Obviously, children learn their early behaviour from their parents. Has any research been done into how parents teach their children, and how responsible parents are with their children?

I wasn't able to do that level of research. That's a 50-person research team, and I hope that's done sometime. However, you may be interested to know that Cambridge University Criminology School have been following delinquent London boys for 30 years, and it's very clear that the kind of families that consistently produce troubled people really don't know how to parent. I don't think that social forces are making it any easier to parent, either.

There are no parenting schools, are there?

No. Grandparents used to be the parenting school. However, the great upheavals of the sixties - tearing down the old buildings and community networks, then rebuilding new towns thus dispersing families throughout the country - were a disastrous social error, not just an aesthetic one. I'm no authority on this, but I would assume that this is one of the many factors which has had a great impact on the nature of parenting.

Although I loved them at the time - everyone was screwing everyone else and having great fun - the sixties were the worst thing that happened for a very long time. That's when the murder rate started going up worldwide. That's when the really profound social dislocations, whether communities or systems of belief or assumptions about civility, occurred. That's when the rot set in, worldwide. The effect of those years has yet to be calculated.

The people who lived through the sixties have lost their stable, central core of values. Those are the basic building blocks of a society which are transmitted through the generations. These people are now the parents, and everything I hear suggests that, in general, they're screwing up more than ever. There is no statistical evidence of this, only anecdotal evidence.

Men Of Blood lists statistics about the number of children who get killed, and their ages when they die. Sole Survivor, an earlier book written by Elliott, is about children who kill their families. I wondered whether there was any connection.

I don't think so. In the UK, the deaths of children are usually caused by depressed parents who then kill themselves. Parents are more of a threat to their children than strangers. If there is a connection, I haven't grasped it yet.

The adolescent, or post-adolescent child who kills his or her entire family is, I think, an entirely different problem. It occurs everywhere in the world, regardless of whether the country has a high or low homicide rate, and there are always one or two each year.

There is an interesting conundrum that a San Francisco social worker named Boggs first drew to my attention - she worked for many years in Watts, a Los Angeles black slum that burnt itself down in the sixties, and then went to Marin County, an affluent white, upper middle-class suburb of San Francisco. She said that in Watts the poor black kids weren't angry at their parents at all, but saw them as equal victims of this brutal society - they were mad at society. Whereas, in Marin County, the kids blamed their parents for everything. It was a brilliant observation.

At that point, I started looking at the ultimate manifestation of being mad at your parents - killing them. There are only a few dozen cases of kids killing their parents, but it was worldwide. A clear pattern emerged, which was that the parents were ferociously ambitious, upwardly mobile, middle class people, who often saw themselves as having failed in their aspirations. They then hoped against hope that their children would make it for them. That's a very widespread, middle-class aspiration, but it's a matter of intensity. For the most intense, this frustration and failure becomes so frenzied that, in extreme cases, the parents dictate every aspect of the child's life to ensure their children's rise. The kids are told which school they go to, who their friends are, what to wear, what kind of cars they drive etcetera.

The control becomes so severe that the kids lose all sense of their own identity - they are obliterated as individuals. In many of these cases, the kids are terrified to assert themselves in any way. The parents begin to devise a whole series of traps to make sure that the child is doing what they want: economic subservience, psychological dependence or both.

The best example I know of is the Ronnie De Freo case. Ronnie was a heroin addict, couldn't stand being at home any more, worked at his father's Buick dealership as a parking lot boy moving cars about, but being paid an enormous sum of money for it, no education, so there is a total financial dependence on his parents. A trap. At twenty-five, he said that if he didn't leave the house he was going to go crazy and kill them all. So he ran away and moved in with his girlfriend. The next morning, his car was gone. His dad had taken it back and said Ronnie had to move back home to get the car and his job. Ronnie went back and, within a matter of days, killed his parents.

A forthright person would just go, leave behind the money and security, but the kids you're talking about just can't survive outside the family.

Exactly. It should be remembered that most kids who exist in this kind of situation escape without it turning into familicide.

In America and the UK, class is defined by money, only in the UK the money tends to be older. In Sole Survivor class is a factor, but is it also a factor for multiple killers?

Certainly. In Hunting Humans, I made a big thing about social class - almost as much as the killers themselves. Someone once said, 'social class is the dirty little secret of American life.' What he meant by that is that, whilst in Britain people talk about social class all the time, people don't like to talk about it or be aware of it in America - that type of conversation is driven underground.

One of the very first things that struck me when I was looking at the memoirs, diaries and interrogations of North American serial killers was that they were obsessed with social class. They talked about it all the time. The Boston Strangler was a working class boy killing in middle class neighbourhoods. He said he was 'putting something over on high class people.' Ted Bundy's mother said he was a terrible snob. Even at the age of ten he was dragging her into the most expensive, snobby shops.

They felt themselves inadequate?

I think so. In the UK, there are some obvious class distinctions, and everyone has someone else of their own class they can talk to and identify with. Everyone has a sense of their own worth because there are others like them. Whereas in America, if you're less than middle class you're just a worthless failure. They don't have any social and cultural support like they have in the UK.

You're defined by how much money you have.

Exactly. America is probably more generous to its winners than any other country, and it's really ruthless to its losers.

Serial killers think of themselves as losers. They're mad at themselves because they're losing. They have a grudge against a segment of society, usually but not always the social class, that they feel has deprived them of their rightful place. They want to get even.

I don't want you to think that Americans are more materialistic than Europeans - in many ways it's the opposite, I think. Go to any European city and you'll see many Rolls Royces, Lambourginis, fashionable addresses, incredibly expensive shops and restaurants. It makes Americans look like Jesuits.

The point is, I think Europeans are every bit as materialistic as Americans, but the difference is with the feeling of being a total loser without any support.

A lot of this work you are talking about and doing is new. There's lots of fumbling about in the night. Nothing's set in concrete.

The human being is such a complex animal that we don't know how it works. And study of human beings is fumbling, whether it's highly developed, like family studies, or undeveloped, like the study of homicide. People stumble through, trying different approaches and ideas. There's no coherent direction. I usually write the first book on a subject then go on. That was the case with *Hunting Humans* and *Sole Survivor*, and *Men Of Blood* is only the third national study in the work this century. I just hope that my books will continue to spur the interest of other scholars.

ELLIOTT LEYTON

Biography

DR ELLIOTT HASTINGS LEYTON (PhD, Toronto) is the internationally renowned author of many best-selling books on violence and crime, including *Hunting Humans: The Rise Of The Modern Multiple Murderer*, and *Sole Survivor: Children Who Murder Their Families*. The past President of the Canadian Sociology and Anthropology Association, he has taught social anthropology at The Queen's University of Belfast, the Memorial University of Newfoundland, and the University of Toronto. He has long-standing ties with New Scotland Yard, the FBI Academy, and Dutch Interpol in The Hague, and many other police forces around the world.

Elliott once said that murder is a remarkable social act, replete with social meaning yet ignored by social scientists. *"A professor at the University of Toronto, who knows me well, said he was not surprised to learn I was writing about homicide, because 'anyone who knows Elliott for any length of time soon begins to consider murder.'"*

While researching and writing *Men Of Blood*, he was a member of the advisory boards to the departments of psychology at the Universities of Liverpool and Surrey, and a Research Fellow in the Institute of Irish Studies at The Queen's University of Belfast.

For his next book, a study of how doctors act under extreme pressure, Elliott is spending at least a month in Rwanda with the emergency medical aid team Médicins Sans Frontiers. While there, he'll also be studying the nature of genocide, a subject he teaches. *'You're always taking the easy option, aren't you, Elliott?'* I told him. He just laughed and said that he was quite looking forward to writing a book, for a change, which was about selfless people who do good with their lives. There again, he wasn't sure whether he'd be able to stand it for more than a month.

Bibliography

ELLIOTT HAS WRITTEN books for the Memorial University of Newfoundland Press and the Institute of Social and Economic Research about an ancient fishing village in Ireland, among the nouveau riche business people of British Columbia, and worker's compensation board bureaucrats in old St John's.

Dying Hard: The Ravages Of Industrial Carnage (1975)

Not published outside of Canada. This is the study of the effects of an industrial disease on a small mining town where hundreds and hundreds of miners died from breathing poisonous fumes. It details the anguish and effects of the disease on the dying miners and their widows.

The Myth Of Delinquency: An Anatomy Of Juvenile Nihilism (1979)

Not published outside of Canada. Dr Leyton studied kids in reform schools on the Eastern seaboard. *"This was so awful, so filled with manipulation, exploitation and betrayal, that I abandoned fieldwork."*

Hunting Humans: The Rise Of The Modern Multiple Murderer (1986)

(First published in America as *Compulsive Killers*) The seminal text about serial and mass killers - the distinction is important. The serial killer is obsessive, can't help himself. The mass murderer is making a statement. They are rebelling against authority/upper classes/women, achieving celebrity status (we remember those who destroy more than those who create), gaining an identity after being faceless, or simply getting sexual satisfaction.

Sole Survivor: Children Who Murder Their Families

Ambitious, upwardly mobile, middle class parents who see themselves as failures often project all their hopes and dreams onto their children. The children are powerless to assert themselves and, in rare cases, find that the only way they can express themselves is by killing their parents.

Men Of Blood: Murder In Modern Britain (1995)

The first serious examination of who kills who in the UK and why. Surprisingly, it seems that the UK is one of the safest places to live in the world. Not convinced? Read the book.

James Ellroy

**WOOF. WOOF. HEAR THE DEMON DOG BARK.
HE'S GOT A TWELVE INCH WANGER THAT GLOWS
IN THE DARK.
HIS BRAIN IS BIG, BUT HIS DICK IS BIGGER.
HIS RIGHT-WING FINGER'S ON THE NUCLEAR TRIGGER.**

Hello, Mr Ellroy.
Call me Dog.
Okay, Mr Dog.
No...just 'Dog.'
If there's one thing you have to admire about Dog, it's that he puts on a good show. He swears. He digs up his past and shoves it in the faces of his adoring public. He simulates masturbation on stage. He howls like the Demon Dog Of American Crime Literature that he is. What's even funnier is that so many people take this stuff seriously.

I have this vision of Dog arriving home after a hard month or two of touring, slipping off his shoes, falling into a chair and hissing with laughter as he recalls the shocked faces of his audiences. A sort of tall, gangly Muttley who caught that dastardly pigeon.

Besides, what do people expect after reading one of Dog's novels? From Brown's Requiem to American Tabloid, they're full of swearing, racism, drugs, bodily functions, violence, fluids, sleazeballs and hairballs. How could you expect Dog to be anything other than rabid in real life?

The fuel which keeps Dog up nights writing his fever dreams is the unsolved murder of his mother in 1958. His books are full of mother-substitutes, the most famous being Elizabeth Short, the Black Dahlia, a celebrated unsolved murder which occurred in January 1947. It is as though he is trying to deny his mother's reality by treating her as fiction. However, Ellroy has shown a greater maturity with his last novel, American Tabloid, and with the publication of My Dark Places, which details Ellroy's search for his mother's murderer, he hopes to acknowledge his mother, to recognise her for the person she really was.

Paul Duncan talked to James Ellroy.

Barking

A DOG'S LIFE

Lee 'the Big Armando' Ellroy, born 1898 in Germany, came to America with his parents, who died in a hotel fire when he was aged six. He was sent to an orphanage, where he was taught by sadistic nuns fresh off the boat from Ireland. He claimed to have had an affair with Rita Hayworth.

Jean (Geneva) Hilliker was born 1915 in Tunnel City, Wisconsin and had a strict Dutch Calvinist upbringing. Aged nineteen, and a nursing-school student, she claimed to have seen gangster John Dillinger gunned down by the Feds.

They met in 1939, married, lived in West Hollywood, Los Angeles.

James was born March 4 1948 in Good Samaritan Hospital. He learnt to read aged three and has been a prolific reader ever since. In 1954, Lee and Jean divorced. Lee drank Alka-Seltzer for his ulcer and chased women. Jean drank Early Times bourbon and chased men. James drank what he was given and did some middle distance running at school. Result: James lived with his mother during the week and his father most weekends.

Jean worked as a nurse at the Packard Bell electronics plant and went out with men on a regular basis. One, Hank, was fat and had a thumb missing. She was always pissed. James preferred his father. When he turned ten, he was given the choice of living with mother or father - he chose father, his mother slapped him, he called her a drunk and whore.

Three months later, he arrived back from a weekend with his father to find cops at his mother's house. They told him his mother was dead, a cop gave him some candy, a news photographer snapped him at a neighbour's workbench holding an awl - they didn't use the second picture of him clowning, showing off.

James begged off the funeral. Moved in with father, freelance accountant, womaniser, minor hero in the war, bullshit artist, a history of heart disease. Briefly, Rita Hayworth's business manager in late forties.

I grew up very poor with my father, after my mother's death, right on the edge of Hancock Park, a very ritzy WASP enclave. Okay, I had the WASP pedigree but the flipside of WASPhood is white trash and that's what we were basically.

James wondered whether his father was going to be murdered as well. The following year, his father gave him a copy of The Badge by Jack Webb, which included a summary of Black Dahlia case - Elizabeth Short, a starlet tortured and mutilated, found naked and in two halves, reminded James of his mother, neither case solved.

James used to ride over to the spot on Norton Avenue and 39th Street, where the Dahlia's body was dumped, to feel her presence. He had nightmares about her, saw her in daylight flashes. Read crime novels from that time on. True crime too. He talked about the Dahlia case with Randy Rice, childhood friend. Kicked out of school for truancy. Years later, he went to Black Dahlia's grave, felt that he knew her, loved her.

1965, aged seventeen, into the US Army, then father became gravely ill, so James faked nervous breakdown, stammered, to get kicked out. His father died. James was virtually penniless and homeless.

Dog became a peeper around Hancock Park, breaking and entering, sniffing women's panties in South Arden. Bought amphetamines from Gene The Short Queen. When no money, Dog drank cough syrup, or swallowed cotton wads in nasal inhalers to get high. Dog spent nights in Robert Burns Park taking speed and masturbating. This was Dog's life for 11 years, drinking, stealing food, drinking, dropping acid, drinking, shoplifting, stealing drink, smoking Maryjane, living on the streets, lifting wallets, sleeping in dumpsters, flophouses. In and out of county jail more than a dozen times. Had odd jobs, once minded till at a porn shop until his hand was found in it.

Dog caught pneumonia and told abscess on a lung. Coupla weeks later was hearing things from the drink. He knew he'd die if he didn't quit the life. Dog quit. He joined Alcoholics Anonymous.

Today, Ellroy doesn't drink, doesn't smoke, goes to bed early. He's very neat, meticulous, keeps a neat house, is disciplined. He presently lives with his wife, feminist author and critic Helen Knode, in Mission Hills, Kansas.

It's the Hancock Park of the mid-West.

You don't have to break in any more.

I own a house like those, now. The surroundings are restful and physically beautiful and they underscore the silence that I need to work. I abhor outside stimulation.

BROWN'S REQUIEM (1981)

1977, Dog caddying at the Hillcrest and, after punching another caddy, the Bel-Air Country Club for $200-300 a week, whilst living in a $25-a-week room at the Westwood Hotel. Dog got the idea for a private eye novel in 1978 and began writing it January 26 1979.

The story: Fritz Brown, ex-cop turned repo man, who uses the PI moniker as a tax-dodge on his illegal activities, is approached by super-caddy Freddy 'Fat Dog' Baker to watch his sister and the old geezer she lives with.

I've seen you put this book down in previous interviews, but it ain't no dog. I think it's great and much underrated.

I think it's a good book.

It contains all the Dog trademarks: corrupt cops; excessive violence; the Black Dahlia case; our hero getting beaten to a pulp; Tijuana; dogs; wine, women & drugs; the unobtainable woman; and the bittersweet conclusion. The unobtainable woman was a major feature of your early novels.

I wrote that book shortly after I got sober. I hadn't been with a woman for years and years and years. I'd had scant experience with women prior to that and I was looking for *the* woman. I was a big grrr, grrr, grrr, kinda guy and women were afraid of me. I hadn't refined my social act at the time. I was working as a caddy and sober and writing my first book. I wanted a woman, I wanted sex, I wanted all that stuff and I wasn't getting any, and that's what really informs that book.

It was autobiographical. Here's a guy who looks exactly like me, has a German-American background, likes classical music, came from my old neighbourhood, gets involved in a bunch of caddies. All that's me. He was a private eye and an ex-cop and I was neither. I did repos very briefly in 1968, so I know a little about that.

What was caddying like?

It's lowlife, basically. 99% of all country club caddies in America are drug addicts, winos, compulsive gamblers, ex-cons and generally shitbirds. I remember - I got sober in August 1977 - the first winter of my sobriety was 1977/78 when we had tumultuous rains in LA. You couldn't putt on the golf course for rodents, so we were only getting 5 bucks a day rain money and these caddies were spending all their money on cheap wine and cigarettes and jungling up in the two restaurants at the golf course, sleeping in the cars in the parking lot, stealing steaks and barbecueing them. I wasn't because I had a place to stay - I was sober.

Caddying was good tax-free cash and allowed me to get home by 2pm and write books. I caddied right up to the sale of my fifth book. I can afford to join the best country club in town now. There are three nearby, but I'd only want to join Kansas City Country Club because it's the oldest and most exclusive. But they wouldn't let me in because you need six letters of recommendation - you really have to be established in Kansas City society.

Are you interested in getting involved in society?

No. They don't let Jews or blacks in and that's no good. I wouldn't want to be part of some place that does that. I just think it'd be a kick to join a country club. My mother-in-law's boyfriend is a member so we get to go to the grill room every coupla weeks for dinner.

Besides, I've never taken a golf lesson so I can't really justify joining the Kansas City Country Club, never mind the fact that I can't get in.

I'd join just to cut up the golf course, but that's me.

I'd like to get two bull terriers and walk them across Kansas City Country Club and let them shit on the greens. I know how appreciated that would be.

It's good fertiliser, isn't it? Top quality shit.

From celebrity dogs, no less.

You're often photographed with your bull terrier, Barko.

He lives with my ex-wife in Westport, Connecticut but I see him occasionally. Barko is both immortal and cross-species heterosexual and throughout history Barko has been the lover of some of the world's most beautiful women. As a matter of fact, for any year of the Twentieth Century, I can tell you the woman he was with chiefly.

1924: Gloria Swanson.

1958: Bridgitte Bardot. People have wondered for years why Bridget Bardot became an animal rights activist.

1963: People have been wondering for years what was that little white speck on the grassy knoll in Dallas on November 22nd. Now, was it smoke coming out of a gun barrel? Wrong! It was Barko, the hit dog. Barko assassinated John F Kennedy. He was having an affair with Jackie K and he wanted her all for himself. Now Barko, fickle hound that he is, dropped Jackie about a year and a half later for the beautiful British actress Julie Christie.

Also, Barko, currently: Emma Thompson. Grrr. Grrr. Grrr.

Barko is a very British dog, a pit bull terrier. Have you ever petted one?

I've never attempted to.

They're very friendly to people. They love 'em. They don't like other animals for shit.

Well, I'll be happy to test that one out when you bring him over to the UK.

I don't think so. I'd never subject him to quarantine or anything like that.

CLANDESTINE (1982)

Story: This is a thinly veiled, chronologically altered account of James' mother's killing. Freddy Underhill, rookie LA cop, plays golf, has one night stands. One of the women ends up dead, so Freddy uses this as an opportunity to propel himself up the ladder of ambition. Dog used many of his father's physical attributes when describing the killer, and doesn't know why he did this. There's a young boy in the novel, just like James, but this boy flashes the local girls. This is Dog's first historical novel, set in early fifties LA, and it introduces us to Dudley Smith, who later played a crucial part in the LA Quartet.

BLOOD ON THE MOON (1984)

First Lloyd Hopkins novel. Story: Hopkins is an intelligent right-wing bastard contemporary cop who is often more dangerous than the criminals he hunts. In this novel he sees the link between a series of over 20 murders over the same number of years. The detection, suspense and action are good. The film, Cop, starring James Woods, was based on this novel - watching it you realise how conventional the novel is, but also how extraordinarily compulsive and obsessive Dog's prose style is. (The film title was changed to Cop because Robert Wise directed a western called Blood On The Moon in 1948 and objected to it being used again.)

BECAUSE THE NIGHT (1985)

Second Lloyd Hopkins novel. I read this one in Austria - dark, brooding, oppressive - the book was like that as well. Story: A deranged psychiatrist, John Havilland, is responsible for manipulating the weak-willed to do his bidding. Sex and snuff-stuff are on the menu.

SUICIDE HILL (1986)

Third Lloyd Hopkins novel. Story: Bank robbers find managers with illicit affairs, hold the bit on the side hostage, and steal the money. Simple, until one of the robbers gets randy and goes berserk. Lloyd leads the manhunt and, in doing so, discovers not all is as it seems within the police force he knows and loves. Edward Bunker has done a screenplay for this one so it may, or probably won't, be coming to a multiplex near you.

SILENT TERROR (1986)

Also published as Killer On The Road. *Story: This is the first person narrative of serial killer Martin Michael Plunkett as he travels across America killing all and sundry. It's different from Dog's other books, and far better than some, so it doesn't deserve to be ignored which is what some critics seem to have done. In fact, it's one of the best serial killer books you're likely to come across. About halfway through Martin is caught - then Dog delivers a twist which had me gasping.*

Of other serial killer books, Dog reckons By Reason Of Insanity *by Shane Stevens is* 'a great big beautiful comic book. It's absolutely preposterous, but great fun,' *and that Thomas Harris (*Red Dragon, Silence Of The Lambs*) is* 'about the only guy who can do them and I think even he should grow beyond them now.'

I figured that Ross Macdonald would have been a big influence on Dog - Macdonald's books are all about people with hidden pasts, just like Dog's characters.

Yeah, he is. Raymond Chandler was also an influence early on. He's diminished in my mind now. A lot of his writing is flat-out bad. A lot of the construction is spotty. And I don't think he knew people anywhere near as well as Dashiell Hammett.

Dashiell Hammett is my fave.

Yeah. He's the great realist. Joseph Wambaugh, the LA cop turned novelist, is a big influence too.

He wrote big, sprawling, irreverent novels like you do now. Do you talk to many crime writers?

I'm not real close friends with any crime writers. I know Edward Bunker and Joseph Koenig, who wrote *Little Odessa*, quite well. I'm not friends with writers, period. Most of my friends are colleagues, basically. Some cops.

Are the cops normal?

Yeah. They're not like my characters! Bill Stoner's an amazingly great guy.

Do you read non-crime books?

I don't really read outside of crime and true crime.

I would have thought you'd like some of the Russian authors, Dostoyevsky especially.

I tried to read *Crime And Punishment* once but it was so drearily written I had to put it down.

I think it depends on the translation you get but, also, you have to be prepared to get into the rhythm of the language. I find that your books are the same way, you have to work to get into the rhythm and cadence of the words and speech and, once you have, it's very evocative, mesmerising even. Do you think in this style now? Is it a natural process?

The style of the book is always set, directly linked, directly derived from, the story. *White Jazz* is a frenetic first-person fever dream so that constant staccato be-bop riff style is applicable. *American Tabloid* is a more fully explicated style full of odd syncopations and repetitions of phrases. It's a big book of outrageous events. It's a very funny book, I think, too.

I think your books are very funny, but it's a dark humour that a lot of people don't see. For instance, many people won't think Jim Thompson is funny, but I find him so. He's so ironic, you have to laugh.

Generally, people in America don't understand irony - saying one thing but meaning another - whereas it's quite common in speech in the UK, and it's also in your books. Do Americans have difficulty reading your books on that level?

There's a genre ghetto and people want the sympathetic character, the easy-to-identify-with character. People want that rebelliousness, the one person against the system book. Raymond Chandler created a very easy to adapt style which is why so many people have adapted to it with such great success. In America, you're up against a genre ghetto all the time. I've broken through that - I'm the darling of the deconstructionists, college professors, homosexual media mavens, people in the movie biz, the cognoscenti. These media hounds are capable of digging on irony but American writers take an almost perverse pride in being simplistic, in being proud of their genre roots.

What you see is what you get.

Yeah. Editors, publishers are in business to sell books, so accessibility counts for a lot.

Do you have to write?

Yes. That's why I'm here. I love telling stories. I love doing it. I love the result of seeing the book in print. I love the glory. I love the money. I love the acclaim. But, mostly, I love doing it. I've always forced myself to live in the craft. I'm a perfectionist and, the older I get - I'm arguably ten to twelve years away from my prime - a writer's real prime seems to be their early sixties.

You think of Leo Tolstoy, George Bernard Shaw, Rudyard Kipling, H G Wells all doing great writing past sixty. Painters are the same.

Symphony orchestra conductors seem to hit their peak in their late sixties, early seventies, and I hope that's the way it is with me.

I've always postponed the thrill of recognition. I've always stood aside from it. I like to perform. I'm a powerful character and I've had a colourful past which has been mythologised and I've attempted, to some degree, to demythologise it. My past is tremendously pathetic and really anything but melodramatic. So, I design the books very carefully. I know how to rest whilst writing a book, and how to rest between books. I like to think a lot, I like to brood. I've got absolutely no taste for popular culture. Parenthetically, it's very odd that on the past few trips to Britain, I'm continually questioned about Quentin Tarantino, who I think is a fatuous child. I think *Reservoir Dogs* is garbage and the forty minutes of *Pulp Fiction* that I saw is most excruciatingly naive shtick, boring tedium that I've ever endured. I stand outside popular culture.

My wife is the most brilliant human being I've ever met. We have a disciplined but quiet home life together and I like to think, to brood, to listen to classical music, Beethoven, and it replenishes me, it puts me back in the book.

I write books that I can honestly say nobody else is writing. You've read a million private eye books - there may be some pretty gifted people out there writing private eye books. I've got no time for it. Serial killer books, thrillers, police procedurals... I have set out to write the books that nobody else would write, to take the risks that nobody else would take and to write the books that nobody, frankly, would have the patience to write, and it's paid off for me.

I'll write fewer books, develop less of a hard readership, than other big-name writers in my lifetime and probably earn less money, but it's okay. I'm earning quite a handsome living doing the thing I love. So, I'm always looking ahead, looking to the next book, looking for ways for me to refine the craft.

The object is not the money but the work, to express what you think, to channel all that into a form other people can understand. When I sit down to read your books, especially the last few, I can look up from the page and think a half hour has gone by, but it's only been ten minutes. The information is so dense, the brain activity so intense that reading your books distorts time, which is ironic considering the way you distort history. Do you have a vision of the reader and their reactions when you write, or do you see the reader as yourself?

As myself. I write the books that I want to write, and I haven't compromised on that level of complexity or of brain work. More traditionally minded editors have warned me about losing the reader with the density and complexity and I figure, if I lose 'em I lose 'em. I'm lucky that I've got some great editors in the US, the UK and in France. My American editor, who cut his teeth in Great Britain, is not interested in my reinforcing the genre qualities of my work. He's only interested in what makes me different, which is why he's publishing me in the first place.

Condensing everything down into a solid block of information, you're obviously spending a lot longer writing the book than the people who read it. Is the writing of it as intense as the reading?

It's a very intense experience. Ideally, the books should be read in decent blocks of time, over as short a period of time as possible, so that the reader can retain the information.

I start with a hugely detailed outline - the outline for *American Tabloid* was 275 pages. It's very, very intense experience, very difficult work. I like density and complexity. Every word in *American Tabloid* and the LA Quartet means something. It's all there to advance the plot. There's no rambling. There's no unnecessary scene-setting. If there are discourses, they are essential to the plot. It's why people can't read the book. I'm sure it's why I don't get stratospheric sales numbers despite all the great publicity that I get. My sales are quite substantial on their own, but I doubt that they'll ever be staggering because most people don't have the discipline or the intelligence for the books. If you blink you'll miss something. If you want an intense reading experience, great, I'm for you.

THE BLACK DAHLIA (1987)

First of the LA Quartet. Now, we get serious. Story: Set against the fictionalised account of the hunt for the true-life murderer of The Black Dahlia in January 1947, this is really the story of two death-obsessed cops, Bucky Bleichert and Lee Blanchard. This was the first Dog I read, and it really shocked me. I remember reading it on a train and, after one passage, heart pumping, mind racing, looking up at the other passengers, who were totally unperturbed. For a second, illogically, I couldn't understand why they were unmoved by the book.

After I had established some sort of readership with my first six novels, I wrote the novel of the Black Dahlia case. It tapped into the deepest aspects of my unconscious. It was a book I had been waiting almost thirty years to write. Rather than go back to my tired-ass series character that I was writing at that time, which is what my publisher and agent wanted me to do, about mid-way through *The Black Dahlia*, I realised that I wanted to create a quartet about Los Angeles (my own smog-bound fatherland) between the years of 1947 and 1959.

THE BIG NOWHERE (1988)

Second of the LA Quartet. Story: Moving to 1950, using the red scare commie-bashing investigating team as background, Dog shows us Danny Upshaw, ambitious death-obsessed deputy with a string of mutilated victims on his hands, Mal Considine, ambitious DA creep who wants power to get custody of his adopted kid, and Buzz Meeks, loveable ex-cop pimp for Howard Hughes. Death, deceit and double cross. Lovely.

What is your attitude towards violence? I think because some of your books are obviously violent, and you sometimes go into great detail, people assume that you like violence.

Violence is always very short, swift and to the point in my books. I rarely dwell on it.

Perversely, that makes it more violent. My assumption has always been that people who don't like violence, who are afraid of it, tend to write it better.

That's exactly right. I've never been a violent person. I'm appalled by it. I'm shocked by it. I'm a big advocate of gun control. Violence is at the root of all intrigue, it's the basis of all threat, in history, which makes it so great to write - I enjoy it. My personal relationship to it - I'm attracted to it because I understand it's relation to history, but I'm appalled by it because I know what it costs.

There is a physical violence, which we can all see, experience in your work. There is also a mental violence in the way politicians mess with

society, or people conduct their relationships. There's this unseen violence, which is felt just as keenly, if not more so. Are you interested in that?

The books will become more and more about that as they become more and more about politics. The basic theme for the Underworld USA trilogy is the private nightmare of public policy. It's mostly psychological.

LA CONFIDENTIAL (1990)

Third of the LA Quartet. From an enormous cast of characters, about eighty, Dog focuses a beady eye on three cops: Trashcan Jack Vincennes (media cop for hire), Ed Exley (overshadowed by his famous father) and Bud White (the toughest of tough LA cops, he's haunted by a wife-beating father). The elements: a Disneyland-like theme park under construction, a series of grisly murders, a cop Christmas party that goes horribly wrong and the cover-up that follows, and Hush-Hush *magazine - sleazesheet to the slags with no end of sinuendo. Dog delivered 809 page manuscript which his agent Nat Sobel advised to cut by taking out unnecessary words. Resulted in clipped cadence style which sounds like a rhythmic psycho-beatnik rap.*

I am a fiend for darkness, sleaze, groovy twisted sexuality. I'm especially interested in this around the late fifties, early sixties, at the time of my emerging sexuality. I recall being holed up with a copy of *Confidential* magazine looking at a picture of Clorine Calvey for about three hours on a hot summer night before I even knew what masturbation was. And I like to go back and relive those times, the time of darkness in my life and explicate it.

I don't like to practice these things, but I'm curious about them. I like to retain an immunity from it which is why I live a very quiet, blissfully monogamous life in Kansas. I love to watch boxing on the TV - my wife has turned into a tremendous boxing fan. I go to the movies occasionally. I love the old film noirs. I lift weights. I like to think.

I haven't lived in Los Angeles in fourteen years. I have enough crazy shit going on in my imagination to last me the next forty-seven years of my life. Believe me, I need no outside stimulus whatsoever. But I grew up in LA and my father was a sleazebag on the edge of the movie biz. I knew that Rock Hudson was a fag in 1959 - it was no newsflash when he finally caught AIDS and died eight or nine years ago. I like movies as cheap entertainment. To me, they're like hamburgers. I've ate about ten profound hamburgers in my life and I've probably seen ten profound movies. I'm voyeuristically curious about people's sex lives, about their inner moral workings, and here you have a whole cast of - usually very good-looking - characters, both women and men and all I want to know is who's a homosexual, who's a nymphomaniac, who's a sader, who's got the biggest wang in Hollywood, who's got the smallest, who's impotent, who's the underhung, who's the snap-diver, who's the sword-swallower, who's the peeper, who's the prowler, who's the pimp, who's the pederast and who's the panty-sniffer? Don't put me in some fucking Martin Scorcese/Quentin Tarantino symposium - contemporary movies don't interest me that much. I don't want to know about that. I want to know about the stars, what they're up to: Tom Cruise, Nicole Kidman, Keanu Reeves, Brad Pitt, Liam Neeson, James Woods, Willem Dafoe...

Dog entertains and shocks by saying libellous things about various well-known movie personalities. He says he's got some well-placed sources in Hollywood, but anyone could say that.

It's true.

You're saying that these are things which everyone knows but no-one can print. Recently I was sitting around talking to friends who work in the media and they were talking about stories involving various personalities and events that they couldn't print, and outright lies they had to print. This is another secret history, only it's social rather than political or criminal.

Whatever story needs to be told will find itself into my imagination.

WHITE JAZZ (1992)

Fourth of the LA Quartet. Star: Lieutenant Dave Klein: lawyer, bagman, slum landlord, mob killer... a very bad lieutenant indeed. Quartet Rollovers: Dudley Smith; Ed Exley; Mickey Cohen. This books has to be experienced, not explained.

White Jazz is definitely a one-off. It's a first-person narration of a very bad man, a cop named Dave Klein, whose life in running down in Los Angeles in the fall of 1958. The book is a fever dream - it's a stream of consciousness style - there are no tricks in it - everything is quite literal but, if you blink, you will miss things. You have to get into the rhythm of Dave Klein's head or you won't get the book at all. There are many people who didn't understand the book. The book did not sell as well as the three previous volumes of the LA Quartet. It was a risk I took - I think the risk is worth it. The important thing with me is always the book, not the sales. I did it for that one book and I returned to a more fully developed style for *American Tabloid*, and I will never go back to *White Jazz* again. I've done it.

Each book, I think, is darker, more dense, more complex and more stylistically evolved than the previous book. I have finished the LA Quartet. It is considered a monument of some sort - I consider it a great monument, like Mount Rushmore, and so does my dog, my wife, my agent and my current publisher. Others are not so charitable, but fuck 'em because they don't have to be. The bottom line is this: if you don't like my books you can kiss my ass.

Doing a series based in the past, even the recent past, a past you lived in, must have involved some research.

I did extensive research on the Black Dahlia murder case because it is fully the historical case laid out, in detail, before I digress fictionally. On *The Big Nowhere*, which is about the Red scare in Hollywood in 1950, I read half a book on the subject, realised I could make the rest of the shit up, and threw the book away. *LA*

Confidential - I only researched the Bloody Christmas police scandal of 1951 and tossed the rest of the books away. *White Jazz* - no research.

Essentially, for a long, long time I had been obsessed with LA during that era, and if a person has talent and brains and some kind of self-knowledge and insight, then the chances are that the things you are obsessed with will be the things you will be good at. It all comes down to: can I make the public believe it? And I could.

DICK CONTINO'S BLUES (1994)

A collection of short stories set during the LA Quartet. Title novella - serial killer wants Dick as partner in crime. Stories: Lee Blanchard; Buzz Meeks; Stan Klein.

The short story form does not interest me. I wrote short stories at the behest of editors that I owed favours to and, luckily for me, because I'd recently been divorced, I saw that I had collected enough short stories to sell a short story volume and make some very quick cash with minimal effort. So I wrote a novella to stand as the frontispiece of this collection, called *Dick Contino's Blues*.

Dick Contino was a big star in America in the late forties and early fifties. He was a handsome Italian guy who played the accordion and nobody ever played accordion like this motherfucker. He humped it, he wolfed it, he waggled it, he gyrated with it, he orbited it like a fucking dervish flying on benzedrine, maryjane and glue. He was a handsome guy. He really banged that box. He had 400 fan clubs nationwide and 5000 fan-letters a week. But he was a fearful young kid and in 1951 his handsome ass was about to get drafted and sent to Korea. He told the draft board that he was really scared and didn't want to go to Korea. This was the wrong thing to say at the height of the Red scare in America. The draft board and Hearst newspapers throughout America took the stand 'Hey Dick, you're getting more ass than a toilet seat, you're making five Gs a week and you're 21 years old - we're gonna draft your ass.' So, Dick's ass was drafted. He was sent to basic training at Fort Ord, California. So Dick ran for 24 hours, went home to his mom and dad, turned himself into the Feds, got slammed, took it right up the rump-ramp for this one in the worst way. Got six months in the federal penitentiary at McNeil Island, Washington and was then drafted and sent to Korea, where he served with distinction. He came back to find the accordion somewhat passé and his career completely derailed. He went from being a big star and a main room guy, to a lounge act and the star of a very sleazy B-movie called *Daddy-O*.

I have some very dim recollections of Dick Contino from the late fifties, and after finishing the LA Quartet I was suffering some separation pangs from Los Angeles, so I decided to do a picaresque, light-hearted farewell to LA in the fifties, hence the novella.

Dick and I are still in touch. Dick is presently undergoing romantic troubles. He's 65 and is going out with the daughter of one of the members of his original fan club. There is only a 37 year age difference between Dick and this woman. She's an Italian woman from upstate New York. She's divorced. She has had several kids by several different men. I think Dick has picked a black marble with this woman. I think Dick is still, many, many years after his great fame and a few years after his resurgence via me, perpetuating the same patterns with bad women. So, in his way, Dick Contino is a noir character.

When you talk about rewriting history, and the whole glitzy fifties era, it reminds me of *Crime Story*. I thought it was great the way they rewrote history, Vietnam, the A-bomb, the Kennedys etc. and had the characters interact with history. It's one of my favourite TV shows.

Mine too. I'm very good friends with Anthony Dennison - he played the villain, Ray Luca. I never saw the show originally but Anthony Dennison and Jeff Stein, who directed a couple of episodes, optioned *Dick Contino's Blues*. They've written a brilliant screenplay from it and are trying to get it made. I've since got all the *Crime Story* episodes on video. The show is great in Chicago, when it's a serial with a continuing storyline, but it goes to hell in the Las Vegas episodes when it becomes discursive and episodic.

I liked the Las Vegas stuff. It was over the top, camp, outrageous. It was great fun.

Yeah, a lot of people liked the outré design.

The characters and designs seemed like they were from the fifties, but the plots were from the sixties. It was a weird mix.

Anthony and I discussed this and he said it actually started set in 1963, but it seemed like 1958. I kept waiting for references to the Kennedy assassination to set things in perspective but it never occurred.

I think Dennis Farina as Lieutenant Mike Torello is just a force of nature. When the hatred between him and Anthony Dennison fuels the plot, it's great, it's epic, but after a while it just goes to hell.

All Dog's books have been optioned for film, including his non-fiction memoir My Dark Places, *except* White Jazz, Killer On The Road *and* Because The Night. *They are in various stages of development - Edward Bunker has done a script for* Suicide Hill, *for example - but will any of them be filmed? Dog doubts it.*

However, the short story Since I Don't Have You, *which is in the* Dick Contino's Blues *collection, was adapted for the* Fallen Angels *TV series. Was it the Dog's delight?*

It was interesting. I thought Gary Busey was a bad Buzz Meeks, James Woods an ineffectual Mickey Cohen and Tim Matheson was great as Howard Hughes.

AMERICAN TABLOID (1995)

First of the Underworld USA Trilogy. The legal: Kennedy; Hoover; CIA. The illegal: Trafficante; Marcello; Giancana. The legbreakers: Pete Bondurant; Kemper Boyd; Ward Littell.

Everybody has written about the Kennedys, but I hadn't done it.

When I finished the LA Quartet, I realised that that was then and this is now. I never wanted to do another novel that could in any way be categorised as a thriller, a mystery or a book based around police work or, specifically police investigations. I realised, what I wanted to do was write a trilogy - three books with fifteen years of American history broken down into five year increments. I wanted one theme to pervade these works and that is politics as crime and the private nightmare of public policy. The genesis of all this is reading Don DeLillo's novel *Libra*, a brilliantly fictional take on Lee Harvey Oswald and the Kennedy assassination.

Now, I was fifteen when Jack 'The Haircut' Kennedy got whacked in 1963. I was never fond of the Kennedys - I never loved them nor hated them. I was unmoved by Kennedy's death even though he was very much of my youth. But now, all of a sudden, after reading *Libra*, I was obsessed by the Kennedy assassination and the events which I viewed to be the harbingers of it.

I began to see that *Libra* precluded me from ever writing a novel specifically about the assassination but what I could do was write a novel wherein the assassination was but one murder in a long series of murders. I decided that this book would be my first novel that would, in no way, be driven by psycho-sexual plots. Some of the action would take place in LA, my chief locale, but most of it wouldn't. I would go one on one with history and recreate that era to my own specifications, so I did.

I hired a researcher, a magazine editor friend of mine. She compiled chronologies and factsheets for me so that I wouldn't write myself into factual error. I extrapolated from those facts. I show all the real life characters in the book - the Kennedy brothers, Jimmy Hoffa, Howard Hughes and the key gangsters of the era - Santos Trafficante, Carlos Marcello, Sam Giancana - in a totally fictional context. You don't need to show Kennedy giving his inaugural speech or having his brains blown out. We've seen it eight million times. Lee Harvey Oswald does not appear in the book. The assassination is 12-15% of the overall text. If you have the stones to say I can rewrite history to my own specifications, I can populate this book with fictional characters, the minor minions of the time, and make them more interesting and more perversely apathetic than the Kennedys, J Edgar Hoover, Howard Hughes and the rest, then you can get away with it.

I have stopped writing psychosexual driven plots. It's the covenant of consciousness. I think writers can get better and better and better and better. I think good writers can bring a thematic unity, an innate talent and a certain native intelligence embedded in his/her unconsciousness and that can see you through any number of books. Three, four or five. There are then the implications of editors - write a series character, a sympathetic private eye, British inspector, innocent person who keeps getting caught up in violent intrigue, so that readers can have somebody to come back to and come back to and come back to. I have decided to ignore that rule and forge my own territory.

For me, my big thematic journey is Twentieth Century American history and what I think Twentieth Century American history is, is the story of bad white men, soldiers of fortune, shakedown artists, extortionists, legbreakers. The lowest level implementors of public policy. Men who are often toadies of right wing regimes. Men who are racists. Men who are homophobes. These are my guys. These are the guys that I embrace. These are the guys that I empathise with. These are the guys that I love.

Now, parenthetically, a number of critics have called me a fascist, a racist, an anti-semite, an anti-papist because my characters are like that. These are the characters who are portrayed as multi-faceted human beings. The reader, on some level, is meant to empathise with them, and I certainly do. I think what angers critics is that the racism, and homophobia and anti-semitism and everything else that these characters express is not fundamental to their character - they are just casual attributes that they possess because they are men of the time.

So I write books of the time, in the language of the time in the first and third person, refer to Jews as kikes, homosexuals as faggots, and blacks as niggers. People don't know how to take it. I love the American idiom. If I can dip into the American idiom I would rather use it, as profane and ugly as it sometimes is than so-called normal King's English.

The bottom line is that Twentieth Century American crime fiction is the story of bad white men and I'll go to my grave thinking that.

With all these bad men to play with, Dog does find time for one good one in *American Tabloid*.

As much research as I've done, one fact stands fast - I think Robert Kennedy was a great man, perhaps the chief crime fighter of the Twentieth Century in America, and a paragon of moral rectitude. Parenthetically, he did not play bury the brisket and pour the pork with Marilyn Monroe. He did not dip the schnitzel with her.

I used to be friends with Shakedown Freddy Ottash, private eye to the stars in LA circa 1955 to 1965. God bless him, Freddy died recently at the age of 71. He was having a heart attack and called a cab rather than an ambulance.

Freddy Ottash was the guy that you saw in 1955 to 1965 LA if you wanted to hotwire a homosexual bathhouse, if you wanted to pull a sex shakedown, get your wife's lover's legs broken, get your wife an abortion, get a dope cure, fix a drunk/driving, or get a picture of Rock Hudson with a dick in his mouth. You went to see Freddy Ottash.

Now Freddy Ottash was too cool to drool. Freddy Ottash would leave you reamed, steamed, and dry cleaned, tied, dyed swept to the side, screwed, blued, tattooed, and bob-gung-gooed.

Shakedown Freddy was the guy hired by Jimmy Hoffa in the Fall of 1961 to hotwire Peter Lawford's fuckpad where Jack was playing bury the brisket with Marilyn Monroe. Now, hepcats, again, parenthetically, off the record, on the QT, and very hush-hush, Jack Kennedy was a two point four minute man. Shakedown Freddy timed a half-dozen Jack Kennedy/Marilyn Monroe assignations and averaged them out. A coupla times Jack couldn't make it to two minutes and he was always citing his bad back, which is why in *American Tabloid* he's known as Bad Back Jack.

Freddy told me he is convinced that Bobby Kennedy never had an affair with Marilyn Monroe that, at the time of Marilyn's death, Bobby was interceding on Jack's behalf, trying to get this crazy fucking woman to quit calling the President of the United States at the White House. She just kicked off coincidentally.

Dogs nips at the heels of historical figures and manages to tear chunks out of them. Doesn't this, er, lead to certain legal...

I have never gotten into trouble using real people in my books because they are dead and can't sue me. In America, their surviving families can't sue. I don't get feedback. The Kennedys, for instance, would never sue. So much is written about them that, if they were to sue, they'd be in court all day, every day, and that way they wouldn't have time to [text deleted].

America likes history because it has so little of it. It likes to define itself by its history, its ancestry, its battles, its fights for truth justice and the American Way. Like most countries, it rewrites history from the winners' viewpoint. Dog rewrites from the point of view of the losers.

America seems very self-centred, like a child in some ways, reacting to what happens without considering its actions first. It also thinks it's a moral leader, as though it can dictate what others think and say and do. It has no myths it can call its own - myths are based on history and are an extension of the consciousness of the society - so America mythologises the near-present. Systematically, Dog demythologises the near-present, this century - his world is closer to Bad Lieutenant *than* Dragnet.

As a kid, I always sensed history going on all around me. I knew I was part of it in some odd way. And I knew there were human stories to be told within it, but I didn't know what those stories were.

I remember, for instance, harkening back to *American Tabloid*, the Cuban missile crisis. I remember going to the store to get some canned goods because the old man thought the atom bomb might drop and we should be well-supplied, and finding the shelves stripped clean, and running into our neighbour, Big John Kilbright, a notorious drunk, stocking up on liquor.

It's wonderful to be able to go back to rewrite history to your own specifications, to fill in the human stories within the real context of history, and link them to actual historical events.

I have the real life characters doing things they didn't do in real life. The one question I never answer specifically about *American Tabloid* is what's real and what's not. You have to keep things ambiguous for the reader. You don't want them to know specifically where the dividing line between fact and fiction ends, or you destroy your verisimilitude. One of the ways I accomplish this in *American Tabloid* was to show the real life historical characters in fictional situations. *American Tabloid* is historically valid. The real life events happened similarly to the ways they did. Beyond that, it's all fiction.

Do you see the real-life people as people or as characters?

As characters. Characters to be manipulated.

Good. People tend to think that what's printed is the absolute truth, that if it's in black and white it must have happened. They don't seem to think beyond that.

Ironically, Dog uses newspaper, magazine, radio and TV broadcasts to explain things that happen, but also to give his fiction a feeling of reality, of truth.

One of the themes of *American Tabloid* is the disparity between reported historical fact and what really happened. You've got *Hush-Hush* magazine in there distorting the truth in a hilarious fashion I think, and you've got the outward Kennedy front which is complicit of everything even though you don't see them advancing that front too much, and then the real-life Kennedys, Hoover and Howard Hughes. Basically it's a secret history.

But it's your secret history. Although, as you said earlier, you're not going to say what is and isn't real, you're appealing to the idea of the conspiracy theory people, tapping into the idea that people are afraid of big organisations, whether they be political, commercial or criminal.

I'm not afraid of the corporations, specifically. I think my central theory is valid - John Kennedy's murder is a conspiracy between renegade CIA men, crazy Cuban exiles and organised crime. This is hardly novel. I got the idea from *Libra*. I think something like this happened. Did it happen specifically in this way? It couldn't have - I invented it.

From the perception of the other characters, Bobby Kennedy is the villain.

That's a good point. I think he's a good guy, basically.

I'm not denying that. What I'm saying is that you write your bad guys as sympathetic and they hate Bobby Kennedy. If you sympathise with the bad guys, then you hate Bobby Kennedy too.

Exactly right. I want my readers to have a vigorous response to some of my characters, to identify with them on the basis of their hidden agendas. Bobby Kennedy was a man, heavily compromised by his family situation, and morally upright in many ways. I think he had essential Oedipal problems that got his brother Jack killed. Bobby recognised Joe Kennedy Sr for what he was, and took his vengeance, once removed, on organised crime. This is what cost John Kennedy his life. Arguably Bobby Kennedy himself - I don't know much about the Robert Kennedy assassination. Robert Kennedy has ideals, and that's what these very tainted men can't stand.

The bad men can't stand someone standing up and making themselves heard and willing to die for their ideals.

The specific tragedy of this book is that it's Bobby who gets Jack killed.

Brother killing brother is the theme of *American Tabloid* - Peter Bondurant and Kemper Boyd accidentally killed their respective

brothers. **You've made a career of getting inside the heads of unsympathetic characters and making us understand them. It's terrible and it's exhilarating. This conflict of emotions brings out things in people that perhaps they didn't really want to feel. Are you trying to get inside people's heads?**

I'm trying to get to them on that level. I didn't realise that that's the course of my design until I'd written the LA Quartet.

Do you know the unsympathetic characters that are in your books?

They are all in my head. Other that a couple of characters in *Brown's Requiem* and *Clandestine*, nobody's based on real life characters. I invent the stuff - even the characters based on historically real characters. It's all a work of imagination.

You're moving from the crime of the forties and fifties to the politics of the sixties and seventies. This reminds me of the ways films stopped being film noirs and started to become counter-culture political conspiracy/suspense/paranoia films. Is there a link there, since you grew up in that era and may be emulating its concerns and culture?

I think there an obvious need to explicit your past. What are you, thirty-five?

Thirty-one.

Right. You get to be my age and you're in no way old, but you've been around for a long time. It's an interesting age. I remember the early sixties, just before you were born, quite vividly. I was not in any way moved by the tumult in the sixties. I had long hair because everyone else did. All I wanted to do, basically, was use drugs. I was so inept as a human being that I couldn't get laid during the Summer of Love. Now I get to go back and recreate it.

Are you reliving it because you didn't live it properly the first time around?

No. I think, to one degree or another, the more curious we are about existence the more curious we are about the past. Not necessarily our own past, but the historical past because it's a codified means of saying that this is who I am and this is how I got here. So, to be able to go back to the past and decode it is tremendously seductive.

But it's all about bad men and bad things. You're saying, in your books, that America is built on corruption. Do you actually like America?

Yeah. I love it, whatever corruption is inherent there. Again, I'm not entirely sure how factually valid my books are. My LA Quartet books are certainly a hyperbolised view of police work in the 1950s.

What I write about are the worlds within worlds. This is the insider world.

The *Hush-Hush* world.

Yes. Politics meets show business meets the para-military meets the big money meets organised crime. This is the world of the next two books. It's a tabloid sensibility, which is why *American Tabloid* is called just that and why, the whole trilogy is called the Underworld USA trilogy. (I'm also a bit of a Samuel Fuller fan -

his film *Underworld USA* came out 1961.)

I've been to America a few times: LA, San Francisco, San Diego. It's such a positive place.

America is a very positive place. I'm very optimistic about America's future, too. We only learn the hard way, so we've some hard lessons to come. They are often the best, most viable lessons, so I hope we learn from them.

But all the things you talk about in the books are the bad things about America.

Yeah, but the bad things are tremendously exhilarating to me. It annoys me when people say that my books are depressing because they're not. I think they're exhilarating. I think they are easily the most passionate crime books ever written and I'm a relentlessly positive, hopeful, optimistic, almost utopian person and I have a great laugh. I'm happy for it, and I'm grateful for it. I think noir, in many ways, is dead for me. And I think the dividing line, for me, will be the non-fiction book that I'm doing next. After that, I think my books will express a greater diversity of character and motive.

All your books have conspiracies at one level or another. Is this your world-view, or does it just make good copy?

I enjoy connecting events. I enjoy filling in the blanks of history and I enjoy plotting. This is very satisfying for me. Do I think conspiracies exist? Yes. I love writing the psychology of men in packs. I am a laureate of bad men and I enjoy the shifting cabals of bad men and putting them together.

My view is much more of a chaos theory of life, where each person does their own little bit and doesn't know the whole picture, and the whole picture sometimes naturally creates a form no-one has any control over. People don't have the ability to stop it or the power to control it. Your characters are completely driven to do the things they do, and they have no control over the big picture.

They are extremely wilful, obsessive men, self-serving men, selfish men and they don't understand that there are forces at work which are very much bigger than them, unless they know something specific. Pete Bondurant, for instance, knows you don't fuck with organised crime. He's a man who wants out of the life - he's getting older, he's met a woman - but self-destructively he forces himself out of the life by pulling a drug heist, and it's only by the grace of God of organised crime that, at the end of the book, he's left standing.

The single thing I hate most about crime fiction is the Raymond Chandler sensibility - *'Down These Mean Streets A Man Must Go.'* Down these mean streets the single man who can make a difference must go. There is an institutionalised rebellicusness to it that comes out of a cheap liberalism that I despise. It's always the rebel. It's always the private eye standing up to the system. That doesn't interest me. What interests me are the toadies of the system.

The people who have to do the dirty work.

That's right. The unsung legbreakers of history.

You write about wilful people, people who go out and do things. These are the people you need to drive plots. Specifically, their wilfulness make them crime-orientated books. Have you ever considered writing about other types of people?

It's their wilfulness, their tormented psyches, which makes the books unpredictable too. The characters' actions are linked to their psyches. If there was no history, they would still be valid as characters. Books of violent intrigue, books of men doing things are the only types of book I want to write for the foreseeable future.

What about women doing things?

I can't add it. I think, perhaps, again, the dividing line between one phase of my writing and another will be attempting to recognise my mother in *My Dark Places*. I think it all keeps coming back to her. My women are aggressive, they're intelligent. My men are attracted to them on the basis of their strength. When you set this in a pre-women's liberation time, where there's no established dialogue for that type of woman, you get some interesting stuff. My wife thinks my women characters are great and I think she's right.

MY DARK PLACES (1996)

Saturday, June 21 1958, 8pm, Jean Ellroy was drinking at the Desert Inn (11271 East Valley Boulevard, El Monte) with a man (dark-haired, fortyish, swarthy Caucasian, thin, between five feet nine and six feet tall) and a woman (white, blonde hair tied back in ponytail, in her late twenties). A drunk at the bar was told the man's name but could not remember it later. The three left together at approximately 10pm. Jean's car (1957 Buick, registration KFE 778) was left in the parking lot.

10.20pm, Jean and Swarthy Man, in man's car (1955/6 dark green Oldsmobile), arrived at Stan's Drive-In. Jean had a grilled cheese sandwich. Swarthy Man had a coffee. They ate in the car, talked, obviously had had a few drinks, left at 10.50pm.

Sunday, June 22 1958, 2am, Jean and Swarthy Man, in man's car, arrive at Stan's Drive-In. Swarthy Man, quiet, sullen, bored, had a coffee. Jean, happy, chatting, was dishevelled and looked as though they had been petting. They left at 2.45am.

Jean was attacked at an unknown locale. She was hit on the head several times. Blood, skin and beard fragments under her fingernails indicated she clawed at her assailant's face. She was strangled to death. After she died, her killer took off one of her stockings and tied it loosely around her neck. She was dumped by bushes beside the Arroyo High School, a mile and a half from the Desert Inn.

11am, Geneva Hilliker Ellroy's body discovered by children. Her murder remains unsolved.

Early in 1994, a friend of mine, a newspaper writer in Los Angeles said that he was going to write a piece about five unsolved, uncelebrated St Gabriel Valley homicides and that he was going to the office of the LA County Sheriff's homicide bureau and review the open files on these five homicides - my mother's among them. He was going to see my mother's files, something that I had never done. I decided, shit, I have to see this file myself.

There had to be, of course, a reason for it, a carrot. So I talked to Paul Scanlon, my editor in America for *GQ*, and said I want to go out and read my mother's homicide file and write about the experience in 5000 words for *GQ*. Paul Scanlon said 'Go Big Daddy, do it.' So I flew out to LA and saw the file and it was just as shocking an experience as you would think it would be. I saw the pictures of my mother nude on the morgue slab. I saw pictures of her dead, a nylon stocking around her neck, where her body had been dumped. And a little click went off in my head, and it meant that this wasn't over. Also, there was a little sub-click that meant 'oh.' And what that 'oh' means is 'You've exploited the similarities between your mother's death and the Black Dahlia murder case for many years, you've exploited your mother's death because it made you a crime writer, and now you have to come back and embrace this woman for the first time, you have to acknowledge her, you have to pay the debt, you have to find out who she is, and to do this you have to find the man who killed her, as unlikely as your success in this endeavour could ever be.'

The man who showed me my mother's homicide file was a brilliant, very humane, soon-to-retire LA County Sheriff's homicide detective named Bill Stoner. A man who'd been a homicide cop for fourteen years. A man who had nothing to do with my mother's case. In fact, wasn't even a cop at the time of my mother's death. We got to be good friends. I wrote the piece for *GQ* in America and in Britain and it was a finalist for the National Magazine Award in America. I spoke to my editors and said that I wanted to expand this piece into a full-length memoir. The book would be my autobiography, Bill Stoner's biography, my mother's biography and Stoner and I would attempt to find the man who killed my mother 37 years after the fact. So that's what I've been doing for the past ten months, looking for the man who killed my mother.

We've been getting a lot of publicity for it. There was a significant incident in the case - my mother was seen leaving a bar with a man who presumably killed her, and a blonde woman. That blonde woman as well as the man have never been identified. Chances are that the blonde woman told numerous people that she was out with a couple of people and the man ended up killing the woman. In these bar scene, alcohol fuelled, lust killing milieus this often happens. The material witnesses often talk. Chances are there are a number of people out there who either know the entire story or elements of it and can help us put it together, especially as we garner all this publicity. So far, we've been unsuccessful.

What's daunting about this, more than anything else, is not any inherent emotional danger, but not being able to make it up. The basic dramatic thrust of the book is that first I recreate the investigation of the death using records and the testimony of surviving witnesses, then Bill Stoner and I reinvestigate the case.

JAMES ELLROY

We've interviewed many old people, many of them with faulty memories. They hem and they haw, they digress off the point. It's not linear. It's not like the bullshit homicide investigations you read in my books and the books of crime writers good, bad and indifferent. One thing does not lead to another. It's one dead end after record check after unsatisfying interview after another after another. But facts about my mother and her life are being gleaned en route. Stories and sub-stories are weaving themselves into the tapestry.

Like other authors before you, your life story makes great copy and you've used that for publicity purposes and to get attention. Do you regret that?

It's true. It's a true story. I've always tried to deflate myself as a dangerous persona. Maybe to some crime writers, most of whom are notoriously wimpy, I am a dangerous guy. But I've never been a dangerous guy except maybe to myself. I've never been violent. I was basically self-destructive and pathetic. I go to great pains to explain this to interviewers and it somehow comes out different when I read the pieces written about me. So now I can set the record straight with this memoir and basically never answer any questions about my past life again, I hope.

You'll just refer them to page so and so of the book.

Yeah. Buy the book. So, no I don't regret using my past.

I was going to ask you questions about your family life, but if it's going to be in the book...

I never had a family life.

That was going to be my point. You didn't have a mother, and your father was an absentee. It must have been a very traumatic time.

It was. I learned self-sufficiency very early on because I did not expect people to take care of me. There's a cold side to me, a tremendously ruthless side to me. But, really, I only try to be ruthless with myself.

I want to sum my life up in this memoir, and I want to pay homage to my mother, and I want to recognise her. I want to find out who she was as much as I can and the way to do this is to attempt to locate her killer. I will never stop looking for her killer, but I will not let it run my life. Bill Stoner and I have become very close friends - he is easily the best friend I've ever had and, outside of my wife, the person I will love the most in this life. He's morally, spiritually committed to this case but we're not going to let it eat up our lives. I think that if we do not find the guy by the end of the year, when I go home to write the book, then it's highly unlikely that we'll find him for the rest of our lives. After that, we'll get together for a couple of weeks every year and run down leads.

Did you find her old friends?

We haven't found any yet. We found my old landlady from the late fifties. My mother was an alcoholic and a very secretive woman. She'd be eighty if she was still alive. We're up against the passage of time - she was killed thirty-seven years ago.

Do you feel as though you've missed out?

I feel like the luckiest man in the world.

UNDERWORLD USA

After *My Dark Places* I will return to the finish the Underworld USA trilogy of which *American Tabloid* is the first volume. That book runs from 1958 to 1963. The two subsequent volumes will run from 1963 to 1968 (Howard Hughes' Las Vegas, Vietnam War heroin deals, Jack Ruby and Lee Harvey Oswald - it starts five minutes after Jack gets the bullet in the head), and from 1969 to 1973 (Nixon and Watergate). Thus, fifteen years of dark American history broken down into three books.

At the end of *American Tabloid* you get two of the three main characters surviving, however tenuously. I want to show these men getting older as they interact with history, and becoming humanised and becoming frailer, and becoming more morally ambiguous. I want to show eroticism and monogamy with Pete and Barb. It's very easy to show the first tumultuous meeting between a man and a woman and a lot of hot sex early on - that's easy as dirt.

It's lust, not love.

Yes, it is. But, to show Pete and Barb sticking it out over the course of five years in the next novel is something else.

After I finish the Underworld USA trilogy, I'm going to jump around a lot. I'm going to write a very long, *a very long*, novel about the Wisconsin State police and my German-American roots. After that, I don't know. I'll never write anything again that can be categorised as a straight thriller or crime novel.

I'm very interested in the America's involvement in Mexican war back in the Nineteenth Century, where America basically held Mexico to ransom and, as a result, got the cattle, oil and gold it needed to finance and feed the nation to become a major world power. It's a very dark period of American history. Does this interest you at all?

No. I'm an urban man. I'm interested in the intrigue. It's the clash of wills. It's the pitting of one man against another and then in packs against each other, more than anything else. It's the changing cityscape. It's the forces of greed and lust that shape a city. It's growing up in Los Angeles during a time it underwent a lot of change.

I don't like noise. I live in Kansas City, in the ritziest enclave in Kansas City, in Johnson County, Kansas. I like peace and quiet. I like quiet, affluent surroundings and well-behaved people. I got enough craziness in my own mind to last me the rest of my life. But my curiosity still rages and continue to rage.

Do you haunt the places where you used to live?

I go to LA a lot, especially recently to do *My Dark Places*. It's a real memory bank for me. It's got a lot of force, a lot of power, but I can't live there any more.

Where does this power come from?

I've lived an extraordinary life and I've done some amazing things. I've been around for 47 years and seen a lot of history, and I've been introspective from the gate. I've had a very impoverished life and a very full life, and I'm grateful for it, and you'll see this as you get older, and your curiosity gets richer and richer, and you can become haunted by your own past and the way that it relates to the overall past. It's just fascinating to touch the fabric of the physical places.

Do you see yourself linked with history? In your novels, everyone has a past, something that drives them on, something they want to keep hidden, that they don't want to face. You talk as though you're directly linked to your own history, and that your own history is directly linked to the history of America. Do you feel that way?

Yeah. I feel that way and, I think, in many ways, my mission in life is to explicate it through the writing of the novels.

Is the writing of the novels a way for you to define your own identity?

Yes. I see it as therapeutic - not in the sense that it's something I want to overcome, because I don't think this curiosity, these drives of mine, are neurotically derived. As I get older, I divide humanity into two camps. There are the people who are neurotically derived and there are the people who have transcended the fearful aspects of their personality and the aspects which are holding down their imagination, holding them down from enjoying life to the fullest. My greatest teacher, the only person I've ever met who has a bigger fucking hard-on for life as I do, is my wife. I'm having a blast. People, especially in France, expect me to be fucking tormented. And I have to say, 'Au contraire, Froggy.'

I'm still choked up from last night - I was in a room full of smokers.

I can't believe I'm picking my nose in a fucking interview.

Just be pleased we're not being filmed.

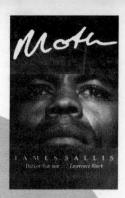

THE BEST AUTHORS
FROM *NO EXIT PRESS*

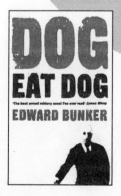

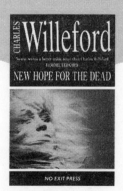

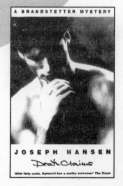

JAMES ELLROY